Reforming Air Pollution Regulation

The Conservation Foundation is a nonprofit research and communications organization dedicated to encouraging human conduct to sustain and enrich life on earth. Since its founding in 1948, it has attempted to provide intellectual leadership in the cause of wise management of the earth's resources. The Conservation Foundation is affiliated with World Wildlife Fund.

Reforming Air Pollution Regulation

The Toil and Trouble of EPA's Bubble

Richard A. Liroff

The Conservation Foundation
Washington, D.C.

Reforming Air Pollution Regulation:
The Toil and Trouble of EPA's Bubble

Typography and cover design by Rings-Leighton, Ltd.,
   Washington, D.C.
Printed by Wickersham Printing Company, Inc.,
   Lancaster, Pennsylvania

The Conservation Foundation
1255 Twenty-Third Street, N.W.
Washington, D.C. 20037

Library of Congress Cataloging in Publication Data
Liroff, Richard A.
   Reforming air pollution regulation.
   Bibliography: p.
   Includes index.
   1. Air—Pollution—Law and legislation—United States.
   2. Air—Pollution—Government policy—United States.
   3. United States. Environmental Protection Agency. I. Title.

| KF3812.L57 1986 | 344.73′046342 | 86-13550 |
| ISBN 0-89164-072-X | 347.30446342 | |

Contents

Foreword

Over the past 15 years, our country has made tremendous strides in reducing the threats of air pollution to public health and the environment. Thanks to the Clean Air Act, automobile emissions have dropped even though Americans are driving far more today than they were 15 years ago. The Clean Air Act has spurred the cleanup of old industrial plants and encouraged the development of new technologies to curb air pollution.

This record of achievement has not come without costs. Indeed, some analysts have suggested that the burden on industry and taxpayers has been excessive because of inflexible regulatory programs and rigid pollution abatement requirements. Moreover, improvements have come many years later than deadlines initially set in the Clean Air Act. It now appears that even the most recent amendments of those deadlines will not be met in many cities.

It was in the context of a debate over the economic impacts of environmental programs, in the last part of the 1970s, that the U.S. Environmental Protection Agency pioneered novel air pollution control strategies intended to integrate pollution control and economic concerns. These strategies—now called emissions trading—aim to promote greater use of economic incentives to reduce pollution control costs and also to spur greater technological innovation in meeting the goals of the Clean Air Act.

In his 1980 report, *Air Pollution Offsets: Trading, Selling, and Banking*, Conservation Foundation Senior Associate Richard A. Liroff examined the first wave of promising policy initiatives. In this new report, *Reforming Air Pollution Regulation: The Toil and Trouble of EPA's Bubble*, Dr. Liroff focuses on a further evolution in emissions trading, the so-called bubble policy. This policy permits trade-offs between easy- and hard-to-control emissions within a plant,

ix

provided the total amount of pollutants leaving an imaginary "bubble" over the facility has an impact on air quality equal to or better than would have been possible under conventional regulatory requirements.

Dr. Liroff's study of emissions trading reflects The Conservation Foundation's continuing interest in the role economic incentives and nonregulatory alternatives can play in promoting environmental quality. His analysis of the pros and cons of emissions trading leads him to conclude, on balance, that this strategy can produce improved environmental quality at reduced cost. But the rules governing trading, he concludes, must be tightened to prevent its abuse. Unlike trading's harshest critics, however, he advocates continued use of trading as a practical, useful supplement to conventional regulatory approaches.

Reforming Air Pollution Regulation is helpful on another level as well: it is a revealing tale about the difficulties in reforming complex laws, programs, and institutions, and the perseverance and determination needed on the part of regulatory reformers if they are to succeed in making even modest gains.

Further progress in meeting air quality goals requires that the nation find additional emission reductions. How can this be done in a cost-effective manner? Can it be done in a cooperative spirit? Over the past decade, The Conservation Foundation's Business and the Environment Program, under the auspices of which Dr. Liroff's report is published, has examined many of the nation's environmental laws, identifying opportunities for improving their effectiveness while taking into account economic and social impacts. Through research on procedures for siting industrial facilities; the founding of a new non-profit organization, Clean Sites, Inc.; and the convening of dialogue groups of business representatives, environmentalists, and others to discuss toxic substances control and similarly sensitive issues, the Foundation has searched for practical ways to improve the environment while meeting the country's economic agenda.

Dr. Liroff's research was made possible by generous support to The Conservation Foundation's Business and the Environment Program by the Charles Stewart Mott Foundation. Additional support was provided by donors of unrestricted funds to The Conservation Foundation.

William K. Reilly
President
The Conservation Foundation

Preface

The Clean Air Act is a symbol of America's determination to clean up its dirty air and to keep its pristine air from being fouled. Billions of dollars have been spent to reduce pollution from industry and automobiles, and much progress has been made. But the ambitious cleanup goals the act originally set have not been met, and in some locations it is not clear if and when they can be. Moreover, the easiest steps may be behind us.

The Clean Air Act is controversial and complex. The administrative mechanisms implementing it have major shortcomings. Regulators' information about pollutants being discharged into the air is incomplete, and their ability to assure compliance with requirements is limited. The federal courts have considered numerous legal challenges by industry and environmentalists alike, alleging regulatory actions to be either too lax or too stringent.

Amid this controversy, many observers have suggested that the United States could achieve its pollution control goals at far less cost. They suggest that regulators, rather than dictating cleanup solutions, should give industries increased flexibility to develop solutions of their own. Not only might this save money, but it would give industries a greater incentive to clean up rather than litigate and might promote the technological innovation necessary to assure continued progress in preventing pollution.

"Emissions trading" gives industry flexibility to develop new control strategies. It has been promoted by the U.S. Environmental Protection Agency (EPA) as a promising means to save money, encourage innovation, remedy weaknesses of existing regulatory programs, speed compliance, and meet the ambitious pollution control objectives of the Clean Air Act. By encouraging a "market" in pollution privileges—allowing industries to lease or sell the "emission reduction credits" they can earn by making their operations cleaner than required by law—emissions trading permits industry to profit from controlling pollution. While appealing on its face, however, emissions trading has proven to be quite controversial, and those promoting it within EPA have had to struggle to keep it alive. The fight over emissions trading illustrates why it can be so difficult to change regulatory policy, why reforms that seem promising on their face can be quite hard to put into practice, and why reforms, like so many government programs, do not always deliver all that they promise.

By tracing the genesis, evolution, and impacts of emissions trading, this report carefully examines the pros and cons of the EPA proposal. A detailed history of the Clean Air Act's implementation since 1970 is provided to demonstrate some strengths and limits of both the existing regulatory approach and emissions trading and to describe the difficulties inherent in trying to reform the existing system by adding emissions trading to it. The conclusions presented here may be disconcerting to the critics and to the supporters of emissions trading. The report downplays some of the critics' concerns about the environmental impacts of allowing certain dischargers to forgo installing some advanced technologies that the Clean Air Act requires. But the report also suggests that some of EPA's statements about the environmental benefits of emissions trading may have led the unsophisticated public to believe that trading spurs additional reductions in emissions; actually, the reductions often are nothing more than administrative recognition of past emission reductions that simply were made in response to conventional regulatory requirements. In many cases, emission trades do demonstrate true environmental or financial benefits, but the legitimacy of emissions trading has been undercut by several emissions trades that EPA initially proposed for approval but later disapproved after environmental groups noted flaws in them.

This report recommends clearer representation by EPA of trading's environmental consequences (a "truth in trading" program), strengthening the information base that is so essential to the sound functioning of both the traditional regulatory strategy and emissions trading, and tightening the rules governing trading. It is better to tighten rules and reduce the number of trades than to have the program's credibility threatened by questionable trades. To its credit, EPA has amended its representations of trading's environmental consequences and is planning to tighten its rules. Nevertheless, controversies are likely to persist, as critics try to restrict trading further.

Because so much time has passed since the start of research on this report in 1980, the risk of accidentally neglecting to acknowledge important contributors to it is enormous. Therefore, I will refrain from listing the several dozen individuals who played a crucial role in production of this report. Some, principally at the U.S. Environmental Protection Agency, provided unimpeded access to their files. Others patiently sat through long conversations, first to educate a novice in Clean Air Act matters, and then to set that novice straight once he thought he had figured everything out. Some sat through even longer sessions because they still hadn't gotten through to him. One individual patiently line-edited lengthy drafts of this manuscript. Several wrote lengthy mini-essays commenting on errors, omissions, and additional problems in earlier versions. Others examined portions of the manuscript, making important suggestions about tone and accuracy. There may still be embarrassing errors in this manuscript, but due to the patient efforts of countless friends, colleagues, professional acquaintances, and interested parties, I know they are fewer than they otherwise would have been.

At The Conservation Foundation, editor Bradley Rymph dramatically improved the quality of the text; Marsha White and Debbie Johnson contributed to its production; and Terry Davies and Gordon Binder made important editorial suggestions.

Many of those who are familiar with earlier drafts of this report should derive considerable satisfaction from the changes made in response to their comments. But there also are those who drew great satisfaction from the first draft's extremely critical view of emissions trading, and these individuals probably will find the muting of this criticism in the final manuscript disconcerting. Proponents of trading may continue to believe that I am insufficiently kind to emissions trading and insufficiently critical of conventional programs for implementing the Clean Air Act.

Some may believe that I have overemphasized some facets of trading at the expense of other more important facets and, as a result, have provided an unbalanced picture of trading's history and impact. But, just as the blind man's perception of an elephant's shape

will depend on the part of the elephant he touches, so too will percep-
tions of trading be shaped by the stake individuals have in both the
existing system and in making emissions trading work, and in their
philosophical views of how the nation's air resources should be managed. Throughout this report, readers will see the very sharp, often
acerbic, differences of professional opinion regarding the impact of
emissions trading. Even if readers disagree with the balance I've struck
in representing trading's pros and cons, I hope that, by the end of
the report, most will have a better understanding of how the Clean
Air Act and emissions trading function and of why emissions trading
has been so vehemently argued over. Of course, the usual disclaimer
applies: I bear sole responsibility for errors of fact and interpretation.

Executive Summary

BACKGROUND

For many years, a pitched battle has raged within and around the U.S. Environmental Protection Agency (EPA) over "emissions trading," a regulatory reform intended to reduce the cost of meeting the national air quality goals established by the Clean Air Act. Emissions trading encourages industries to control pollution more than they are required to, at points where reductions can be achieved most inexpensively, while allowing companies to forgo more expensive reductions that otherwise would be required elsewhere at a facility.

Emissions trading, say its proponents, should reduce costs, encourage innovation, increase cooperation between regulators and the regulated, and promote administrative flexibility—all while helping meet the nation's air quality objectives. To its critics, however, emissions trading poses a threat to the environment, one that allows industries to avoid needed controls and take advantage of loopholes in the regulatory system.

The fight over emissions trading has taken place in the context of growing recognition that it may be increasingly expensive to achieve further reductions in air pollution beyond those already accomplished. Emissions trading is seen by its proponents as a way of promoting additional reductions cost-effectively, at a time when regulators' ability to identify and force reductions is in doubt. Emissions trading is also viewed by its proponents as a means of reducing barriers to modernizing industry, since it should encourage the replacing of older, heavily polluting facilities with relatively cleaner ones.

Critics, however, continue to place faith in relying on regulators to identify new pollution reduction opportunities. They do not regard barriers to new industrial development as being so high and believe that trading will lead to new plants being less effectively controlled than they otherwise would be.

Reforming Air Pollution Regulation: The Toil and Trouble of EPA's Bubble examines the history and impact of emissions trading, focusing principally on the "bubble policy" for existing sources of pollution. The bubble policy allows industry to be excused from pollution controls at one or more emission points in exchange for increasing controls at other emission points—as if all points were placed under an imaginary bubble. The emissions from each bubble must have an impact on air quality equal to or better than the impact of the original controls. The report also examines emissions trading proposals for new and modified sources, including "bubbles" for new sources and "netting" procedures that enable modified sources to avoid some of the Clean Air Act's more onerous requirements.

Much of the controversy in emissions trading has occurred over thorny implementation issues: Are trading proposals legal? What are their consequences for enforcement? Will the proposals, in fact, produce equivalent or better environmental results than existing requirements? What administrative safeguards are necessary to preclude or reduce abuse? What is the appropriate balance between placing constraints on trading to limit abuse and making sure rules are flexible enough to yield the benefits trading should produce?

The fight over emissions trading illustrates how difficult it can be to change regulatory policy, how reforms that seem quite sensible on their face can be quite hard to put into practice, and how reforms, like the promise of so many government programs, do not always deliver all that they claim.

CONCLUSIONS

Reforming Air Pollution Regulation explores the competing arguments for and against emissions trading through case studies of more than a dozen of the approximately 40 bubbles for existing sources proposed for approval by EPA. Drawing also on the research of others, it offers the following conclusions:

1. A few bubbles have reduced pollution more than compliance

with conventional regulatory requirements would have. In many other cases, however, the emission reductions attributed to bubbles appear not to have been the result of the opportunity to trade. Rather, the emission reductions under the bubble merely represent regulators' acknowledgment of companies' past responses to conventional control requirements, where the companies had controlled more than required without the incentive provided by trading.

2. A few bubbles have sped pollution abatement, producing reductions in emissions faster than would have occurred in response to conventional control requirements.

3. Bubbles have produced significant cost savings. Even if one were to discount claims of savings by a 20 to 50 percent "skepticism" factor, the savings have been considerable. This cost-rationalizing element of bubbling is vulnerable to criticism in communities whose ability to meet air quality standards is in doubt, for cost savings have resulted from forgoing previously identified controls that these communities may need to reach the standards.

4. Bubbles have added some useful flexibility to the Clean Air Act's administration even though their environmental benefits and detriments on the whole have been unremarkable.

5. The bubble policy has inspired virtually no technological innovation.

6. The participation of environmental and public interest groups has been vitally important in promoting disapproval of bubbles whose environmental benefits have been misrepresented by applicants. Participation has also encouraged more thorough review and assessment of proposed rules governing emissions trading.

RECOMMENDATIONS

EPA's rules governing bubbles for existing sources have swung from restrictive to permissive. To gain benefits from bubbles and other trading concepts while avoiding some of their worst abuses, a middle-ground approach is EPA's best policy.

As EPA develops the next set of rules, the agency should take certain steps to ensure that (a) emissions trading can continue to help correct problems in the conventional regulatory system and (*b*) short-comings evident in past trades are precluded in the future. Specifically, EPA should:

- tighten trading rules;
- clarify the risks of trading, by providing improved information to the general public about what impact trading might have on efforts to attain national air quality goals;
- systematically monitor and evaluate state trading activity;
- adopt a "truth-in-trading" policy, by disclosing more clearly the actual environmental impacts of trading; and
- improve monitoring of emissions and ambient air conditions.

When it reauthorizes the Clean Air Act, Congress should allow EPA to continue its experiments with emissions trading, including trades for new and modified sources. Even though emissions trading has not yet produced the results that its most enthusiastic promoters once expected, it continues to hold promise as a strategy for promoting more cost-effective pollution control. If, after all the years of regulators' trying to make it work and with evidence that it sometimes does produce results not attainable by conventional approaches, emissions trading were scuttled, Congress would send the wrong signal to would-be innovators in the public and private sectors.

Trading has been the victim of unduly high expectations. While it has produced some notable benefits, a vibrant national market in emission reductions is a long way off. If efforts to foster and improve emissions trading are abandoned, further benefits will be lost.

Glossary

Ambient air quality standard—see *National ambient air quality standard*

Applicability bubble—An emissions trade that permits modified points in a plant to avoid New Source Performance Standards if their increases in emissions are balanced by equal decreases elsewhere in the plant. (An applicability bubble can also be labeled "netting out of NSPS.")

Banking—An administrative system for recording and storing emission reduction credits, designed to facilitate the exchange of such credits among dischargers.

Baseline—The level of emissions from which emission reduction credits are calculated.

Best available control technology (BACT)—An emissions standard applied to major new and modified emitting facilities in areas that have attained the national ambient air quality standard for particular pollutants. BACT standards are supposed to be set on a case-by-case basis and to be at least as strict as New Source Performance Standards. (For a fuller definition of BACT, see box in chapter 2, "Selected Technology Standards of the Clean Air Act," and, for the industry facilities subject to this standard, see box in chapter 5, "Industrial Operations Subject to Permit Requirements of the PSD Program.")

Bubble policy—First issued in 1979, and incorporated later into EPA's Emissions Trading Policy Statement, this policy permits existing stationary sources to use alternative approaches to come into compliance with the emission limits set in state implementation plans. An imaginary "bubble" is placed over the emission points for which the alternative strategy is developed. Under the bubble, companies can control most the points that are cheapest to clean up and control least those that are the most expensive. This alternative combination of emission limits must, in terms of ambient impact and enforceability, be equal to or better than the original emission limits dictated by regulators.

Command-and-control system—The existing regulatory scheme, based on rules that usually apply specific uniform emission limits— generally based on known feasible control technology—to every emission point within a regulated process. These emission limits, generally established by regulators, are "commands" to which dischargers must respond.

Compliance bubble—Similar in effect to the bubble policy for existing sources, the compliance bubble permits new sources of pollution to develop more cost-effective strategies for meeting New Source Performance Standards.

Emission reduction credits (ERCs)—The units used in emission reduction transactions. Dischargers can earn credits for controlling pollution at specific points more than required by regulations and can use those credits in bubble, offset, and netting transactions.

Emission standard—Limit set for the amount of a given pollutant a particular source may emit into the air.

Emissions trading—A supplement to the command-and-control system, emissions trading permits dischargers to receive credits for reducing pollution beyond levels required by regulators at particular emission points. These credits can be used in various forms of emissions trades, such as netting, offsets, and bubbles.

Emissions Trading Policy Statement (ETPS)—EPA's general guidance governing emissions trading, first issued in 1982.

Increment—The increase allowed in concentrations of sulfur dioxide and particulates in areas whose air is cleaner than the national ambient air quality standards for these pollutants. (See *Prevention of Significant Deterioration.*) (See figure 2.3 for a summary of the standards.)

Lowest achievable emission rate (LAER)—The emission standard applied to major new and modified sources of a pollutant in areas that have not attained the ambient standard for that pollutant.

Theoretically more stringent than New Source Performance Standards, LAER is defined in the Clean Air Act as the most stringent emission limit contained in any state implementation plan or achieved in practice. (For a fuller definition of LAER, see box in chapter 2, "Selected Technology Standards of the Clean Air Act.")

National ambient air quality standard—A federal standard that sets maximum levels for concentrations of a common pollutant in the air. Primary standards protect human health; secondary standards protect public welfare (plants, animals, aesthetics). (See figure 2.1 for the current standards.)

Netting—A procedure whereby dischargers can avoid some of the Clean Air Act's most demanding administrative and technological requirements—those triggered by increased emissions from modified points in stationary sources—by taking credit for reductions of emissions from other points within these sources.

New Source Performance Standard (NSPS)—An emission limit applied to new stationary sources. It is supposed to reflect the use of the best demonstrated control technology and to take into account costs, energy requirements, and other factors. EPA sets the standards on an industry-by-industry basis. (For a fuller definition of NSPS, see box in chapter 2, "Selected Technology Standards of the Clean Air Act," and, for a list of industries for which standards have been set, see box in chapter 5, "Sources Subject to New Source Performance Standards.")

Nonattainment area—An area dirtier than the national ambient air quality standard for a given pollutant.

Offset policy—Rules that allow a new or expanding major pollution source in a nonattainment area to be sited. The operator of a source arranges to eliminate emissions from existing sources by an amount greater than the emissions added by the new or modified source. This "offsetting" of new emissions by reductions in existing emissions allows economic development even while an area continues to reduce its pollution.

Prevention of Significant Deterioration (PSD)—Program that protects areas cleaner than the national ambient air quality standards for a given pollutant, by limiting the amount of pollutants new sources may emit. (See *Increment.*)

Reasonably available control technology (RACT)—The emission standard usually applied to existing stationary sources of a pollutant in an area that has failed to attain the national ambient air quality standard for that pollutant. RACT represents the emission limit a particular source is capable of meeting by applying control technology that is reasonably available considering technological and economic feasibility. (For a fuller definition of RACT, see box in chapter 2, "Selected Technology Standards of the Clean Air Act.")

State implementation plan (SIP)—A plan prepared by a state, for the approval of EPA, that outlines strategies for achieving the national ambient air quality standards. If a state plan is inadequate, EPA is authorized to promulgate an adequate plan.

Volatile organic compounds (VOCs)—Substances that can contribute to formation of ozone. Reductions in VOC emissions are central elements of state and local strategies to attain the national ambient air quality standard for ozone.

Chapter 1

Understanding the Basics

At first glance, the emissions trading policy proposed by the U.S. Environmental Protection Agency (EPA) seems to make great sense. By giving industries increased freedom in choosing how they comply with the Clean Air Act, without compromising the statute's environmental goals, it appears to be an appealing regulatory reform promising more innovative, cost-effective control of air pollution.[1] Unlike earlier pollution control efforts that relied exclusively on regulators' technological judgments and dictates, emissions trading rewards dischargers of pollutants who find new, inexpensive ways of reducing their emissions. Those dischargers receive credits when they reduce pollution beyond the levels required by regulators at particular emission points and can use those credits to relax their obligations to abate pollution at other points. If they choose, dischargers can sell or lease their credits to others to assist them in meeting their obligations.

Economists and policy analysts long have contended that development of a market in emission credits will foster more efficient solutions to the nation's air quality problems by encouraging companies to find less expensive means to meet environmental standards. The companies might even reap a profit from cleaning up more than regulations require. Advocates of emissions trading have argued further that this decentralized search for solutions to air quality problems will speed compliance, encourage innovation, and reduce incentives for industries to litigate environmental requirements.

1

Beneath emissions trading's apparent logic, however, have lain many disturbing questions about its actual effects and the motives for its advancement. One of the proposal's principal critics has charged that it has "been twisted primarily into a polluters' charter for evading emission control responsibilities" and has become "a positive obstacle to solving the pollution problems of . . . cities with unhealthy air."[2]

THE ECONOMIC RATIONALE FOR EMISSIONS TRADING

Emissions trading finds its intellectual roots in the economic literature on transferable discharge permits for pollution control.[3]* The literature on these permits is substantial,[4] so only a brief description of the relevant economic theory is offered here.

The costs of reducing pollution differ from source to source. Yet, because the time and money available for obtaining detailed information about those variations is limited, regulators who use the traditional "command-and-control" approach toward dischargers of pollutants cannot take cost factors into account very well when they are fashioning strategies for meeting environmental goals.† Regulators often make judgments about control strategies on the basis of incomplete information, based at best on analyses of just a few plants and technologies. Moreover, regulators may be heavily dependent on the polluting industries themselves for information about costs, and the industries have every incentive to overstate costs so as to encourage regulators to adopt weak standards. Increasing those incentives to withhold information from regulators is the understandable fear among plant managers that, if they do discover alternative emission-abatement methods that are less expensive than the methods dictated by regulators, their companies could be forced to implement the new approaches *in addition to* those demanded by

*Most conventional regulatory systems assign industries permits indicating the amount of pollution they are allowed to discharge. These permits are specific to individual sources and cannot be shifted to other sources. Transferable discharge permits, in contrast, can be shifted from one industry to another, thereby allowing one industry to shift its pollution allowance to another.

†"Command and control" is policy analysts' shorthand for a system of government regulations that requires industries or other regulatees to act in a way determined by regulators.

regulators. Because of these information problems and fears, spending under "command-and-control" approaches may be greater than is necessary to achieve environmental goals.

By overcoming some of these obstacles, transferable discharge permit systems can promote more cost-effective pollution control. Within boundaries established by regulators to assure achievement of environmental goals, emissions trading encourages companies that can control most cheaply to do so, knowing they can profit from performing better than standards require by selling or holding for future use the emission reduction credits (ERCs) they accumulate. Other companies are likely to purchase ERCs when the credits are cheaper than the abatement processes the purchasers would otherwise have to install. These transfers can reduce the total cost to society of achieving environmental goals.

The cost-effectiveness of any transferable permit system will be limited by the constraints placed on trades by regulators. These may be a response to concern that trades may produce overly high concentrations of pollutants in some places and to the need for regulators to monitor and enforce emission reductions subject to trades. How well the market for ERCs functions will also depend on the availability of information, numbers of buyers, numbers of sellers, and amounts of credits sought and for sale.[5]

A BRIEF OVERVIEW OF TRADING PROPOSALS

Emissions trading proposals come in many different forms. These have emerged, one by one, in response to special circumstances of diverse programs established by the Clean Air Act. Their distinctive roots make understanding their relationship to one another—their similarities and differences—that much more difficult.

To comprehend some of the debates over trading requires mastery of an exceedingly specialized vocabulary, one that can be quite confusing even to cognoscenti. To make matters more difficult, this vocabulary, which includes such terms as *bubbles, netting, offsets,* and *banking,* is layered on top of an already complex vocabulary of acronyms and standards derived from the original Clean Air Act. The following paragraphs introduce the major terms of emissions trading. The remaining acronyms and standards of the Clean Air Act are introduced in chapter 2.

Bubbles

EPA's bubble policy* derives its name from the placing of an imaginary bubble over multiple emission points of pollutants. The level of emissions allowed from the one opening in the imaginary bubble is the sum of the emissions that would result from placing traditional controls on individual points under the bubble. The company operating the points is then free to adjust the level of control among the individual points so it can reach that sum at least cost.† It has the opportunity to control most the points that are the cheapest to clean up and to control least those that are the most expensive.‡ As the company reduces discharges more than is required at some points, it earns ERCs that can be applied against other points where controls will be less stringent. The company's savings can be substantial. For example, if using methods traditionally dictated by regulators to reduce total emissions at a facility from 100 tons to 60 tons would cost a company $5 million, the company might be able to achieve the same reductions in emissions by using an alternative approach that cost only $3.5 million (figure 1.1).

In theory, the bubble's flexibility provides a powerful incentive for companies to develop new, less costly means of pollution control or to find the least expensive mixes of readily available control technologies and production changes. Presumably, plant managers know their plants more intimately than do regulators and thus have better senses of where novel abatement opportunities lie.

Originally, EPA developed the bubble policy for use in regulating existing sources of pollution. In the last few years, however, EPA has tried to expand the concept to new sources of pollution. Under bubble policies it has adopted for new sources in some industries,

---

*The "bubble policy" for existing sources once was a discrete statement of EPA policy, but it was later merged into an "emissions trading policy statement" that included principles for bubbles, netting, offsets, and banking.

†Only emissions of the same pollutant can be traded. For example, increases in sulfur dioxide can be traded only for decreases in sulfur dioxide and not for decreases in particulate matter or nitrogen dioxide. Moreover, the ambient impact of these changes—their impact on concentrations of the pollutant in the air— must be equivalent.

‡To ensure the revised limits are enforceable by regulators, the new emissions limits for individual points under the bubble are supposed to be incorporated into a new permit for the company's facility.

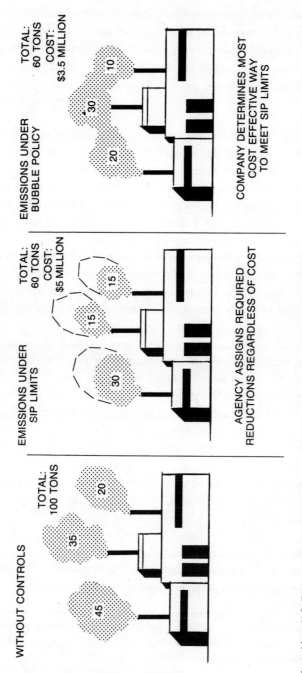

Figure 1.1
EPA's Bubble Policy for Existing Sources

Adapted from U.S. Environmental Protection Agency, *Controlled Trading: How to Reduce the Cost of Air Pollution Control* (Washington, D.C.: U.S. Environmental Protection Agency, 1981), p. 5.

EPA has written emission standards for groups of emission points rather than for individual points. It has also considered, but not yet adopted, general principles for new source bubbles and has proposed approving a bubble that revises the emission standards for a new power plant in Illinois.

Netting

Among the most demanding administrative and technological requirements of the Clean Air Act are those triggered by increased emissions from modified points in sources. However, a company can avoid or reduce these requirements when it compensates for those increases by reducing emissions from other points within that source and thereby earning ERCs. Because this trading approach causes the net emissions from the entire source to stay at the same level as they were before the modifications, it is commonly known as *netting*. For example, if modification of one point in a source would increase that point's emissions by 100 tons per year, and such an increase normally would require a control technology that removed 98 percent of the emissions at that point, the company might be able to avoid installing the control technology—and to save some money—by reducing emissions by 100 tons at another point within the source. Although, in some cases, the company might still have to install some emissions control at the point of increase, it would not necessarily be to the level specified by the otherwise-applicable emission standard.

Netting and the bubble are conceptually similar, in that increased controls at one point are traded for decreased controls at another. However, the bubble initially was developed to ease the obligations of companies to reduce emissions from existing sources. Netting, in contrast, was intended to reduce the administrative and pollution reduction obligations of sources being modified.

Offsets*

In regions of the country where the total amount of emissions from existing sources must be reduced to meet national ambient standards†

---

*This report does not discuss the offset policy as fully as other elements of emissions trading. For a more in-depth treatment, see the companion report, Richard A. Liroff, *Air Pollution Offsets: Trading, Selling and Banking* (Washington, D.C.: The Conservation Foundation, 1980).

†Ambient standards specify permissible concentrations of pollutants in an area's air. These standards are distinguishable from emission standards, which govern the amount of pollution allowed from particular points.

for air quality, current trading policies allow industries to construct new or modified major sources of pollution if they offset those sources' emissions by reducing emissions from existing sources by even greater amounts (figure 1.2). In other words, industries can construct those sources if they can generate ERCs from their own existing sources or acquire ERCs that other dischargers of pollutants have earned for reductions they have made in the area.

This offset policy differs from netting in several respects. First, it applies to both new and modified sources, not solely to modified sources. Second, it was developed originally for areas whose air is dirtier than ambient standards, whereas netting operates in areas both cleaner and dirtier than the ambient standards. Third, netting merely requires existing emissions to be reduced by amounts equal to new emissions, whereas the offset policy requires existing emissions to be lowered by an amount greater than the new emissions added.*

Banking†

The transfer of ERCs from one discharger of pollution to another is facilitated by another major component of EPA's emissions trading policy, banking, which allows ERCs to be recorded in a central administrative ledger for future use in the same area. The ledger usually is maintained by state or local air pollution control officials. If a company that has earned ERCs chooses, its credits can be purchased or leased by another discharger of the same pollutant for use in a bubble or offset transaction. By giving geographically proximate industries ready access to confirmed credits so that the companies do not have to search widely for them, ERC banks may facilitate emissions trading. The banks may also encourage companies to reduce their own emissions, since they may believe that the credits they could earn would be more readily marketable than would be the case without a bank.

Other Trading Approaches

Trading has developed or been suggested for specific industries, independent of EPA's formal emissions trading policy. For example, a special system for trading "lead rights" has been established to help refiners comply with Clean Air Act requirements that they reduce

---

*Chapter 5 discusses additional distinctions between netting and offsets.

†This report gives limited attention to banking. For a fuller discussion, see Liroff, *Air Pollution Offsets*.

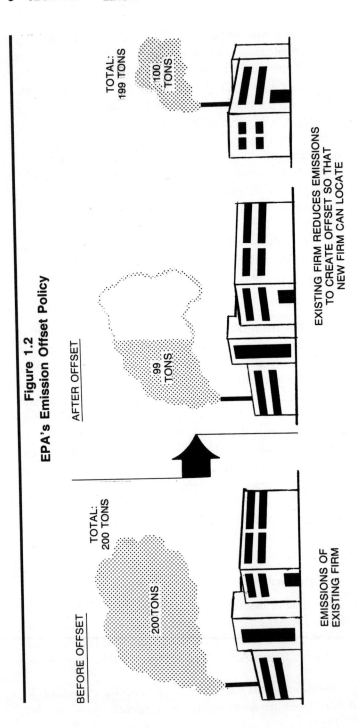

Figure 1.2
EPA's Emission Offset Policy

BEFORE OFFSET

TOTAL: 200 TONS

200 TONS

EMISSIONS OF EXISTING FIRM

AFTER OFFSET

99 TONS

EXISTING FIRM REDUCES EMISSIONS TO CREATE OFFSET SO THAT NEW FIRM CAN LOCATE

TOTAL: 199 TONS

100 TONS

Adapted from U.S. Environmental Protection Agency, *Controlled Trading: How to Reduce the Cost of Air Pollution Control* (Washington, D.C.: U.S. Environmental Protection Agency, 1981), p. 5.

lead in gasoline,[6] and averaging of emissions from several classes of car and truck engines (that is, trading of emissions among those classes) has been proposed to promote compliance by manufacturers with emission control requirements for new trucks and automobiles.[7] Emissions trading reportedly can reduce the cost of programs proposed to reduce acid rain; emission limits can be established on a state-by-state basis, and industries can agree on the most cost-effective reductions under such statewide bubbles.[8] Trading has also been proposed by EPA in its new "tall-stack rules" as a means for utilities to reduce the costs of compliance.[9] These rules would forbid utilities from using extra-tall stacks to avoid emission reduction requirements. The common denominator of nearly all these additional applications of trading is the desire of regulators to lessen the financial impact of regulations. Trading enables industries to reduce their emissions in a more cost-effective manner.

WHY THE FUROR?*

Many regulators and environmentalists fear that emissions trading could undermine the existing regulatory system and retard progress toward cleaner air. They have challenged proponents of trading, including many reform-minded regulators, who contend that increasing flexibility for dischargers would not necessarily be inconsistent with continuing progress toward clean air. The pro-trading forces argue that trading could improve the existing system and speed progress toward attaining current national ambient air quality standards.

Differing Philosophies

Just beneath the surface of many of the disputes over legal, technical, administrative, and environmental aspects of emissions trading lie fundamentally different philosophical views of what should be society's commitment to reducing air pollution. To some, pollution is morally wrong. They view clean, breathable air as a commodity that cannot or should not be priced and believe that public health and welfare should not be left dependent on the whims of the marketplace. In their eyes, emissions trading might, in the name of efficiency, unfairly or inappropriately redistribute the burden of pollution abatement. But to others, pollution control is more a resource management problem. They contend the existing regulatory system acknowledges

---

*The points made in this section are explored more fully in chapters 3-5.

that some pollution is acceptable and believe procedures must be developed to reduce pollution to those socially acceptable levels in a more cost-effective manner.

One political scientist, Brian Cook, interviewed opponents and proponents of emissions trading and found that, for some persons, trading proposals "raise problems of equity and distributive justice, . . . raise questions about who ought to own objects valued by society, . . . [and] raise the issue of how value ought to be assigned to social objects."[10] Cook found that disagreements over political and philosophical concerns were more vigorous than those over implementation issues and that conflicts over implementation issues were most intense when they most reflected underlying philosophical concerns.

Implementation Issues

In addition to philosophical disagreements, several implementation issues have also contributed to the furor surrounding emissions trading proposals. A basic comprehension of those issues is necessary before one can effectively understand why trading has been so controversial.

Fixing the System—Minimalist and Expansionist Approaches

Proponents and opponents of trading have tangled over a wide range of implementation issues. A major focus of disagreements is the amount of flexibility states have, subject to EPA oversight, in developing and revising "state implementation plans" (SIPs) to attain the ambient standards. These plans require industries to reduce their emissions. A related source of controversy is the credibility of the plans, even those that have received EPA approval. SIPs are only as good as the assumptions underlying them, and considerable room exists for technical disagreements about the assumptions. Because the plans contain inventories of industries' emissions and emission reduction strategies targeted at them, these documents are, in a sense, accounting mechanisms. Accounting accuracy is essential to the smooth operation of both the existing command-and-control system and emissions trading. The poor quality of many inventories and the questionable validity of many planning assumptions yields heated disputes over whether emissions trading should be permitted in many areas. Both proponents and critics of emissions trading agree that problems in inventories and assumptions make the command-and-control system flawed, but they disagree on the role emissions trading can play in remedying the defects.

The arguments over the role of state plans in implementing emissions trading suggest that proponents of trading, within and outside EPA, might conveniently be labeled "command minimalists." Command minimalists, primarily officials on EPA's Regulatory Reform Staff, tend to emphasize that states have considerable flexibility in developing air management strategies and that EPA has exercised its oversight responsibilities as fully as the Clean Air Act requires. The minimalists acknowledge that state plans are problematic. But they contend that the requirements of EPA-approved plans should be deemed appropriate bases for trading, until EPA formally reverses itself and determines that state plans are, in fact, inadequate. These reformers contend that regulators should define "stopping points"— regulatory requirements they will not tighten—that provide firm bases on which industries can rely in making trading decisions.[11] They claim that, if these bases are established, industries will have an incentive to identify new abatement options, without fear of having these new ones added to, rather than substituted for, existing ones. Industries will then propose cost-effective bubbles, thereby improving inventories in state plans and helping the nation to achieve the Clean Air Act's goals more quickly.[12]

Command expansionists, including officials in EPA's air programs office* and environmentalists in organizations like the Natural Resources Defense Council generally agree that the existing regulatory system is flawed. They recognize that emissions trading may have a role to play in improving inventories and other elements of the existing regulatory system. But expansionists contend that, unless the rules governing trading are fairly strict, they will only enable industries to "game" regulators. That is, industries will use trading opportunities to exploit weaknesses in state plans. Expansionists tend to use information from proposed trades as evidence of a need to tighten existing regulations and to deny industries that propose trades any benefits from them.†

---

*There is no EPA "Air Programs Office," per se. References in this report to the air programs office are to those several offices within EPA administering Clean Air Act programs and reporting to EPA's assistant administrator for air and radiation.

†Expansionists also take a broad view of EPA's authority vis-a-vis the states, suggesting that EPA can be more demanding of states than minimalists contend.

Expansionists might concede that, by urging the disapproval of many trades proposed by industry, they might discourage trading. But, rather than lamenting the loss of prospective trades, expansionists more likely would view them as "abusive" efforts by dischargers to take advantage of the system's flaws. Expansionists claim that they only want to make sure that EPA does not, by acceding to industry requests, unintentionally encourage dischargers to misuse trading. Minimalists respond that, if EPA structures its trading policy so that limits are placed on the rewards industries can reap through trading proposals or so that industries coming forward with new proposals end up with even tighter regulatory requirements, industry proposals probably will dry up and increased cost-effectiveness, improved state implementation plans, and other benefits from trading will be destroyed.

Expansionists agree with minimalists that it is useful to provide industries with incentives for developing cost-effective abatement techniques, but expansionists are much less forthcoming with such incentives than minimalists are. Expansionists tend, for example, to oppose giving industries rewards for emission reductions that "would have happened anyway" for business reasons. Especially in areas that have not attained the national ambient standards, expansionists support only trades that promise to produce new reductions in emissions, as opposed to mere adjustments on paper of emission reduction requirements. Expansionists view many of these adjustments on paper—labeled "paper credits"—as methods for avoiding controls that actually might be needed to attain ambient standards. Reluctant to concede any stopping points to regulation, expansionists see industry-identified control options as supplements to, rather than substitutes for, existing requirements.

Expansionists often are reluctant to approve of trades that are consistent with EPA-approved state plans for attaining national ambient standards. They argue that the plans frequently are flawed and that the ambient standards will not be met as states project. Minimalists, by contrast, tend to assign greater credibility to the state plans. Arguing that EPA-approved state plans are the recognized legal basis for abatement obligations, minimalists suggest that so long as trades are consistent with state plans, they should be acceptable, even if (a) they are mere paper adjustments of requirements or (b) even if they reflect abatement actions that industries still would have taken in the absence of the trading opportunity.

Legality

Because of federal court interpretations of the Clean Air Act, whose complex language governs emissions regulations, some trading policies may be illegal. If the Clean Air Act's provisions require the reduction of emissions from a particular point, for example, it may be illegal for regulators to allow a company to avoid that requirement, even if an equivalent reduction could be achieved more cheaply elsewhere. EPA's ability to permit companies to avoid having to meet emission standards for particular points by grouping those points with others for regulatory review depends on whether the language of the Clean Air Act forces EPA to insist on those standards' application at those individual points.

EPA must constantly bear in mind how courts might view any rules it makes for trading. In drafting the Clean Air Act, Congress did not use such terms as *source, plant,* and *facility* clearly or consistently in telling EPA which points should have controls applied to them. As a result, environmentalist, industry, and EPA litigators have tangled many times over just what those terms mean.[13]

Federal appellate judges have made herculean but largely unpersuasive efforts to reconcile appeals court opinions that sometimes have approved trading and other times have not. The result has been great uncertainty over the legality of trading policies. But, in June 1984, the U.S. Supreme Court declared that, since Congress was ambiguous in drafting the Clean Air Act, EPA should have substantial administrative discretion to decide which points to regulate.[14] This decision lifted much of the pall the appeals courts had cast over trading. Nevertheless, if EPA continues to attempt novel applications of emissions trading, legal battles surely will follow.

Technology Forcing

Trading's critics fear that its netting component would permit some sources of pollution to modify and expand without having to be as tightly controlled as they would be with more traditional approaches to pollution control. The permissiveness behind netting runs directly counter to a basic component of those traditional approaches, "technology forcing," a complex set of techniques designed to force dischargers to use advanced technologies on major new and modified sources of pollution. Technology forcing is intended to allow ambient standards to be met in both the short and long terms and to reconcile them with continued economic development.*

The arguments over technology forcing have provoked numerous claims and counterclaims. Proponents of netting advance three basic arguments. First, the standards for major new and modified sources are so costly that they discourage new investment and encourage dischargers to continue using dirtier old facilities. This may interfere with attaining the ambient standards in the short term. Second, nationwide the contribution of major new and modified sources of pollution to areas failing to meet ambient standards is slight, so that allowing those sources to avoid the most technologically stringent standards makes little environmental difference in the short term; attaining ambient goals requires cleaning up or closing down the far more numerous existing sources. Third, the most stringent emission standards that a netting source would avoid are, in practice, no more stringent than emission standards to which the source would remain subject, so netting would not in practice have a significantly adverse environmental impact.

Netting's critics reply to these arguments as follows: First, investment decisions are based on many factors, so it should not be assumed that new facilities are discouraged simply by the environmental standards that would be applied to them. Second, so long as ambient standards are unmet, human health is threatened, so *both* new and old sources should be strongly regulated. Third, if additional emissions from new sources are allowed in areas where ambient standards are being violated, older sources must be regulated that much more stringently to attain the ambient standards.

Enforcement

Because of their novelty, dischargers' trading plans may place particularly great administrative burdens on regulatory personnel. The

---

*In theory, economic development will not threaten air quality in the future, because new and modified plants will be tightly controlled and will replace substantially dirtier older plants.

plans may require considerable scrutiny because they require operating procedures to which regulators are not accustomed; they may
also pose unusual monitoring and enforcement problems. In addition, critics worry that, by allowing dischargers to seek additional
compliance time to develop bubble proposals for problem facilities,
recalcitrant polluters may be given further opportunity to drag their
feet in abating emissions. Proponents argue that, rather than undermining the integrity of the regulatory system by making enforcement more difficult, trading proposals can help disclose information
useful to improving it. For example, trading proposals may provide
new data on how well pollution control devices are working in practice. Moreover, contend those proponents, specific trading plans may
be accompanied by innovations in monitoring and enforcement, and
monitoring and enforcement safeguards can be written into permits
governing proposed trades.

Credit Calculating

Another factor that complicates the merging of trading policies into
the existing regulatory system is the difficulty that exists in determining what emission decreases should qualify for ERCs. Disagreements over calculating credits are a major component of the conflict between minimalists and expansionists. One of the most disputed
matters is the definition of the "baseline" from which to calculate
decreases in emissions—whether it should be some existing administrative requirement, some variation on that requirement, or a discharger's historic emissions level. Critics say that selecting an inappro-
priate baseline might have adverse environmental consequences,
because credit might be given at one point for emission reductions
that exist only on paper, thereby allowing otherwise forbidden emissions elsewhere and squandering an opportunity to clean the air. For
example, a state plan might assume a plant operates at full capacity
and allows some point to emit 100 tons per year. But, if the plant
has never operated at full capacity and has never emitted more than
80 tons per year at the point, the 20-ton difference might be used
by the plant owner to avoid cleaning up 20 tons of actual emissions
from another point. In such a case, actual emissions from the plant
would increase as a result of the trading opportunity.

The baseline issue also arises in a second context. A state plan
might require a plant owner to install a pollution control device to
meet a 60-ton-per-year emission limit, even though the regulators

and the plant owner expect that the device will never emit more than 40 tons per year. The extra 20-ton-per-year reduction, not developed in response to the trading opportunity but having occurred in response to the conventional regulations, might be used by the plant owner to avoid a 20-ton-per-year abatement obligation at another point. Critics contend that if this extra 20-ton reduction beyond requirements occurred as a result of standard industry pollution reduction practice, no credit should be given for it, and it should not be used to avoid control requirements elsewhere.

Proponents respond that, even if using a particular baseline would permit avoidance of otherwise applicable requirements, trades should be approved when their baselines are consistent with existing administrative strategies for achieving ambient standards in an area.

Credits for shutdowns of facilities are as hotly contested as baselines. In fashioning trading proposals, regulators have found it difficult deciding whether ERCs should be available for shutdowns. Critics of emissions trading argue that liberally granting credits for curtailments or shutdowns of factories near the end of their useful lives could reduce substantially the obligation of those building major new and modified facilities to employ advanced technologies and to minimize new emissions far into the future. In the words of one prominent critic, "A plant which has but five years of life left and curtails emissions by 100 tons per year nevertheless generates a 100 ton credit that lasts forever."[15] Critics also contend that, since most shutdowns would occur anyway for economic reasons, no ERCs to industry should be given for them; the cleaner air from the shutdowns simply should benefit the public. Proponents respond that, if regulators have not relied on reductions from such shutdowns in their local plans for attaining the ambient standards, then credits should not be denied. In their eyes, a pound of pollution is a pound of pollution, regardless of how it is eliminated from the air, and giving credits for shutdowns encourages earlier shutdown of older polluting facilities.

In addition, regulators have been concerned with other questions that would automatically follow a decision to grant ERCs for shutdowns: how many years should such credits (as well as those from other sources) remain available for use, and should the value of credits awarded in one year be "discountable" in future years to promote attainment of national ambient standards? Regulators do not want to create too concrete a "property right" in emissions credits, one that would require that a company be compensated if the value of its ERCs was reduced. However, the more regulators limit the long-term value of credits, or increase uncertainty about their value, the less companies may wish to employ emissions trading.

Environmental Impact Modeling and Other Administrative Requirements

Another implementation issue arises from the need to assess the environmental equivalence of trading proposals. Regulators must decide what procedures dischargers must follow to demonstrate that the combination of increases and decreases proposed under a bubble will not harm the environment or endanger human health. Some pollutants (for example, the organic compounds that contribute to smog) add to a regional air quality problem but without identifiable effects in a small local area. For those pollutants, regulators usually do not demand sophisticated modeling* of air quality impacts, so trades may be relatively easy to execute. But, for pollutants that have significant localized effects, such as sulfur dioxide and particulates, the impact on air quality must be modeled to assure that individuals downwind from the points of increase are not subjected to significantly higher or more harmful levels of emissions. Substantial modeling may be required where the points involved in trades are very far apart and where the heights of the points involved in the trades differ.

Regulators' decisions on such technical matters will determine how great an administrative burden will be placed on dischargers. The heavier the burden of proof, the costlier the demonstrations of equivalence, the more substantial the monitoring requirements—all these will reduce the cost savings available through trading and, hence, its attractiveness.

Intergovernmental Relations and Interstate Equity

Trading proposals raise questions about intergovernmental relations and interstate equity. One issue is how free from EPA's guidance and review state regulators should be in their efforts to implement

---

*Modeling is a mathematical technique for predicting ambient air pollutant concentrations resulting from specific emissions. Starting with information on meteorology, terrain, and present air quality, the effect on the ambient air of adding or changing a source of air pollutants can be predicted.[16]

trading. Critics wary of trading have sought to maintain considerable federal oversight of trades approved by states, while proponents have tried to reduce such oversight because it can be cumbersome.

Another concern is the possibility that trading involving new and modified sources would reduce the uniformity among states that nationally established technology-based standards are intended to provide. Critics of trading and many state officials stress the importance of uniform emission standards, so that states will not use relaxed environmental requirements as a means for competing for new industry. But proponents of trading note that many such standards are set on a case-by-case basis and, even where the standards are uniform, states may have widely varied but not readily documentable attitudes about how strictly such standards will be enforced.

ASSESSING EMISSIONS TRADING

Emissions trading should not be assessed solely in absolute terms (that is, how it works in practice against how it is supposed to work in theory). If one were to judge emissions trading solely by how it is supposed to work in theory, it would be easy to find substantial shortcomings. But it is also true that, if one were to assess the existing command-and-control system by comparing theory to practice, similar shortfalls would be easy to find. It is more appropriate to assess emissions trading in relative terms: how much does it enhance or undercut achieving the environmental goals of the existing system? Assessing emissions trading by examining its interplay with the existing system helps identify its strengths and limits in practice and also helps identify problems common to both approaches that must be remedied to provide sounder management of the nation's air resources.

Chapter 2

The Clean Air Act— Implementation Problems and the Rise of Emissions Trading

The Clean Air Act is the basic statute governing the United States's national effort to maintain and improve air quality. Originally enacted in 1963 and amended substantially in 1970 and 1977, it mandates an action-forcing regulatory strategy directed toward achieving pollutant-specific national ambient air quality standards by specific dates.[1] Those standards specify maximum allowable concentrations of common pollutants in the air, with any levels above the standards considered threats to public health and welfare. The act both provides for cleaning up regions that fail to meet those standards and protects from significant future deterioration areas whose air is already cleaner than the standards, particularly large national parks and wildernesses.[2]

The Environmental Protection Agency (EPA) published its initial ambient air quality standards in April 1971. Since then, both it and the states have worked diligently to meet them. As specified in the Clean Air Act, the states are supposed to develop pollution abatement programs to achieve the standards.[3] EPA reviews, approves, and financially assists those state programs. If a state fails to act or develops an inadequate program, however, EPA can withhold federal aid for the state air pollution control program, for highway construction and for construction of sewage treatment plants.[4] EPA also can ban awarding of permits for construction of major new and modified sources of the pollutant for which an area has not attained the standard. In addition, EPA can produce its own plan for an area.

EPA also establishes national technology-based emission standards for new sources of pollution and for modifications of existing sources.[5] States are expected to use these standards as they establish and administer their programs. These standards are supposed to be much stricter than standards for existing sources and are intended to dictate the use of advanced control technologies. In theory, not only do these standards encourage advances in such technologies by providing a government-mandated market, but, as noted previously, they also help reconcile future economic development and environmental quality goals. The EPA standards also preclude states from competing with each other for new industry by using weakened emission standards as a lure.

State programs under the Clean Air Act typically incorporate some basic elements:

- inventorying of emission sources and monitoring of air quality for the purpose of planning pollution control strategies;
- issuance of permits to existing sources specifying permissible levels of emissions and, if reductions are necessary, dates by which reductions must be achieved;*
- monitoring of sources' compliance via inspections, reviews of records, or sampling of emissions and fuels;
- enforcement action against noncomplying sources; and
- review and permitting of proposed new sources of pollution.

The Clean Air Act is a typical command-and-control statute. EPA and the states tell dischargers, usually in great detail, how pollution should be abated. Considerable discretion is left by EPA to the states, although states often rely heavily on federal recommendations on how reductions in emissions could be achieved.† What flexibility

---

*In planning to achieve the national ambient standards for ozone, carbon monoxide, and nitrogen dioxide, states benefit from strict federal emission standards for new cars and trucks.

†If they choose, state and local governments are free to establish requirements stricter than those imposed by the federal government. Some states and cities have chosen to exercise that option, although other states' legislatures have forbidden their environmental regulators from being any tougher than EPA requires.

dischargers have under the existing system derives from their negotiations with regulators over the form and stringency of proposed emission standards.

IMPLEMENTING THE CLEAN AIR ACT, 1970-1976

National ambient air quality standards were established initially for sulfur dioxide, carbon monoxide, nitrogen dioxide, particulates, hydrocarbons, and photochemical oxidants.[6] Since then, a standard has also been established for lead, and the standard for photochemical oxidants has been revised and changed to a standard for ozone, the principal component of smog. The standards are somewhat complex (figure 2.1). For some substances, two different standards have been set: primary, to protect the public health, and secondary, to protect the public welfare as measured by effects of pollution on vegetation, materials, and visibility.

After EPA published its initial ambient air quality standards, state governments had nine months to prepare state implementation plans (SIPs) describing how the primary standards would be met by the statutory deadline of mid-1975. SIPs were developed for 247 planning areas, "air quality control regions," into which the United States was divided. In theory, to devise an ideal, cost-effective plan for each region, a state would have had perfect knowledge about all emission sources in the region, about the relationship between emissions from those sources and ambient air quality in the region, and about the costs of control and technologies available for reducing emissions. The state could then have processed that information and devised economically efficient programs for achieving ambient standards in each region.

The reality, however, was far from the ideal. Critics of the Clean Air Act have noted that devising an economically optimum implementation plan in nine months "would have taxed [even] a large, well-prepared, and technically first-rate organization."[7] Those critics have further noted that most state agencies were neither large nor technically very expert, did not have relevant data readily available, and were required to make some gross judgments about the need for reductions in emissions from stationary sources to reduce ambient levels of pollutants.[8] Often, using data provided by existing monitors of ambient conditions, state agencies estimated the percentage reduction in emissions needed to achieve a national ambient

Figure 2.1
National Ambient Air Quality Standards

Pollutant	Primary (health-related)		Secondary (welfare-related)	
	Averaging time	Concentration	Averaging time	Concentration
Particulates	Annual geometric mean	75 µg/m³	Annual geometric mean	60 µg/m³
	24-hour	260 µg/m³	24-hour	150 µg/m³
Sulfur dioxide	Annual arithmetic mean	(0.03 ppm) 80 µg/m³	3-hour	1,300 µg/m³ (0.50 ppm)
	24-hour	(0.14 ppm) 365 µg/m³		
Carbon monoxide	8-hour	(9 ppm) 10 µg/m³	None	
	1-hour	(35 ppm) 40 µg/m³		
Nitrogen dioxide	Annual arithmetic mean	(0.053 ppm) 100 µg/m³	Same as primary	
Ozone	Maximum daily 1-hour average	0.12 ppm (235 µg/m³)	Same as primary	
Lead	Maximum quarterly average	1.5 µg/m³	Same as primary	

These standards are further categorized for long- or short-term exposure. Long-term standards specify an annual or quarterly mean that may not be exceeded; short-term standards specify upper limit values for 1-, 3-, 8-, or 24-hour averages. With one exception, the short-term standards are not to be exceeded more than once per year. That exception is the standard for ozone, which requires that the expected number of days per calendar year with maximum hourly concentrations exceeding 0.12 parts per million be less than or equal to one.

Source: U.S. Environmental Protection Agency, *National Air Quality and Emissions Trends Report, 1983* (Research Triangle Park, N.C.: U.S. Environmental Protection Agency, Office of Air Quality Planning and Standards, April 1985), pp. 2-1, 2-2.

standard. Then, reviewing their inventory of existing emissions, they developed combinations of technology-based requirements for reductions of emissions from existing sources. With limited capabilities to model the impact of sources' emissions on ambient air quality, and with only rough indications of existing air quality from monitoring stations of uncertain reliability, states had to employ crude, simplifying assumptions as they established limits on emissions and devised plans to achieve the national ambient air quality standards. As a result, controls on individual sources may have been either tighter or looser than was necessary to achieve the ambient standards.

There were political factors at work also. In cases where considerable popular pressure for pollution control existed, states may have adopted some unduly stringent control requirements. In areas where the pressure was less intense, there may have been undercontrol, especially where state agencies had limited resources and where industry was in a good position to negotiate abatement requirements.

As state governments completed their SIPs, the plans had to be submitted to the EPA administrator for approval or disapproval. As the administrator made his decisions, both industry and environmentalists filed large numbers of lawsuits. Industry was inclined to believe either that unduly strict plans had been approved or that sufficiently strict plans had been disapproved, while environmentalists believed that unduly lenient plans were approved when they should have been disapproved.[9]

As part of its implementation of the Clean Air Act, EPA began developing two trading proposals that would serve as forerunners to the emissions trading policy. For one, EPA began work in the early 1970s on New Source Performance Standards (NSPSs), industry-by-industry standards for new and modified sources of pollution. (A box, "Selected Technology Standards of the Clean Air Act," compares NSPSs and the other technology-based standards of the Clean Air Act.) It was in the context of a suggestion in 1972 that smelters be allowed to net out of NSPSs that conflict over emissions trading began.[10] (See box, "Evolution of EPA's Emissions Trading Policies.") The controversy, described more fully in chapter 5, culminated in a court ruling that declared that netting out of NSPSs, at least in the manner EPA defined for the smelting industry, was contrary to the Clean Air Act's purposes.[11] This decision cast a shadow over subsequent trading proposals.

Selected Technology Standards of the Clean Air Act

Lowest Achievable Emission Rate (LAER). Theoretically the most stringent of the emission standards listed here, this standard applies to new and modified major sources of pollution in nonattainment areas. As defined in Section 171(3) of the Clean Air Act, 42 USC 7501(3), LAER is the rate of emissions which reflects (a)the most stringent emission limit contained in the implementation plan of any state for a category of sources, unless the owner or operator of a proposed source demonstrates that this limit is not achievable, or (b)the most stringent emission limit achieved in practice by a class of source. The most stringent of these two alternatives is applied to the proposed new source subject to LAER. LAER must be at least as stringent as a New Source Performance Standard that might otherwise apply to a proposed new source. LAER determinations are made on a case-by-case basis.

Best Available Control Technology (BACT). This emission standard applies to new and modified major sources proposed for PSD areas. As defined in Section 169(3) of the Clean Air Act, 42 USC 7479(3), BACT means an emission limit based on the maximum degree of reduction of emissions, taking into account energy, environmental, and economic impacts, and other costs. BACT must be at least as stringent as a New Source Performance Standard that might otherwise apply to a proposed new source. BACT is theoretically less stringent than LAER, because it gives greater weight to economic impacts. BACT determinations are made on a case-by-case basis.

New Source Performance Standard (NSPS). This emission standard applies to new and modifed sources. As defined in Section 111(a)(1) of the Clean Air Act, 42 USC 7411(a)(1), an NSPS reflects the emission limit achievable through the use of the "best technological system of continuous emission reduction which . . . has been adequately demonstrated." In setting an NSPS, the EPA administrator must take into consideration the cost of achieving the emission reduction, along with non-air-quality health and environmental impacts and energy requirements. NSPSs are established by EPA on a category-by-category basis.

Reasonably Available Control Technology (RACT). This emission standard applies to existing sources in areas that have not attained the national ambient air quality standard for a particular pollutant. RACT has been defined by EPA as representing the lowest emission limit that a particular source is capable of meeting by the application of control technology that is reasonably available considering technological and economic feasibility. EPA has prepared, or is in the process of preparing, industry-specific Control Technology Guidance documents. Focusing on industries emitting the volatile organic compounds that contribute to ozone, the documents contain the emission standards that EPA believes reflect RACT. If states deviate from these EPA recommendations in their state implementation plans, EPA expects the states to document their reasons for doing so. The guidance documents for various industry categories notwithstanding, EPA recognizes that RACT standards should be set on a case-by-case basis for individual sources. Theoretically, RACT standards are the least stringent of those listed here.

Second, when many areas of the country failed to meet the Clean Air Act's mid-1975 deadline for attaining ambient air quality standards, EPA started formulating its "offset policy."[12] This policy allowed major new and modified sources of emissions to site in areas where the standards were not met (labeled "nonattainment areas"*). It thus enabled EPA to avoid imposing politically unpopular bans on the construction of major new and modified sources of pollution. To obtain permits to construct major new sources and modified sources, companies had to find ways to use very advanced technologies that produced the "lowest achievable emission rate" (LAER) ("Selected Technology Standards" box) at those sources and also had to offset whatever additional emissions still resulted. LAER standards were expected to be more stringent than any NSPS established for a source, the rationale being that tough demands should be imposed on anyone wishing to add potentially large amounts of new emissions to areas whose air quality is considered a risk to human health and welfare. As a result, regulators were not expected to give much consideration to cost factors as they established LAER standards.[13]

THE 1977 AMENDMENTS AND THEIR IMPLEMENTATION

In 1976 and 1977, Congress considered major revisions to the Clean Air Act and, after lengthy hearings and heated floor debate, enacted them into law in August 1977.[14] The wide-ranging amendments included extension of the deadlines for achieving the national ambient standards to 1982 and, in some circumstances, to 1987.[15] Existing sources in nonattainment areas were obliged, at a minimum, to apply "reasonably available control technology" (RACT) ("Selected Technology Standards" box). RACT standards were expected to represent "the lowest emission limit that a particular source is capable of meeting by the application of control technology that is reasonably available considering technological and economic feasibility."[16] RACT standards could be less demanding than the NSPS and LAER standards for new sources. Theoretically, RACT was supposed to be set on a case-by-case basis for individual sources. In practice, however, both EPA's RACT guidelines and states' RACT regulations often have

---

*"Nonattainment" is determined on a pollutant-by-pollutant basis. An area may be designated "nonattainment" for ozone, but "attainment" for sulfur dioxide. Most nonattainment areas are violating the ozone standard. Some areas are "nonattainment" for more than one pollutant.

Evolution of EPA's Emissions Trading Policies

1971 EPA publishes initial NSPS rules; no netting provided.

1974 EPA's initial PSD regulations allow netting in attainment areas by defining many sources as "plants."

1975 EPA adopts revised NSPS rules; some netting allowed. Industry and environmental groups file suits.

1976 EPA promulgates emissions offset policy for major new and modified sources in nonattainment areas.

1977 Congress amends Clean Air Act, modifying EPA offset policy and PSD program.

1978 In *ASARCO, Inc.* v. *Environmental Protection Agency*, D.C. Circuit panel rules against netting allowed by EPA in its NSPS regulations.

EPA issues revised PSD rules, allowing limited netting for modified sources in attainment areas. Industry and environmental groups file suits.

1979 EPA issues revised offset policy and rules for nonattainment areas; allows netting only in areas having EPA-approved SIPs. Manufacturing Chemists Association files suit.

EPA proposes "alternative emission reduction option", a bubble policy for existing sources subject to SIPs.

In *Alabama Power Company* v. *Costle*, D.C. Circuit panel

holds netting opportunities should be broadened in attainment areas.

EPA issues "final" bubble policy for existing sources, liberalizing proposal issued earlier in year.

1980 EPA reorganizes staff, brings separate "bubble" and "offset" staffs together in one office. EPA-convened regulatory reform conference airs grievances about obstacles to wider use of trading.

Responding to *Alabama Power* ruling, EPA revises PSD rules, broadening netting in attainment areas. But its revised rules for nonattainment areas disallow netting, even in areas with approved SIPs.

1981 Outgoing EPA Administrator Costle issues press release announcing liberalization of bubble policy for existing sources.

EPA approves New Jersey's "generic bubble" rules, making it easier for existing sources to use bubbles.

EPA redefines "source" in nonattainment areas, thereby allowing greater use of netting. Natural Resources Defense Council files suit.

1982 EPA publishes proposed interim Emissions Trading Policy Statement setting out general principles for bubbles, offsets, and netting; further liberalizes trading rules.

In *Natural Resources Defense Council* v. *Gorsuch*, D.C. Circuit panel holds that EPA's redefinition of *source* in nonattainment areas violated Clean Air Act. Court opinion outlaws netting in nonattainment areas.

1983 EPA solicits public comment on rules governing trading in nonattainment areas lacking approved SIPs.

EPA issues NSPS rules allowing "compliance bubble" for tape and label coating industry. No suits filed.

1984 In *Chevron, U.S.A.* v. *Natural Resources Defense Council*,

U.S. Supreme Court reverses D.C. Circuit's *NRDC* v. *Gorsuch* decision, and criticizes D.C. Circuit for second-guessing EPA's interpretations of Clean Air Act.

1985 A "fourth draft" of a "final" Emissions Trading Policy Statement, to replace 1982 interim policy, circulates for review within EPA.

1986 EPA Administrator Lee Thomas decides major emissions trading issues. "Final" Emissions Trading Policy Statement scheduled for publication in the *Federal Register* in mid-year.

been issued on an industry-by-industry basis. These practices have led to disputes over emission trades using RACT as a baseline (see chapters 3 and 4).

The amendments required states to develop revised SIPs for nonattainment areas by January 1, 1979. Failure to meet that deadline would have meant federal sanctions, such as a ban on the construction of major new and modified sources of air pollution.[17] The states were somewhat better prepared for this planning exercise than they had been six years earlier, when they had to submit their original SIPs to EPA, because of the increased experience they had gained. But they also were considerably understaffed and once again were under enormous time pressure.[18] EPA, for its part, faced a considerable political backlash if it applied sanctions broadly. So EPA readily approved many plans and constructed the concept of "conditional approval" to give states additional time to remedy many deficiencies. The National Commission on Air Quality, established by Congress to assess implementation of the 1977 amendments and to make recommendations for further amendments, eventually reported that EPA accepted virtually all of the states' projections that they would meet air quality standards—even though officials at all levels of government acknowledged privately that the projections "often were based on imprecise emission inventories, inadequate projection techniques and, in general, were overly optimistic."[19]

The inadequacy of emission inventories in many states was highlighted by a consultant to the National Commission on Air Quality, who found that outdated and unverified emission inventories were used repeatedly in state plans; much of the unverified data originated directly from industrial sources.[20] The same consultant also noted how the stringency of abatement requirements for sources depended heavily on the models state regulators used in their planning. For example, in Ohio, plans were developed for reducing emissions in eight cities. As figure 2.2 shows, two different analytical techniques were used to calculate the percentage reduction in emissions required to achieve the ambient standard for ozone for each of those cities. With one exception, the technique selected for use in the state's plan for each city was the one that required the least amount of emission reductions. The consultant added that it was reasonable to believe that other areas of the country made similar choices among analytical techniques.

These differences in abatement requirements, so dependent on the model used by regulators, underscore the fictional nature of SIPs. As products of scientific uncertainty and administrative accommodation, assumptions and calculations may have only the most tenuous relationship to actual air quality and emissions, and projections of attainment may be worth little, despite the dedicated hard work of the regulators who prepare them.

This uncertainty about state plans has been a major contributor to emissions trading controversies. As discussed more fully in chapters 3 and 4, those most critical of emissions trading, worried about phantom reductions and threats posed to attainment, have looked askance at using many SIPs as bases for calculating emission reduction credits. Proponents of emissions trading, in contrast, have argued that, if a plan projects attainment and has been approved by EPA, it is appropriate to use that plan as the basis for such calculations. Trading advocates claim that the roughness of those plans can itself justify using emissions trades to adjust control requirements, suggesting that it makes sense, first, to employ more cost-effective alternatives and, later, to use more expensive controls if they are needed.

Another feature of the 1977 amendments was their elaboration of a detailed program for Prevention of Significant Deterioration (PSD) of air quality in regions designated as attainment areas.[21] The

Figure 2.2
Percentage of Reductions Required in Emissions of VOCs,
Based on Analytical Techniques
Selected for Ohio Implementation Plans

City	Technique 1[1]	Technique 2[2]	Technique selected
Cleveland	67%	50%	1
Akron	35%	18%	2
Toledo	47%	25%	2
Columbus	43%	25%	2
Canton	22%	10%	2
Youngstown	64%	44%	2
Dayton	61%	40%	2
Cincinnati	40%	50%	1

1. Known as "EKMA."
2. Known as "Rollback."

Source: Adapted from Pacific Environmental Services, *Study of the 1979 State Implementation Plan Submittals* (Elmhurst, Ill.: Report prepared for U.S. National Commission on Air Quality, December 1980), p. 7-12.

program was established on a pollutant-by-pollutant basis. The amendments themselves defined the permissible "increments" (increases) in sulfur dioxide and particulate concentrations (figure 2.3) and left it to EPA to define the limits for other common pollutants.* (This program is described in greater detail in chapter 5.)

When EPA issued regulations in 1978 implementing the PSD program, some observers worried that modifications to existing plants would be able to avoid both the PSD program's administrative requirements and the program's new technology-based standard, known as "best available control technology" (BACT), by taking credit for reductions in emissions elsewhere within those existing plants. Once again the issue was resolved in the courts. This time,

*EPA's program for the other pollutants has languished.

Figure 2.3
Allowable Increases in Concentrations of Sulfur Dioxide and Particulates in Attainment Areas with Comparisons to National Ambient Air Quality Standards

Pollutant	Maximum allowable increases			NAAQS	
	Class I	Class II	Class III	Primary	Secondary
Particulate matter					
Annual geometric mean	5	19	37	75	60
24-hour maximum*	10	37	75	260	150
Sulfur dioxide					
Annual arithmetic mean	2	20	40	80	—
24-hour maximum*	5	91	182	365	—
3-hour maximum*	25	512	700	—	1,300

All figures are in micrograms per cubic meter.
* Short-term maximums may be exceeded no more than once per year.

Source: Committee on Prevention of Significant Deterioration of Air Quality, Environmental Studies Board, Commission on Natural Resources, National Academy of Sciences. *On Prevention of Significant Deterioration of Air Quality* (Washington, D.C.: National Academy Press, 1981). p. 8.

unlike the decision a year earlier involving NSPSs and smelting, netting was found permissible.[22] The reviewing court concluded that, in the PSD program, Congress was interested in technological improvement primarily in regard to construction of new sources, not in regard to existing sources whose changes produce no increase in emissions. Thus, the court said, netting was an appropriate element in determining whether modifications subject to PSD requirements had occurred.

The "bubble policy" for existing sources was another product of EPA activity designed to implement the 1977 amendments. The policy, first published in January 1979, was intended to promote cost-effective pollution control in the newly revised SIPs. Beginning in 1980, the many trading policies for different types of sources—offsets, netting, bubbles, and banking—converged into an EPA program initially labeled "controlled trading." This was renamed "emissions trading," and EPA worked to develop an integrated set of trading principles. An interim Emissions Trading Policy Statement was published in mid-1982. As of January 1986, because of a host of controversies, EPA had not yet published a final version of the statement.

ACCOMPLISHMENTS AND OUTSTANDING PROBLEMS

The Clean Air Act was enacted at a time when skepticism of industry concern for the environment was rampant, when the federal government was often called on to solve major national social problems, and when environmental problems seemed much simpler than they do today. The act emphasized government-developed solutions and downplayed the importance of economic considerations because Congress feared that industry would advance claims of infeasibility and expense as an excuse for foot-dragging.

Times have changed, and the hopes and ambitions of the early 1970s have become the missed deadlines and hard realities of the late 1970s and the 1980s. More and more observers have noted the limits of the command-and-control approach, the need for greater concern with cost-effectiveness, and the usefulness of giving industries more positive incentives to develop control strategies. Even though the 1982 deadline for compliance with the national ambient air quality standards has passed, Congress has failed to adopt comprehensive new amendments to the Clean Air Act that would legislatively modify that deadline and make other needed changes. EPA has developed some clever interim strategies for working with states that failed to meet the deadline and has begun working on programs for areas that received an extension of the deadline to December 31, 1987, but are likely to miss it. Yet the agency still lacks definitive guidance from Congress on future strategies for cleaning the nation's air and on how emissions trading should figure in them.

The command-and-control system of the Clean Air Act does have significant accomplishments to its credit. EPA estimates that emissions of several conventional pollutants have either declined or held steady despite increased activity in polluting sectors of the economy; major U.S. cities continue to benefit from cleaner, less unhealthful air, at least with respect to the pollutants for which standards have been set.[23] These conclusions about progress and the regulatory system's role in reducing emissions are not universally accepted, however. Both EPA's emission estimates and the index for measuring air quality in large cities are problematic, and critics of the command-and-control system are eager to credit energy conservation, reliance on cleaner fuels, and economic downturns as significant contributors to environmental progress.[24]

One clear problem that cannot be overstated is the complexity of the regulatory system that EPA implements, particularly with respect to the review of new and modified sources. For example, a single proposed industrial project may be subject simultaneously to requirements of the offset, PSD, and NSPS programs if the project would emit large amounts of pollutants for which ambient standards have been set and the area where it would be located exceeds some of the standards and not others.* If the project would emit organic compounds (contributors to ozone), sulfur dioxide, and particulates and the area were nonattainment for ozone, the project would be obliged to meet the LAER standard and to offset the remaining ozone-forming organic compounds it would emit. Even if it were to net out of the LAER and offset requirements, the project still would be obliged to apply NSPS technology to its emissions, since netting out of NSPS is not allowed. If no NSPS had been developed for the emission points in question, they might still be obliged to satisfy some less demanding abatement requirement.

If the same project's proposed site had attained the ambient standards for sulfur dioxide and particulates, the project's emissions also

---

*Although this example is an extreme one, to be sure, it illustrates the plethora of requirements a proposed project could encounter.

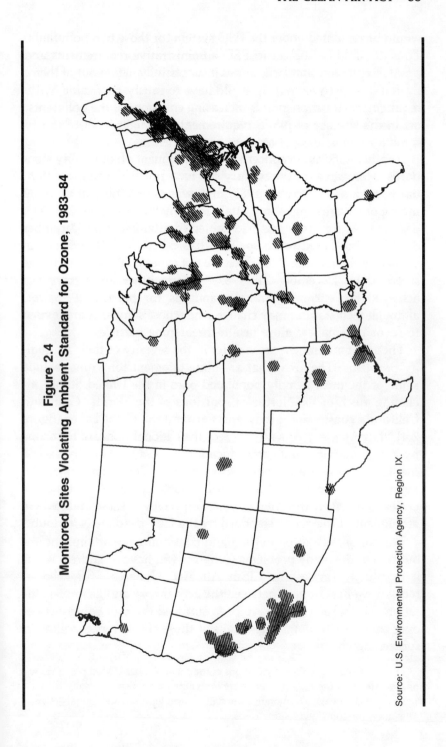

Figure 2.4
Monitored Sites Violating Ambient Standard for Ozone, 1983–84

Source: U.S. Environmental Protection Agency, Region IX.

would be regulated under the PSD system for those two pollutants. Thus, it could be subject to PSD administrative requirements and a BACT emission standard, unless it successfully netted out of them. Even if it were to net out, it would have to satisfy applicable NSPS requirements for those points increasing emissions of the pollutants, or, in the absence of NSPS requirements, it might have to satisfy some less-demanding abatement requirement.

Another continuing concern is nonattainment of air quality standards. Many areas of the country still have not achieved those standards, and, as of October 1985, EPA was estimating that up to 32 metropolitan areas might not attain them by the December 31, 1987, deadline. As for areas that had projected attainment by December 31, 1982, but failed to do so, EPA has called for SIP revisions in 16 metropolitan areas, 7 of which are not expected to meet the ozone standard by December 31, 1987.[25] Many other areas have not achieved the current national standards for particulate matter, although their statuses may change when those standards are revised to focus on smaller, more health-threatening particles.[26]

These nonattainment areas differ in the severity of their air quality problems. The areas that are nonattainment for ozone include some of the most heavily populated ones in the United States, including much of the Northeast, portions of the Florida, Gulf, and California coasts, and urban areas around the Great Lakes (figure 2.4).* Los Angeles frequently exceeds the national standard for ozone by a high margin, while other locations across the country exceed the standard less often and by a lesser degree.[27] Continuing nonattainment problems in heavily populated regions fuel efforts by trading's critics to restrict netting and bubbles, especially in those areas where attainment of the ozone standard by the 1987 deadline is in doubt.

The complexity of permitting and continuing nonattainment are but two of the many problems Congress will have to address when it eventually revises the Clean Air Act. Congress will need to recognize a host of gaps between the act's theory and its implementation. Many such gaps have been surfaced through controversies over emissions trading. The details of those controversies follow in succeeding chapters.

*Figure 2.4 shows monitored violations of the ozone standard. Most places showing violations on the map probably are designated administratively by EPA as "nonattainment areas." The monitored nonattainment locations and formal designations may not coincide in some cases.

Chapter 3

The Evolution of the Bubble Policy for Existing Sources

As the Environmental Protection Agency (EPA) has worked to make the bubble policy for existing sources the centerpiece of its efforts to promote emissions trading, it has had to cope with considerable controversy both within and outside the agency. Within, the policy has been the principal vehicle for regulatory reformers who recognize the limits of the command-and-control system and seek a way to promote innovation and eliminate cost-ineffective elements of state implementation plans (SIPs). Those reformers, however, have faced challengers in EPA's air programs office who fear that the bubble policy will undermine enforcement efforts, interfere with attainment of the national ambient air quality standards, and place additional administrative burdens on regulators. Outside EPA, the regulatory reformers have had to struggle to overcome a wide variety of misgivings: the initial reluctance of state regulators to take on added, unfamiliar responsibilities while still coping with EPA's conventional regulatory demands; initial wariness by businesses that suspected EPA of using trading as a means of further tightening regulatory screws; and persistent claims by environmentalists that trading creates huge holes in the regulatory safety net.

In developing the bubble policy for existing sources, EPA has had to balance frequently competing objectives as it has felt its way, often making policy judgments with uncertain technical foundations. In that process, EPA has sought to uphold the integrity of the existing regulatory system while providing enough flexibility for businesses to have an incentive to advance bubble proposals. Perhaps the most significant concern in recent years has been the use of bubbles in nonattainment areas that may not meet the extended statutory deadline of December 31, 1987, for achieving the national ambient air quality standards, and in areas that had expected to meet the December 31, 1982, deadline for attainment but did not.*

The agency has also focused on such questions as:

- What baselines should be used for calculating additions and reductions, and what relationship should those baselines have to the "reasonably available control technology" (RACT) standards that are supposed to be met by existing sources in nonattainment areas?
- Should a polluter who is currently subject to an enforcement action be eligible to use a bubble for compliance, and, if so, under what conditions?
- How much proof, in the form of modeling and monitoring data, should sources have to provide to demonstrate that their bubble strategies are environmentally equivalent to conventional control strategies?
- What conditions should be imposed on bubbles to assure that they are as enforceable as conventional control strategies?
- What minimum conditions should state rules for bubbles be required to meet to reduce the need for federal reviews of individual bubble proposals approved by state regulators under those rules?

The major trend in EPA's policies issued between 1979 and 1982

---

*The emphasis placed in this chapter on two types of nonattainment areas—those that expected to meet the 1982 deadline and did not, and those that may not meet the 1987 deadline, is a simplified representation of more complex circumstances. There are many, finer distinctions among SIP situations—for example, areas that have never projected attainment by 1987, areas that project attainment by 1987 but whose projections are suspect, areas that originally projected attainment by 1982 but that failed to carry out their adopted plans, and areas that projected attainment by 1982 but whose fully implemented plans proved to be inadequate.

was broadened eligibility of areas and dischargers for trading. On one hand, this trend caused an increase in the number of bubbles being proposed, provided empirical evidence of some of trading's benefits, and underscored some of the gaps between the theory and the practice of the command-and-control system. On the other hand, however, it contributed to criticisms that bubbles undercut enforcement, interfere with prospects for attaining and maintaining air quality standards, and enable dischargers to exploit gaps in the command-and-control system. Since 1982, when it issued an interim Emissions Trading Policy Statement (ETPS) that took effect immediately, EPA has been grappling with development of a final policy.* Conflicts over bubbles proposed and approved under the liberal 1982 policy have been quite heated. A final policy still had not been issued as of early 1986, in part because of the controversies. The final policy, now expected to be released in mid-1986, will tighten the rules for trading.

This chapter traces the evolution of the bubble policy for existing sources, from its genesis in the late 1970s, through the interim Emissions Trading Policy Statement, to the current controversies that have delayed publication of the ETPS in final form. The chapter does not focus on specific bubble applications but traces the political and bureaucratic history of trading and selected arguments made by its supporters and critics. Because some of the competing sides' arguments are rather abstruse, particularly those over baselines, chapter 4 examines the bubble policy in practice in an attempt to make these ethereal arguments more tangible.

THE GENESIS OF THE BUBBLE POLICY, 1977-1978

The bubble policy evolved from the desire of some EPA officials and some companies to find less expensive ways for existing dischargers of pollutants to comply with the requirements of SIPs. The earliest proposals for bubbles for existing sources were floated around 1977. Within EPA, they were pushed by the Office of Planning and Management in parallel with efforts to promote trading under the offset policy.† Outside EPA, they were advocated by Armco Inc., a steel company.

---

*As noted in chapter 1, the "bubble policy" for existing sources was subsumed in the Emissions Trading Policy Statement issued in 1982.

†One of the Office of Planning and Management's principal responsibilities is evaluating and suggesting improvements in EPA's programs.[1]

The domestic steel industry had been targeted by EPA for a special enforcement effort. In 1977, EPA had identified steel producers, along with utilities and smelters, as especially lagging in their compliance with Clean Air Act requirements;[2] nearly half of the emission sources in the steel industry were in violation of applicable standards.[3] The steel industry's record was later noted by *Business Week*: "The industry has fought the air and water cleanup regulations every inch of the way, and it has increased its costs substantially by postponing compliance in a time of swiftly rising prices."[4]

At the time, however, the steel industry was financially troubled because of foreign competition and many other factors. Government actions allegedly had contributed to the industry's decline, so a special interagency task force (the Solomon committee) had been established in 1977 to review federal policies. As part of an administration-wide effort to respond to the committee's December 1977 report, senior EPA and steel industry officials held several meetings in early 1978.*

In those and other meetings, Armco promoted a bubble for its Middletown, Ohio, steel mill. The company, which had a better environmental reputation than many other steel companies, wanted to forgo expensive controls on particulates from some of its facilities and to substitute inexpensive controls on particulate matter blown from unpaved roads and storage piles.[6] Armco claimed that it could save millions of dollars in capital and operating costs, while reducing particulate emissions beyond levels required by conventional regulations.†

Many concerned parties greeted the bubble concept with skepticism. Environmentalists and many officials of EPA's air program‡ feared the bubble's adverse consequences for enforcement, because the idea was being promoted by an industry that had fought many battles with EPA over environmental regulations. Environmentalists

---

*Although the Solomon committee had not urged a major relaxation of environmental requirements, topics discussed by EPA and the industry included ambient air quality standards, SIP revisions, compliance dates and penalties, and the bubble.[5]

†Chapter 4 discusses the details of Armco's bubble.

‡One of the principal skeptics within EPA was David Hawkins, EPA's assistant administrator with responsibility for air quality programs. Hawkins had been an attorney with the Natural Resources Defense Council before he was appointed to his EPA position by President Carter. He returned to NRDC after leaving EPA.

viewed the bubble idea as a political statement that EPA was backing down on regulatory requirements and expected the states to follow suit. The Natural Resources Defense Council (NRDC) was particularly disturbed by EPA's consideration of the bubble concept. In a May 1978 letter to EPA Administrator Douglas Costle, NRDC suggested that, were a bubble policy to be adopted, it should incorporate rules to assure its enforceability.[7] NRDC worried about administrative burdens resulting from bubbles. It suggested that, unless a source proposing a bubble bore the full cost of review and monitoring, many states would be pressured either to provide a lax review or to divert resources for a more thorough review from existing enforcement efforts.[8]

Many state regulators also were uneasy with the bubble concept. Some regarded the idea as coming at a particularly inopportune time, when states were busy updating, revising, and tightening their SIPs for nonattainment areas. Others believed that they already had the authority to use bubblelike approaches, if they so chose, and they preferred not to have yet another set of EPA directives, including federal review of individual bubble proposals, placed on them.

In mid-1978, EPA established a task force to assess the feasibility of the bubble concept and to suggest an approach for implementing it. The task force's principal criteria for evaluating the bubble concept included legality, enforceability, environmental acceptability, and economic efficiency.[9] The impact of the bubble on sources' existing obligations to abate their pollution was an especially important concern for several reasons: many areas had failed to attain standards, sources' noncompliance with obligations was a major contributor to nonattainment, and revised SIPs would be making further demands on many sources.

In its September 1978 report, the task force recognized that bubble proposals ought not to hinder those enforcement efforts that were already under way, particularly in states where SIPs then in effect were being revised. The task force noted concerns that bubble proposals would open to litigation matters that were not then litigable and that the most recalcitrant sources might propose bubbles to escape tough requirements they had repeatedly sought to avoid. In response to those concerns, the task force recommended that only sources currently in compliance with existing SIPs or on a compliance schedule be eligible to bubble their emissions.

For bubble proposals to be environmentally acceptable, the task force said, they should cause neither increased total emissions nor deteriorated air quality.[10] Undesirable tradeoffs, such as compensating for increases in hazardous pollutants with decreases in nonhazardous ones, should be precluded. There should also be constraints on the trading of emissions between emission points of different heights, because of differing ambient impacts, and limits should be placed on trading among several categories of particulates. (See box, "Controlling 'Hazardous Substances' and Judging Environmental Equivalence of Control Strategies.")

The task force concluded that the bubble concept, while permitting continued stringency in environmental control, could provide industry with an incentive to innovate and that such innovations could be the basis for more rigorous control efforts in the future. Moreover, the task force believed that industry efforts to identify novel control opportunities could help state regulators improve their inventories of emission points.[11] The task force suggested a series of limits on bubble proposals to ensure their legality, enforceability, and environmental acceptability.

Although the task force's report endeavored to demonstrate that NRDC's concerns could be addressed through appropriate regulatory safeguards, NRDC was not appeased.[12] In a letter to EPA, NRDC contended that states were already able to use the bubble under some provisions of the Clean Air Act, had not used it, and, therefore, had reservations about the concept. NRDC concluded by stating that the bubble was "more likely to call forth innovations in evasion than in technology."[13]

Some EPA staff, particularly those in the air programs and enforcement offices shared a concern expressed by NRDC that the steel industry would use an EPA endorsement of the bubble concept to undermine state and local regulatory efforts. In a June 1978 meeting with the steel industry, EPA officials had contended that they would not encourage states to revise existing regulations to permit bubbles unless EPA received assurances that the industry would not use such changes to slow compliance.[14]

After the task force completed its work, the dispute over the bubble continued within EPA. The policy could have been applied to many industrial sources, but debate within the agency focused heavily on the steel industry. Those wary of the policy contended that no assurances had been received from that industry and that any policy issued by EPA would be seen as a political statement aligning EPA

Controlling "Hazardous" Substances and Judging Environmental Equivalence of Control Strategies

The Clean Air Act provides for special treatment of substances labeled as "hazardous." Under Section 112 of the act, EPA is required to list such substances and establish national emission standards (but not ambient standards) for them. EPA, however, has listed and set emission standards for very few substances under Section 112.

Some compounds that might be controlled under Section 112 are members of families of substances for which national ambient and emission standards have been set under other sections of the Clean Air Act. As discussed in chapter 2, emission standards have been set for volatile organic compounds (VOCs) that contribute to ambient levels of ozone and for the particulates that contribute to ambient levels of particulates. But these standards often do not take into account the different degrees of risk to environmental quality and human health caused by the different substances that can be classified as VOCs or particulates. (A revision in the national ambient standard for particulates, proposed in 1984, would recognize that larger particles are less risky to human health than smaller particles, but it has taken years to move toward this revision, and disagreements continue over whether the distinction it makes among different sizes of particles is appropriate.)

The bubble policy and the Emissions Trading Policy Statement, in their myriad forms, have repeatedly referred to the importance of "equivalence" in trades. But, because existing conventional strategies to control VOCs and particulates mix so many different substances in undifferentiated fashion into these two large categories, it is difficult to judge precisely the environmental equivalence of bubble and conventional control strategies. Assessing the environmental risk of allowing VOCs or particulates to be traded under a bubble at a particular plant depends on the specificity and accuracy of emission inventories, models, and other elements of the existing regulatory strategy. States with good emission inventories accustomed to making fine distinctions among emissions are in a better position to evaluate equivalence than are states with poor inventories that are less accustomed to distinguishing among different types of organic compounds and particulates.

with the steel industry's efforts to ease its compliance obligations.[15] Looking back on the underlying reasons for this opposition within EPA, Michael Levin, the current head of the Regulatory Reform Staff,* has commented:

[The bubble proposal] evoked massive resistance from the agency's Air Programs and Enforcement offices, [which had] large investments in the status quo, direct accountability to suspicious environmentalists, and perspectives formed by past dealings with recalcitrants.[16]

---

*The Regulatory Reform Staff is a component of EPA's Office of Planning and Management. It was created in late 1979.

EPA'S BUBBLE POLICY PROPOSAL—JANUARY 1979

EPA published its proposed bubble policy in the *Federal Register* in January 1979, about the time states were supposed to be submitting their revised SIPs to the agency. The document, titled "Recommendation for Alternative Emission Reduction Options within State Implementation Plans," reflected the tug-of-war within EPA between bubble proponents and opponents.[17] It indicated that the agency had decided to give great weight to concerns about enforceability and the equivalence of trades, even if that meant reducing the number of trading opportunities.

EPA invited comment on the entire proposal, explicitly stating its interest in the resource burden that final adoption of the policy might place on state air pollution control agencies and inquiring whether the administrative costs of the bubble would outweigh its benefits. EPA also encouraged the states to be receptive to individual bubble requests. The agency argued that SIPs were less economically efficient than they might be and that savings from the bubble were one of the few positive incentives available for innovation.[18]

The proposed policy's terms indicated that, while EPA reformers had prevailed in having a policy issued, the agency's traditionalists had successfully made sure that the conditions under which bubbles would be permitted would be quite stringent. The objectives of the Clean Air Act were not to be compromised in any way. EPA insisted that several air quality- and enforcement-related conditions be satisfied.

First, all air quality standards were to be met. The bubble would only be available in states having approved SIPs projecting attainment of standards by statutory deadlines. Emissions could not be increased, and, if air quality would be adversely affected by controlling one point less and another more, then the trade could not be approved. Regulated industries would be responsible for quantifying emission changes and demonstrating that their proposed alternative emission reduction plans would be equivalent to standard plans in pollution reduction, enforceability, and environmental impact. The more unusual a proposed alternative, the more detailed the demonstration of air quality equivalence would have to be.[19] All demonstrations would have to be paid for by the discharger.

Second, the pollutants traded under any alternative proposal would have to be comparable. Trades could not be made among different pollutants for which national ambient air quality standards had been set (for example, particulates could not be traded for sulfur dioxide) and, within those categories of pollutants, those with different health or ambient air impacts could not be traded against one another. Thus, carcinogenic particulates could not be traded against noncarcinogenic ones, nor could hydrocarbons designated as hazardous be traded against other hydrocarbons. Further, emissions from open dust sources like roads and storage piles could not be traded against industrial-process emissions.* EPA contended that industrial process emissions differed in character from road dust and that open dust sources did not contribute significantly to ambient concentrations. Moreover, because of the difficulty of calculating emission rates from open dust sources and modeling their impact on ambient air quality, acceptable demonstrations of equivalency were effectively precluded.

Third, bubbles would not be able to replace existing SIP provisions. The bubbles would be treated as *alternative* SIP provisions— that is, as additions to a SIP—and would have to undergo federal review. By treating the bubbles as alternatives to, not replacements of, existing SIP provisions, regulators could continue to enforce the existing SIP provisions even if the new ones were not approved or were delayed. Where SIPs were being revised by states because the ambient standards had not been attained, companies would be able to propose a bubble in anticipation of new limits being proposed in a revised SIP.

Fourth, each emission point would have to have a specific emission limit tied to enforceable testing techniques.

Fifth, no noncomplying source would be allowed to submit a bubble proposal. Sources that had thus far deferred compliance would not be given an additional opportunity to defer compliance until a bubble was approved. Sources would have to be in compliance, on a compliance schedule, or subject to a court decree specifying compliance deadlines.

Sixth, existing compliance dates would not be extendable. To ensure that the policy would not be abused, sources proposing bubbles would have to agree in writing not to seek either stays of compliance with existing requirements or avoidance of sanctions if bubbles were delayed, disapproved, or otherwise not made effective.[20]

---

*This condition, had it remained in effect, would have outlawed Armco's proposed bubble.

Finally, no delays of existing enforcement actions would be allowed. States would be expected to continue to seek compliance with the requirements of existing SIPs as expeditiously as possible. This requirement, like the others related to enforcement, was meant both to make continued unlawful pollution less likely and to reduce the benefits that might accrue to sources from their continuing noncompliance.

Despite these attempts by EPA's regulatory reformers to accommodate the agency's internal skeptics and external critics, NRDC, joined by the Sierra Club Legal Defense Fund, continued to have reservations about the bubble concept.[21] NRDC again noted that the bubble policy had been proposed by the steel industry and that the industry was using EPA endorsement of the bubble to promote eased implementation requirements at the state level. NRDC preferred that EPA not adopt the policy but, if the agency were to adopt it, add even more conditions to it.

Environmentalists were not alone in their concerns about the political implications of EPA's endorsement of the bubble concept. In a December 1978 letter to EPA Administrator Costle, Harry Williams, the head of the State and Territorial Air Pollution Program Administrators (STAPPA) and director of Indiana's air pollution control program, commented that the timing of the bubble proposal "was extremely poor."[22] He stated that that was the consensus of the 29 states represented at a STAPPA meeting at which a draft of the bubble proposal had been presented. Williams said that many of the states "are strongly of the opinion that industry may utilize the proposal to 'force' changes to revised SIPs at a very inopportune time." He added that the states had serious staffing problems that might be compounded by a bubble policy.

Williams, while noting that many states supported the bubble as a concept, reiterated his concerns at a March 1979 public hearing.[23] It was the considered opinion of many of the 24 states responding to a questionnaire on the bubble proposal that the states already had used the bubble concept "to a degree" in their existing SIPs and that the timing of the EPA proposal was "less than desirable." Quoting another state official, Williams added that the proposed policy did not provide the states with any more flexibility than they had previously had, that it was likely to be followed by additional guidance documents, and that, in view of states' existing authority to use the approach, no further guidance was needed and the proposed policy was unwarranted and unnecessary.

EPA's Levin has described the state reactions somewhat differently:

> State agencies saw resource drains behind every rock and asserted that they already possessed SIP authority to use bubble approaches, ignoring the fact that previous bubbles had been used solely as bargaining chips that rewarded recalcitrant firms engaged in drawn-out compliance negotiations.[24]

The Williams and Levin comments highlight the fact that one of the great unknowns in the battle over bubbling has been how and to what extent states used it before it was formally proposed by EPA. No one knows for certain to what degree the possible pitfalls NRDC and other critics found in bubbling, or the benefits proclaimed by its proponents, already existed in earlier, lower profile state permitting actions. Regardless, the net result of all the conditions EPA attached to its proposed policy was not only to prevent the bubble's use by those with a history of recalcitrance but also to restrict its availability and attractiveness to those who had acted in good faith in the past and wished to do so in the future.

Supporters of the bubble concept also submitted comments on the EPA proposal. Armco and some other commenters contended that EPA should allow trades between open dust sources and industrial-process emissions. These commenters submitted detailed studies to EPA arguing that fugitive dust from roads, storage piles, and other open sources did contribute to violations of standards in industrialized nonattainment areas and that such dust contained the fine particles of greatest health concern.

Other pro-bubble commenters argued that treating individual bubble proposals as SIP revisions was not necessary to ensure federal enforceability. These commenters preferred, among other things, for bubble proposals to be processed as changes to state-issued permits and for states to include in their individual SIPs "generic bubble regulations"— that is, permitting programs containing trading features. These permitting programs would be state-level analogues of the federal bubble policy, setting forth general rules under which bubbles would be allowed by state regulators. Proponents of this approach claimed that, because such regulations would be part of SIPs, permits issued under them automatically would be federally enforceable, so EPA review of individual bubble proposals as SIP revisions would not be necessary.

EPA would be able, however, to audit permit changes at a later date to ensure the general state rules were being applied reasonably to individual bubble applications. Because federal review of proposed SIP revisions was so time-consuming, the proponents of state generic bubble rules viewed such rules as an important shortcut to getting individual bubbles approved.

EPA'S REVISED BUBBLE POLICY—DECEMBER 1979

After making important revisions to its January 1979 proposal, EPA issued and put into effect a bubble policy in December 1979.[25] The revisions loosened some of the proposed restrictions, often in response to comments that the restrictions would be environmentally counterproductive, were of questionable legality, or were not technically defensible on the basis of existing information.[26] Major changes included permission for bubbles over multiple plants, extensions of compliance deadlines in some circumstances, increases in total emissions from under individual bubbles, and trades involving open dust sources. Additional changes eliminated still other constraints and deleted an earlier suggestion by EPA that controls developed under bubbles would provide a basis for tighter regulation in the future. And, in response to comments received from state officials, EPA also tried to reduce some of the January 1979 proposal's administrative demands.

One of the most noteworthy changes by EPA was on the fugitive dust issue. EPA deleted its earlier statement that open dust sources did not contribute significantly to violations of ambient air quality standards, and the agency left open the door for the trading of controls between industrial processes and unpaved roads under specific, fairly narrow conditions. While relaxing its policy, EPA observed that ensuring equivalent effects on air quality from trades of open dust was extremely difficult because too much uncertainty existed in determining emission rates, in predicting the effectiveness of control technology, and in modeling ambient impacts.[27] EPA claimed that the economic benefits a company could gain by placing controls on open dust sources instead of process emissions could not outweigh the risk to society of the agency's approving trades that might not adequately protect air quality standards.[28] For these reasons, EPA said that, until air quality models were improved and verified, it would approve no proposals for trades between open dust and industrial sources, if those proposals were based solely on modeling. The agency did, however, leave open the opportunity for dischargers to demonstrate, through monitoring, the equivalence of trades between open dust and industrial sources. Dischargers could pave roads, cover storage piles, or otherwise control open dust, although their obligations to satisfy existing SIP requirements would not change until the results of the monitoring were known.[29] In allowing such demonstrations, EPA recognized Armco's willingness to monitor the results of its proposed controls on open dust.

The revised EPA policy retained many restrictions designed to assure enforceability and protection of ambient air quality. Perhaps the most significant of the retained limitations was the insistence that each proposed bubble be processed as a SIP revision,[30] since, as SIP revisions, individual bubble proposals would each be subject to federal review and approval.* In retaining this restriction, EPA rejected commenters' arguments for state generic bubble regulations. It insisted that case-by-case SIP revisions were necessary for bubbles to be federally enforceable and that periodic audits would not be a practical means of oversight since any errors found would not be readily reversible. To some observers, EPA's insistence on treating bubbles as SIP revisions was an important backstop, to prevent state regulators from being too lax in revising permits.

Although, on balance, the revised policy, with its easing of many restrictions on the use of the bubble, seemingly would indicate a victory by the agency's regulatory reformers, the victory was largely symbolic. The policy was not accompanied by the financial and personnel resources that would have been necessary to make it effective. EPA's Levin has commented that the agency "formally assigned just three staffers to implement the policy, . . . made no organizational or funding changes to back its rhetoric, and had only the foggiest notion of the resources that full-scale national implementation might entail."[31]

---

*Even before announcement of the bubble policy, dischargers could seek changes in the terms of their permits by obtaining revisions to SIPs. But obtaining a SIP revision was widely viewed by dischargers as equivalent to running a gauntlet. The bubble policy explicitly encouraged dischargers to come forward with changes in the terms of their permits, but, by requiring SIP revisions for individual bubbles, perpetuated gauntlet running.

LOWERING HURDLES AND DROPPING
RESTRICTIONS—1980-1981

The bubble policy remained problematic for many industries. In several areas, bubble opportunities were still unavailable. Gross delays in the SIP revision and review process meant that many states lacked federally approved, revised SIPs that projected attainment of ambient air quality standards by statutory deadlines. In addition, EPA's requirement that dischargers take steps to satisfy existing SIP requirements while their bubble proposals were being reviewed led some plant managers to feel that any potential savings from bubbles might be wasted meeting existing obligations.

EPA committed itself to rapid review of SIP revisions for bubbles, but this assurance carried little weight when placed in the context of the agency's numerous delays in reviewing SIP revisions. As late as 1981 (prior to an EPA effort to streamline the SIP revision process), the typical SIP revision took approximately 220 workdays at the agency and involved 24 steps.[32]

The SIP revision issue came to a head when New Jersey proposed revisions to its air pollution regulations. New Jersey had developed a generic bubble regulation that permitted existing sources of volatile organic compounds (VOCs), which New Jersey called "volatile organic substances," to use bubbles for compliance purposes. New Jersey proposed to review dischargers' plans but would not submit them to EPA as SIP revisions.

In March 1980, when it conditionally approved other portions of New Jersey's revised SIP, EPA declined to act on the proposed bubble regulation.[33] EPA's inaction was challenged in court by the Chemical Manufacturers' Association, some of whose members had existing plants in New Jersey that could have benefited from plant-wide bubbles. Those plants were under pressure to meet SIP requirements, and it appeared that, if EPA insisted on an individual SIP revision for each proposed bubble, the plants would have difficulty using bubbles to meet compliance deadlines.

The SIP revision issue surfaced again at a major national conference on regulatory reform sponsored by EPA in September 1980.[34] EPA's bubble policy had been in existence for nearly nine months; yet few bubble proposals had been made by industry. It became obvious at the conference that the major sticking point was the SIP revision requirement, and state regulators seemed to share industries' concern. Two weeks after the conference, EPA decided to approve New

Jersey's bubble regulation subject to several conditions, the essence of which was that EPA would continue to monitor each bubble proposal closely, even though a formal SIP revision for each would not be required.

In granting that approval, EPA had creatively developed a legal justification—the proposed rule's tight language—that the agency previously had been unable to find.[35] The rule contained sufficient safeguards to assure EPA that bubbles would not interfere with attainment and maintenance of air quality standards. The state would simply perform an essentially mechanical task of adding bubbled VOC emission limits to see whether their sum equaled existing limits. Since VOC emissions have no significant site-specific effects, complicated calculations of site-specific ambient impacts of bubbled emissions were not necessary.

EPA used the New Jersey proposal to signal other states that it would henceforth approve tightly drawn generic bubble regulations.[36] The agency issued its final approval of the New Jersey regulation in April 1981, further explaining the legal reasoning that permitted it to approve the state's rule.[37] EPA also eased its proposed auditing of individual bubble approvals.

The approval of the New Jersey rule was one of several EPA efforts to liberalize the bubble policy in late 1980 and early 1981. Just before he left office with the change in presidential administrations, EPA Administrator Costle approved several changes to streamline administrative review of bubbles and to make them more readily available. The changes were announced via a press release, which noted that a formal *Federal Register* notice detailing the changes was being prepared.[38] The changes included four major reforms.*

First, EPA would make bubbles available in those nonattainment areas for which revised SIPs had not yet been fully approved. The sources would have to agree to definitions of RACT for the points they wished to bubble and could then meet those limits in the most cost-effective manner under their bubble. By making this change, EPA seemed to be providing a defensible baseline for such bubbles, since RACT was the statutory requirement for existing sources in nonattainment areas.

Second, EPA would reduce the modeling requirements for certain sulfur dioxide and particulate sources that wished to bubble. EPA

---

*These reforms were to be supplemented by some additional measures.

proposed a sequence of modeling requirements, making the amount of modeling dependent on the types and location of the sources involved. Enough modeling would be required to provide an assessment of environmental impact in each case; more detailed modeling would be required only if necessary. In places where bubbled points were close together and had similar emission characteristics, modeling would not be required, provided overall emissions did not increase. Where sources were more distant, or varied significantly, more modeling would be required.

Third, EPA would encourage states to submit generic bubble regulations for sulfur dioxide and particulates and would indicate the circumstances under which such rules would be approvable by the agency.* For some sulfur dioxide and particulate bubbles, modeling might not be required because total emissions remained the same and the sources were similar or close together or because emissions of the pollutant involved were less than 100 tons per year. If states adopted generic rules for such bubbles, defining when sources were "similar" and "close," then SIP revisions for specific bubbles could be forgone.

Finally, EPA would provide increased time for plants using bubbles to come into compliance. EPA's new willingness to grant extensions in compliance deadlines for individual sources was intended to allow those bubbles that would produce greater environmental benefits (for example, more control of emissions) than compliance with conventional regulations, but that would also require greater time to execute. In some cases, such as coating operations, such bubbles could encourage the use of low-solvent technologies and less energy-intensive controls.

The September 1980 regulatory reform conference was a major factor in this liberalization of bubble requirements. According to the Regulatory Reform Staff's Levin, the conference's ultimate aim was "to bring sharply to the attention of top EPA management the need for drastic liberalization if the bubble—and the agency's credibility—were to survive."[39] Levin reports that the conference "succeeded beyond its sponsors' dreams."[40] Not only were rules liberalized, but

---

*In approving New Jersey's regulations, EPA had not had to consider whether it should or could approve generic bubble rules for particulates and sulfur dioxide. Unlike VOCs, these pollutants have site-specific impacts, which vary depending on stack height, topography, and other factors.

the agency staff working on the bubble doubled and the bubble's technical assistance budget quintupled. Marketing and technical work on the offset and banking policies were integrated with the bubble policy project under the aegis of the Regulatory Reform Staff.[41]*

The marketing and liberalization of rules continued through 1981. EPA proposed to approve a number of bubbles, including Armco's, and hosted or cohosted national and regional conferences on various aspects of trading.[43] In addition, the Regulatory Reform Staff moved to consolidate all the rules for netting, bubbles, and the offset policy into one document; by May 1981, a draft Controlled Trading Policy Statement had been approved by an EPA interoffice working group.[44] Three months later, a revised draft was circulated for informal comment outside the agency.[45]

THE INTERIM EMISSIONS TRADING POLICY STATEMENT—1982

Publication of the EPA's new emissions trading policy in the *Federal Register* was delayed, in part by the transition in the agency's leadership at the beginning of the Reagan administration. The administration was slow to fill key positions in the agency, and many of the new appointees had little or no knowledge of emissions trading. Not until April 1982, 15 months after outgoing Administrator Costle had promised it, was an official interim policy, with an accompanying "technical issues document," published in the *Federal Register* as the Emissions Trading Policy Statement (ETPS).[46] That statement incorporated the policy changes announced in the January 1981 press

---

*After its creation in 1979, the Regulatory Reform Staff adopted, as one of its largest and most visible projects, a vigorous, multifaceted marketing approach to emissions trading, involving at various times conferences, "how-to" publications, draft editorials, contacts with key business leaders, and solicitation of endorsements from sympathetic observers. Pro-bubble EPA staff members believed that such marketing was essential to overcome the inertia of the command-and-control system and to move emissions trading from invention to implementation.[42]

Although, in many ways, this marketing approach could be regarded as a model for future efforts to launch innovative programs, it came to a halt in late 1981, when the new team of Reagan political appointees at EPA stopped many agency activities in their tracks. Since then, the Regulatory Reform Staff has continued to promote trading, but its efforts are lower key and consist largely of status reports on bubble activity and occasional articles in professional journals.

release and introduced several additional means for broadening trading. EPA characterized the new statement as:

- authorizing state generic trading rules for all pollutants for which national ambient air quality standards had been set;
- extending use of the bubble to areas that lacked approved projections of attainment;
- expanding opportunities for use of bubbles as alternative means of meeting SIP requirements;
- reducing requirements for detailed air quality modeling;
- reducing constraints on trades involving open dust sources;
- allowing sources of VOCs more time to implement bubbles under compliance schedules, consistent with reasonable further progress towards meeting statutory deadlines for attainment;
- allowing sources to use bubbles to come into compliance, instead of having to be on a compliance schedule with original SIP limits to be eligible to bubble; and
- allowing broader use of emission reductions from shutdowns.[47]

The policy statement also declared that only reductions that were "surplus," "enforceable," "permanent," and "quantifiable" could qualify for emission reduction credits (ERCs) and be banked or used in an emissions trade.[48]* These criteria were elaborated on in an accompanying technical issues document. The document reiterated many previously stated requirements such as stipulations that trades be restricted to the same pollutant and that they not increase emissions of hazardous pollutants. In addition, the document stated EPA's principles for evaluating states' generic rules.

In adopting the interim ETPS, EPA accepted command minimalists' argument that states have considerable flexibility in developing their strategies for attaining the national ambient standards, consistent with statutory requirements and EPA regulations, and that, once state plans are approved, it is entirely appropriate for those plans to be used as the bases for trading.[50] Dischargers simply must demonstrate that any proposed trades are consistent with the methods used to develop the state projections.

The principles embodied in the ETPS have been the subject of prolonged and sometimes acerbic controversy. Critics' distrust of at-

---

*These four criteria were not entirely novel, since they were elaborations on principles EPA had developed in the emissions offset and banking project that had operated in parallel with its bubble policy project in 1979 and 1980 (see chapters 2 and 5).[49]

tainment projections of SIPs, fear of forgoing some reductions by granting credits for past reductions not motivated by trading opportunities, and questioning of the suitability of RACT requirements as baselines for trades—all have fueled the dispute. Disagreements over rules for trading have been particularly heated with respect to those areas that may not attain the ambient standards by the extended deadline of December 31, 1987, and those that had projected meeting the deadline by December 31, 1982, but failed to do so.

One of the most fundamental points of disagreement has been over what constitutes a "surplus" reduction. The ETPS, reflecting the command minimalists' view, defined it as a reduction "not currently required by law."[51] In contrast, the expansionists define "surplus" as any reduction not needed for attainment. Because they define "surplus" in this manner, expansionists do not believe trading should be permitted in nonattainment areas lacking approved projections of attainment, since the areas have not yet figured out how they will reach the ambient standards. Even in areas with approved projections of attainment, expansionists are dubious of using existing RACT requirements and other EPA-approved regulations as bases for defining what is surplus, because the expansionists distrust the projections and suspect that additional reductions will be required for attainment.

EPA's ETPS suggested that, in areas lacking approved projections of attainment, trading might nevertheless be permitted if RACT requirements for certain sources could be agreed on. But, both in those areas lacking approved projections and in those having them, expansionists take issue with using RACT standards as baselines for trades. Their arguments against RACT have taken different forms at different times in the several years since the ETPS was published. Often, those arguments have evolved as responses to specific bubbles advanced by individual companies, as those bubbles have highlighted differences between how RACT standards are set in theory and how they are set in practice.

EPA's initial guidance for setting RACT standards, published in late 1976, indicated that such standards were to be determined case by case.[52]* For VOCs, however, regulators established them for en-

---

*The pertinent memo stated that a RACT determination "may vary from source to source" due to different characteristics "of an individual source or groups of sources." The memo indicated that RACT "should represent the toughest controls considering the technological and economic feasibility that can be applied to a specific situation."[53]

tire classes of sources to avoid the administrative nightmare of making individual determinations for thousands of sources.* Because of this practice, expansionists sometimes have questioned whether RACT standards have been set at the statutorily required level for the individual sources seeking to bubble pursuant to EPA's trading policy. When sources have sought credit for already-achieved reductions, expansionists have argued that the technology to control emissions more than required by the industry-wide RACT was, by definition, "reasonably available" to the individual sources wishing to bubble. Therefore, those expansionists have claimed, no credit should have been given for reductions below the industry-wide RACT baseline.

Expansionists' criticism of RACT as a baseline also has taken the form of an attack on emission reductions generated by what the expansionists have labeled "standard industry practice"—that is, a technology that many sources routinely use to meet numerical emission limits in RACT standards. Such a technology may routinely reduce emissions to lower levels than an applicable RACT standard requires, even though the numerical emission limits in that standard may supposedly have been based on that technology. For example, an emission standard may permit only one pound of emissions per unit of production, but the technology may routinely emit only half this amount.

Minimalists accept the emission limits stated in RACT standards as appropriate regulatory stopping points, allowing those seeking to bubble to obtain credit for having reduced emissions more than required. By, contrast, expansionists often claim that the lower levels of emissions achieved by sources should be considered as new baselines, so that no ERCs are given for performing better than the limits in the RACT standards. Expansionists fear that, if the baselines are not lowered in this manner, industries will get credit for reductions they would achieve anyway. The industries would then be allowed

---

*"Control Technology Guidance" (CTG) documents represented EPA's view of the emission rates normally achievable by such classes of sources as bulk gasoline terminals, printing plants, and coaters of cans, fabrics, paper, and autos.[54] EPA essentially required states to adopt these general guidelines as part of their SIPs, taking the position that any state's deviations from the norms "should be adequately documented."[55] States were, of course, free to be much tougher than EPA's guidelines suggested; deviations in the other direction most concerned EPA.

to forgo potential reductions elsewhere that could help areas attain the ambient standards.*

Another locus of disagreement between expansionists and minimalists, in all areas, has been the use of plant shutdowns in trades. Expansionists generally believe that shutdowns occur as a matter of course and should not be credited in trades unless they are done specifically to earn ERCs. Expansionists also believe that the benefits from shutdowns should accrue to the public, not individual companies. Minimalists, however, cite past administrative policies (including EPA's initial offset policy in 1976) to argue that granting credits for shutdowns is consistent with EPA's historic regulatory practices.

In an attempt to deal with these different perspectives, EPA decided in the ETPS to allow shutdowns that were consistent with accounting practices in state plans.† Shutdowns could be considered "surplus" and therefore could qualify for ERCs, so long as they were not double-counted—that is, credit could not be given for shutdowns both as part of a state's general projection of attainment and as part of a specific bubble proposal advanced by a company.[56] EPA suggested that states had at least three options for granting individual sources credit without double-counting:[57] the states could reexamine the credit that had been taken in the SIP for a shutdown and decide not to take that credit; they could allow that credit in the trade only after all the reductions the SIP had expected from shutdowns had occurred; or they could assign to a source credit for only a portion of the reductions from a shutdown, if it could be shown that such credit was consistent with the attainment projection and with reasonable further progress towards attainment. Expansionists wary of attainment projections continued to have a problem with this approach.

EPA SEEKS COMMENT ON MORE NONATTAINMENT AND SHUTDOWN OPTIONS—1983

In August 1983, EPA published for public comment additional policy options concerning the ETPS.[58] These options were prompted by reactions to the ETPS; by the probable failure of many areas to have

---

*The Sohio and Ashland bubble cases in chapter 4 illustrate this controversy.

†In projecting attainment, states might have assumed some shutdowns would occur in certain industries and might have counted those expected reductions as part of their strategy for attaining the national ambient standards.

met ambient air standards by the Clean Air Act's December 31, 1982, deadline; and by a court decision suggesting that bubbles in non-attainment areas are not permissible unless they produce a net benefit for air quality.*

In its request for comments, EPA focused on using ERCs in areas lacking projections of attainment and on crediting reductions from shutdowns. EPA replied to many of the complaints voiced by NRDC and other expansionist critics and argued that emissions trading would be more a help than a hindrance in finding solutions to the nonattainment problem. EPA acknowledged that several areas without approved projections of attainment had yet to determine where all the emission reductions would be made to bring about that attainment. The agency, however, suggested that the only alternative to emissions trading would be a more aggressive search by regulators for reductions and that such a search would be likely "to collide with the very information barriers that discouraged a [projection] of attainment in the first place."[59] In other words, if regulators had earlier had trouble getting industry's assistance in finding sufficient measures to project attainment, that situation was not about to improve if dischargers had no incentives to come forward with voluntary reductions. EPA argued that trading might reduce stonewalling

> by encouraging plant managers to submit data on emissions, modeling, and unregulated or uninventoried emission sources. . . . It may help states develop new RACT regulations for categories of sources, both because of improved information and because opportunity for trading reduces those rules' potential cost.[60]

EPA also claimed that expansionists' suggestion that ERCs be given only when sources are shut down specifically to earn the credits would be "administratively unworkable" because it would require some sort of test to determine a discharger's motives.[61] Such a test, suggested EPA, would either lead to the approval of all shutdown credits, thereby undermining the reason for the motives test, or require so much proof from a discharger that no shutdown credits would be approved.

While defending emissions trading in areas lacking approved attainment projections, EPA decided to hedge its bets, especially on

---

*This decision, NRDC v. Gorsuch, is discussed in chapter 5. The text refers to the "probable" failure of areas to attain, because when EPA solicited further comments in August 1983, it was still uncertain which areas had attained and which had not.

the crediting of shutdowns. It included in its invitation for public comment a new set of policy options, some of which were more environmentally demanding than those offered in the interim ETPS. The options differed primarily in the degree to which they allowed credit for shutdowns and for reductions below RACT requirements. In the middle of the range of options was one that provided that a bubble could be approved only if it promised to produce emission reductions at least 20 percent below the reduction level required by RACT. This "RACT plus 20 percent" requirement, as it came to be called, might be applied, in nonattainment areas lacking approved projections of attainment, either to only those bubbles involving shutdowns or to all bubbles.* EPA suggested that this extra 20 percent reduction could compensate for uncertainties in SIPs and would not prevent a state from requiring further reductions from a source at a later date.

The policy options drew a wide variety of responses, many of which were not surprising. Industry generally favored liberal shutdown credits.[62] NRDC weighed in with a formal response containing yet another set of critical remarks.[63] In addition, the council's David Doniger contended in a speech many months later that the "RACT plus 20 percent" approach would be akin to paying someone eight dollars in cash in return for a 10-dollar check written on an account with no money in it.[64] His criticism was based on NRDC's view that there simply are no "surplus" reductions available in nonattainment areas lacking approved attainment projections.

Sixteen state and local regulatory bodies responded with opinions that ranged across all the options without disproportionately favoring any one.[65] New Jersey, Pennsylvania, and the Dayton, Ohio, Regional Air Pollution Control Agency favored no credits for shutdowns in bubbles for existing sources.[66] Responding to EPA's contention that including shutdowns in individual bubbles would speed

---

*The procedure for using RACT in calculating credits from shutdowns would work as follows: A shutdown would cause 100 tons of a pollutant to be eliminated. But if the facility were to continue operating rather than shutting down, applying RACT would eliminate 80 tons of those emissions. Since if the facility continued operating it could not get credit for those 80 tons of reductions RACT would require, credit would not be given for them if the facility shut down completely. Rather, the baseline from which credits would be calculated would be the 20 tons remaining if RACT had been applied. The "RACT plus 20 percent" requirement might reduce credit from the shutdown even further.

compliance, New Jersey commented that attainment would occur only on paper and that "EPA should be seeking meaningful reasonable further progress [toward attaining ambient standards] rather than making paper compliance easy."[67] New Jersey also challenged EPA's assumption that pollution control costs are very important in business decisions, stating that air pollution control costs are rarely a significant factor in decisions to shut down facilities, that virtually all shutdowns occur regardless of air pollution control requirements, and that allowing shutdowns to be used to avoid the control of other facilities "would be counter to reasonable progress."[68]

At the opposite extreme from New Jersey was the South Coast Air Quality Management District, which manages Los Angeles's air. Voicing its support for shutdown credits, the district noted that its rules require an extremely stringent level of RACT on all existing sources, which makes it difficult for sources to earn ERCs from controls tougher than RACT. The district added that "practically all" ERCs in its area are the result of shutdowns or curtailment of operations.[69]

The balance of the state and local agencies' letters either did not directly address the options offered by EPA or favored one or another of the options that allowed credit for shutdowns. The states' letters, both in their descriptions of state programs and in their responses to EPA's options, also revealed how diverse are state approaches toward developing SIPs and making assumptions about air quality improvements from shutdowns.

THE "ALM RESOLUTIONS" OF 1984-85

The debate within EPA over trading continued into 1984. By this time, the agency had new senior leadership, with William Ruckelshaus replacing Ann Gorsuch as EPA administrator. With comments on its 1983 notice in hand, the agency began moving toward a final decision on trading. The air programs office continued to call for tough restrictions.[70] For example, the office suggested that, in nonattainment areas lacking projections, credits for emissions below RACT limits should not be allowed if the low emission levels were simply the result of routine performance of the technologies that industries employed in response to RACT requirements. It also suggested use of a "but for" test: to get ERCs, applicants would have to show that reductions would not have occurred but for the desire for credits.[71] Air programs staff members felt (a) that EPA should adopt rules that would assure real environmental progress from trades and (*b*) that trades that might produce fewer emission reductions than the conventional SIP should not be permitted.

The regulatory reform staff considered some of the key air programs office proposals to be administratively unworkable, although the staff members were willing to agree to some tightening of the rules. In what came to be known within the agency as the "Alm Resolutions" (after EPA Deputy Administrator Alvin Alm), the top EPA leadership rejected in early 1985 the most stringent of the air programs office's proposals, although they did endorse a substantial tightening of the trading rules. Some of the key provisions of the "Alm Resolutions" for nonattainment areas lacking projections were (*a*) using RACT as a baseline for calculating credits, but taking historical operating hours and other capacity figures into account; (*b*) requiring a reduction in emissions at least 20 percent better than RACT;* and (*c*) allowing no credits for reductions (including shutdowns) occurring before a source applied for a bubble. In addition, EPA regional administrators would have discretion to target some bubble applications for special review.[75]

THE FINAL EMISSIONS TRADING POLICY STATEMENT—1986

Before EPA staff agreed on specific language implementing the Alm Resolutions, and published the revised rules in the *Federal Register*, EPA's leadership changed yet again. William Ruckelshaus resigned, believing he had repaired the worst damage done to EPA during the Gorsuch years, Alm left with him, and Lee Thomas became the new EPA administrator. With the change in leadership, issues that appeared to have been largely resolved by Alm were reopened.

---

*In support of the "RACT plus 20 percent" proposal, the Regulatory Reform Staff compiled figures on the estimated reductions in emissions from stationary sources needed to attain the ozone standard in major nonattainment areas. The staff then applied a "RACT plus 20 percent" standard to those areas, incorporating certain assumptions about the percentage of reductions previously accomplished, the percentage of stationary sources controllable, and the growth in emissions likely to occur.[72] The staff concluded that "RACT plus 20 percent" would be more than sufficient to produce ambient attainment in most areas, if those areas could secure such reductions across-the-board.[73] But the air programs office, noting that only a small percentage of stationary sources are controllable, questioned the credibility of this projection.[74]

The air programs office continued to fight for tighter rules. The office preferred not to have any bubbling in nonattainment areas without projections of attainment. But, if bubbles were to be allowed, the air programs office suggested use of "standard industry practice" as a baseline for calculating credits. The office suggested a host of other tightenings, all designed to limit perceived abuses of trading. The Regulatory Reform Staff responded by suggesting that the Alm resolutions would largely take care of the worst of the problems that had surfaced in past bubbles and would promote continued environmental progress in nonattainment areas lacking projections. Once again, lengthy memorandums were exchanged between the two offices.* Neither the staffs of the two offices nor the assistant administrators in charge of each were able to reconcile their differences.

A final decision on the competing views was left to EPA Administrator Thomas. In early 1986, Thomas invited representatives of the environmental community, state and local regulatory agencies, and industry to present their views on trading, prior to his choosing among the competing suggestions from his subordinates. When he makes his decision on EPA's revised policy, Thomas will have before him not only the competing theoretical arguments of his staff but also the record of the bubble policy in practice. To that record, we now turn.

---

*The discussion above highlights the disagreements over bubbles in nonattainment areas without demonstrations. There also were disputes over bubbles in other areas, modeling requirements, generic state rules, and a host of other issues.

Chapter 4

The Bubble Policy for Existing Sources in Practice

The bubble policy for existing sources has moved forward on three major fronts. In those states that lack generic trading rules, bubbles have been approved by the U.S. Environmental Protection Agency (EPA) as state implementation plan (SIP) revisions. In addition, EPA has approved state rules governing the trading and banking of emission reduction credits. Bubbles have also been approved by those states whose generic trading rules have been approved by EPA. EPA's approvals of bubbles and generic rules slowed in 1985, as uncertainty continued over the contents of the final Emissions Trading Policy Statement.

Experience with bubbles can be assessed in several ways. For one, a broad perspective can be provided by gross figures on bubbles proposed and approved, reductions achieved, and the like. These figures are available from status reports compiled regularly by EPA's Regulatory Reform Staff. A more finely grained perspective can be provided by the regulatory records of individual bubbles submitted to EPA for approval. These often yield detailed information on approaches used, reductions achieved, and controversies between command minimalists and command expansionists. Details can also be learned from reviewing files on bubbles approved under state generic rules. This report's analysis of bubbles in practice focuses primarily on EPA's own bubble approval activity, rather than on activity under state generic rules, simply because information on EPA's own activity is easier to gather and provides sufficient insight into major conflicts.

EPA STATUS REPORTS—OVERVIEWS OF BUBBLE ACTIVITIES

Figures recited by the Regulatory Reform Staff in its January 1985 summary status report are truly impressive, considering the many hurdles the emissions trading policy has had to leap.[1] Observing that bubbles "give firms flexibility to meet pollution control requirements more quickly, make innovative control approaches profitable, and can save companies millions of dollars over the cost of conventional controls,"[2] the report notes that by January 10, 1985:

- EPA had directly approved 40 bubbles and proposed to approve 7 more, saving their users an estimated $300 million over the cost of conventional controls. Of these 47 bubbles, approximately 60 percent produced emission reductions beyond initial requirements.[3]
- Thirty-three additional bubbles had been approved by states under generic rules.[4] As stipulated by EPA policy, these bubbles were not subsequently processed by EPA as individual SIP revisions.
- At least 125 bubbles were under development or review either as SIP revisions or under state generic rules.[5]
- Overall, "more than 200 bubbles [had been] approved, proposed, or under development in 29 states throughout the nation. The total estimated savings from these bubbles [had exceeded] $800 million."[6]
- Generic rules had been approved for 9 states or local areas, and generic rules were being developed by more than 11 states and localities.[7]
- EPA had approved four state or local banking rules and had proposed to approve banking rules for four other state or local areas. Nine other states or localities had adopted banking rules, some of which were undergoing EPA review.[8]

A more comprehensive EPA report shows that, through the end of 1984, the primary metals industry, with 10 bubbles approved or proposed for approval by EPA, had been the principal beneficiary of the bubble policy; almost all of those bubbles were for the steel industry.[9] Nine bubbles were for paper products companies, five each for chemical manufacturers and electric utilities, and the remainder distributed among other industries.[10]

In the future, as more bubbles are approved at the state level, particularly for volatile organic compounds (VOCs), this leading position of the steel industry in bubbling almost certainly will decline. As already is evident in New Jersey, where 26 bubbles have been approved, numerous paper, can, and tape coaters will be availing themselves of less difficult trading opportunities under state generic rules for VOCs.[11]*

EPA's figures also separate bubble proposals by type of pollutant. Through the end of 1984, most of EPA's bubbles were for VOCs (18), followed by particulates (17) and sulfur dioxide (12).[12] EPA records indicate that about half of the bubbles were in attainment areas and about half were in nonattainment areas.[13]

EPA's figures are impressive, but, with respect to their claims about reductions in emissions, they can easily be misinterpreted. Until early 1985, in its status reports and articles based on them, EPA's Regulatory Reform Staff was quite careful in choosing language to give the impression of success in achieving emission reductions. For example, its October 1984 and January 10, 1985, reports noted that approximately 60 percent of the bubbles were producing emission reductions "beyond initial requirements."[14] Its April 1983 report summarizing activity through December 1982 referred to nearly two-thirds of the bubbles as producing "more reductions than required."[15] In a September 1984 article in *EPA Journal*, the Regulatory Reform Staff's Michael Levin noted that nearly 70 percent of the bubbles approved or proposed for approval produce "substantially greater emission reductions than conventional limits, with the rest producing equivalent reductions."[16] An outside observer might easily believe that these reductions have occurred as a result of the trading opportunities. But references to reductions "beyond initial requirements," "more reductions than required," and "substantially greater emission reductions than conventional limits" tell only part of the story.

---

*Not only are there more coaters than steel manufacturers, but trades for VOCs are easier to accomplish than the steel industry's trades for sulfure dioxide and particulates.

For example, in 1981, EPA approved a particulates bubble for a Corning Glass Works plant in Kentucky.[17] The bubble, which was listed in EPA's May 1984 status report as producing a "reduction below baseline" of 8.6 pounds of particulates per hour, covers three glass melting tanks (Tanks T-121 to T-123), all of which had been in compliance with their conventional emission limits (figure 4.1).[18] These altered emission rates under the bubble are the result of periodic nonoperation of one tank (T-122) and, when that tank is not operating, nonoperation of the electrostatic precipitator that controls emissions from that tank and another one (T-123) jointly. The precipitator is not operated at those times because it was designed to cleanse emissions from T-122 and T-123 together and cannot function properly when only T-123 is operating. Corning evidently sought the bubble because uncertain market conditions were likely to reduce its reliance on T-122. But, under the bubble, when the precipitator is not operating, actual emissions *increase* 2.5 pounds per hour.

Figure 4.1
Pre- and Post-Bubble Allowable and Actual Particulate Emissions—Corning Glass Works, Kentucky

	Emission point	Allowable emission rate (pounds/hour)	Actual emission rate (pounds/hour)	Maximum GLC[1] ($\mu g/m^3$) 24-hour
Before bubbling	T121	19.8	10.6	----
	T122	10.8	----	4.8
	T123	0.78	0.5	----
	Totals	31.38	11.5	
After bubbling	T121	19.8	10.6	----
	T122	0.0	0.0	3.2
	T123	3.0	3.0	----
	Totals	22.8	13.6	

1. Ground Level Concentration. Calculations based on the tanks' allowable emission rates.

Source: 46 Fed. Reg. 53409 (October 29, 1981).

This bubble is for an attainment area, so existing levels of pollutants are not a threat to human health. Moreover, the increase in actual emissions is quite small. Indeed, this SIP revision may seem to be a reasonable approach to changing circumstances. At issue here, however, is not the wisdom of the change, but whether the status report's claim of a reduction below allowable emissions tells the full story. It does not.

Under this particular set of circumstances—a bubble in an attainment area, involving a small amount of emissions—highlighting this difference between actual and allowable emissions may appear to be unduly critical quibbling. But, as a number of additional bubbles discussed later in this report suggest, it would be incorrect to infer from claimed reductions in allowable emissions that the bubbles for existing sources are bringing about any changes in actual emissions.

A second example illustrating problems with EPA's claims of emission reductions is provided by a plant operated by E.I. du Pont de Nemours & Company in Kinston, North Carolina.[19] This bubble, approved by EPA in 1983, covers 13 sources of particulates at the plant, 2 of which were previously violating allowable emission limits set by the state. The 28 pounds per hour of reductions below baseline claimed for this bubble in EPA's May 1984 status report tell only part of the story. The bubble raises the allowable emissions rate on the 2 noncomplying sources to bring them into compliance, while reducing the allowable emissions rate on the 11 other sources that historically have emitted pollutants at levels far below their allowable rates (figure 4.2).

The *Federal Register* notice for this bubble notes that it is expected to produce no increase in actual emissions and that the affected plant is in an area that is not exceeding the national ambient standards for particulates. Because there should be no increase in actual emissions, no portion of the Prevention of Significant Deterioration (PSD) increment for this attainment area should be consumed, and full-scale modeling indicates that the bubble will adequately protect national ambient standards for particulates. As a result, this bubble should have no adverse environmental effect. Nevertheless, this example underscores the need to treat EPA's statements of emission reductions with care; they may simply represent administrative recognition of past reductions and not additional efforts by dischargers to reduce their actual emissions.

Figure 4.2
Pre- and Post-Bubble Allowable Particulate Emissions—
du Pont Plant, Kinston, North Carolina

Source	Allowable before bubble	Allowable under bubble	Proposed change
Spinning mill	2.05	5.24	+ 3.19
Spinning mill	3.11	9.61	+ 6.49
Product recovery unit	16.50	6.51	− 10.00
Heated dryer	6.74	3.97	− 2.77
Heated dryer	6.74	3.97	− 2.77
Heated dryer	6.74	3.97	− 2.77
Heated dryer	6.74	3.97	− 2.77
Heated dryer	6.74	3.97	− 2.77
Heated dryer	6.74	3.97	− 2.77
Heated dryer	6.74	3.97	− 2.77
Heated dryer	6.74	3.97	− 2.77
Heated dryer	6.74	3.97	− 2.77
Heated dryer	7.47	5.00	− 2.47
Total:	89.79	62.09	− 27.7

All figures are in pounds per hour.

Source: 48 Fed. Reg. 52056 (November 16, 1983).

In the future, EPA should be able to improve its reporting. In mid-1985, the Regulatory Reform Staff stopped making statements like those singled out above. Moreover, the Regulatory Reform Staff's data management system has been improved so that it can better distinguish between changes in allowable and actual emissions.*

Du Pont's Kinston bubble also is a reminder that a bubble can speed compliance in two ways. One, illustrated by some bubbles discussed later, is for a noncomplying source to reduce its level of actual emissions to levels at or below those required by regulators. The Kinston bubble illustrates a second method: changing regulatory obligations so that existing levels of actual emissions, formerly deemed noncompliance, are redefined as compliance. Such a redefinition can

*However, the data base will still depend heavily for its completeness on the submission of appropriate data by the state and federal regulators processing bubble applications.

be held up by proponents of the bubble policy as an example of increased flexibility. It allows a discharger to save money and, if accompanied by administrative recognition of emission reductions achieved elsewhere, it does not increase environmental harm. But critics such as the Natural Resources Defense Council (NRDC) view such flexibility more skeptically—as spurring innovations in evasion.

LESSONS FROM SPECIFIC BUBBLES

EPA's status reports on emissions trading provide no more than a statistical overview of bubbling. But the sharp conflicts over how the bubble policy for existing sources should be implemented in practice and the reasons for the sharp disagreements over baselines and other such matters are best understood in the context of specific bubble applications. The specific bubbles described below are not a scientifically selected random sample of all bubbles proposed to or approved by EPA, so no statistical inferences can be drawn from them. But they should provide a more concrete sense of the bubble policy's strengths and liabilities.

Two Model Bubbles

Trading advocates contend that bubbles can speed compliance, encourage innovation, save money, and produce environmental results equivalent to and perhaps better than results from conventional regulatory requirements. Skeptics have questioned these claims. Two bubbles—one for a Minnesota Mining and Manufacturing (3M) facility in Pennsylvania, and one for a du Pont facility in New Jersey, illustrate how well bubbles can work in practice.

3M, Bristol, Pennsylvania

Minnesota Mining and Manufacturing (3M), a company with a good environmental record, has developed (and EPA has approved) a bubble for its Bristol, Pennsylvania, tape coating facility. The plant is in a nonattainment area having a December 31, 1987, deadline for attaining the ambient standard for ozone. The bubble employs technological innovation to produce reductions in actual emissions, even beyond those required by conventional control strategies, at reduced cost.

Pennsylvania's "reasonably available control technology" (RACT) regulations would have required a 74 percent reduction in emissions from the seven tape coaters and three tape treaters in the Bristol facility.[20] Pollution control devices had been added to two of the machines previously, but eight more devices would have been required to meet the RACT requirements at a cost 3M estimated to be nearly $9 million.[21] The devices would also have consumed substantial amounts of natural gas.[22]

As an alternative to this conventional approach, 3M proposed replacing one solvent-based coater with a solventless system. At the same time, it proposed continuing the use of the existing two pollution control devices and reducing production at some or all of the remaining machines.[23] The company expected to be able to reduce emissions from the entire facility by an amount at least equivalent to that required by Pennsylvania's RACT regulations. It also projected savings in capital costs of $3 million and annual operations and maintenance savings of between $1 million and $2 million.[24] The company reports that it has succeeded in reducing emissions to about 1,000 tons per year below the levels required by RACT.[25] Its actual emission levels are now many thousands of tons below the uncontrolled levels that predated the existing controls.[26]

To implement its new system, 3M sought and received an extension of the compliance deadline from April 9, 1982, to January 1, 1984.[27]* This was consistent with EPA policy permitting such extensions in nonattainment areas having a 1987 attainment deadline for ozone. The extension seems reasonable when measured against the benefits of installing new technology, conserving energy, and saving money. Moreover, this bubble indicates that it can be environmentally counterproductive to prohibit extensions of compliance dates for proposed bubbles.†

Du Pont Chambers Works, Deepwater, New Jersey‡

A bubble approved by New Jersey for the du Pont Chambers Works also demonstrates the benefits of EPA's bubble policy. The Chambers

---

*Although a compliance extension was required for the bubble, one might also have been required if 3M had tried to comply with the conventional regulations.[28]

†The bubble policy is not a unique provider of compliance extensions under the Clean Air Act. Delayed compliance orders under Section 113 of the act provide some flexibility for extending compliance deadlines.[29]

‡This bubble, unlike the others discussed in this section, was approved under generic state rules. As the first such bubble, and as a success story cited repeatedly by EPA, information about it was readily available.

Works, one of the largest chemical plants in the United States, contains approximately 460 sources of VOCs.[30]* Most of the emissions come from a very small percentage of the sources.

Du Pont evidently began developing its bubble scheme in 1977, when New Jersey was giving preliminary consideration to tightening controls on VOCs. Having estimated it would cost $15 million to meet New Jersey's conventional RACT requirements,[31] du Pont proposed to reduce emissions from some of the largest sources by 99.9 percent while controlling its smaller sources less stringently than otherwise required. Development of EPA's bubble policy and New Jersey's generic bubble rules allowed implementation of the scheme, which du Pont initially estimated would save $10 million in capital expenditures. The capital savings leaped to $13.5 million when New Jersey revised its regulations to exempt certain substances from controls, the reductions required by RACT were changed, and du Pont adjusted the bubble to forgo some previously planned controls.[32]†

Du Pont includes 119 of the 460 sources under its bubble.[34] Of the 119, 3 are the major sources selected for overcontrol, 88 have control systems that remain unchanged, and 28 have no control systems. Du Pont states that these points were selected from among the 460 sources because they would require controls to meet the new RACT regulations or because their existing controls produce emission reduction credits (ERCs) by reducing emissions more than required by regulations.[35]

The reductions at the three largest sources are being accomplished by using their emissions as an auxiliary fuel in furnaces.[36] The original bubble would have reduced du Pont's annual emissions from the 2,769 tons allowed by RACT to 438 tons, a significant 84 percent reduction.[37] Under the revised bubble, the RACT-allowed emissions are 2,489 tons annually, and emissions under the bubble are 1,932 tons annually, or 22 percent below the RACT level.[38] Both the RACT and bubble levels are several thousand tons per year lower than du Pont's actual emissions prior to adoption of the RACT requirements.

The Chambers Works bubble demonstrates that bubbles can reduce emissions below levels otherwise required by RACT, produce earlier

---

*New Jersey labels these compounds "volatile organic substances."

†Du Pont originally proposed to overcontrol seven of its largest sources, including four for which an incinerator would be built. It appears that under the revised bubble, the incinerator is not being constructed, but other controls are being used on the 4 large sources.[33]

compliance because fewer new controls must be planned and installed, and simplify enforcement because a state can focus its attention on the few sources where the most reductions are expected.[39]

The bubble is also noteworthy because it was approved for a plant in a nonattainment area whose SIP had been approved, but which had been granted an extension to December 31, 1987, for attainment.[40] Under EPA procedures, areas seeking extensions to 1987 were obliged to show that implementation of RACT and other reasonable measures would be insufficient to produce attainment by December 31, 1982, but such areas had until mid-1982 to submit supplemental SIP revisions containing the details of how attainment by 1987 would be achieved.[41] As a result, when the du Pont bubble was approved, New Jersey had not finally calculated which sources would provide all its needed emission reductions. The du Pont bubble suggests, therefore, that bubbles can be valuable even in areas lacking complete attainment plans.

Fuel-Switch Bubbles

One relatively common form of an emissions trade approved by EPA is the fuel-switch bubble. With this form of trade, a discharger substitutes one type of fuel for another as part of an emission-reduction strategy. These trades can help reduce reliance on expensive fuels, saving money for companies or consumers.

Narragansett Electric Company, Providence, Rhode Island

A bubble approved by EPA in 1981 for the Narragansett Electric Company is typical of one type of fuel switch.[42] The bubble covers two plants located in an area that has attained the national ambient standard for sulfur dioxide. It is one of the few multiplant bubbles approved thus far. The two electric generating facilities covered by the bubble—the South Street and Manchester Street plants—are located one-quarter mile from each other in Providence, Rhode Island. Prior to this bubble, the plants were required by Rhode Island to burn low-sulfur (1 percent) fuel oil. Under the bubble approved for them, Narragansett Electric is permitted to burn higher-sulfur (2.2 percent) fuel oil at South Street when it either burns natural gas at or does not operate the Manchester Street facility. Company studies (including modeling), submitted when the bubble was requested, estimated that annually sulfur dioxide emissions would decrease by 1,400 tons, fuel-cost savings would equal $3 million, and oil consumption would decline by 600,000 barrels.

Figure 4.3 displays the operating history and emissions from the two plants for the period 1980-1984. Total emissions dropped by 2,463 tons, to 2,926 tons in 1984. But this 46 percent reduction in emissions was partly the result of a 35 percent reduction in power generation, from the 11.96×10^{-12} British thermal units (Btus) in 1980 to 7.72×10^{-12} Btus in 1984.

The best indicator of the consequences for emissions of the change in fuels is the amount of emissions produced per amount of power generated. At the South Street plant, where low and higher sulfur oil are burned, emissions climbed from 1.05 pounds of sulfur dioxide per million Btus to 1.81. At the Manchester Street plant, where natural gas and low sulfur oil are burned, emissions dropped from 0.75 pounds of sulfur dioxide to 0.35 pounds. For the two plants together, the average dropped 16 percent, from 0.90 pounds of sulfur dioxide per million Btus to 0.76. However, this 16 percent decrease in emissions per amount of power generated occurred only in 1984; in prior years, emissions per amount of heat generated were about equal to or were above the levels of 1980.*

Consumption of higher sulfur fuel oil at the South Street plant (not shown on figure 4.3) climbed from zero gallons in 1980 to 8.8 million gallons in 1984, while consumption of low sulfur fuel at the plant dropped from 39.5 million gallons to 5.7 million gallons. Substitution of millions of gallons of cheaper, higher sulfur fuel, with attendant savings, would not have been possible without the bubble.

Tampa Electric Company, Tampa, Florida

Another type of fuel-switch bubble, one for a coal conversion from oil to coal burning, has been implemented at the Tampa Electric Company's Francis J. Gannon station. There, coal is to be burned in four of the utility's six boilers, with compliance with emission standards calculated on the basis of a bubble over all six units. The plant is located in an area that has attained the national ambient air quality standards for sulfur dioxide. No increase in actual emissions is permitted, and conditions attached to the permit are designed to prevent Florida's ambient air quality standard for sulfur dioxide from being threatened.[43]

---

*It is important to note that in the pre-bubble base year of 1980, the Manchester plant had already begun to burn natural gas, so the base year does not represent the burning in both plants of only 1 percent sulfur fuel oil. Moreover, in the absence of a complete analysis of the power company's choices for generating power, an examination beyond the scope of this report, one can only speculate about what the actual emissions might have been had the bubble not been permitted.

Figure 4.3
Energy Generation and Emissions—
Narragansett Electric Company Stations, Providence, Rhode Island

Year	South Street			Manchester Street			Total		
	Btus of heat generated (x10^{12})	SO$_2$ emissions (tons/year)	Emission rate (lbs SO$_2$/mBtu)	Btus of heat generated (x10^{12})	SO$_2$ emissions (tons/year)	Emission rate (lbs SO$_2$/mBtu)	Btus of heat generated (x10^{12})	SO$_2$ emissions (tons/year)	Emission rate (lbs SO$_2$/mBtu)
1980	5.92	3,108	1.05	6.04	2,281	0.75	11.96	5,389	0.90
1981	4.15	2,980	1.44	5.68	1,768	0.62	9.83	4,748	0.97
1982	2.27	1,452	1.28	2.47	1,339	1.08	4.7	2,791	1.18
1983	2.52	2,332	1.85	4.92	962	0.39	7.44	3,294	0.89
1984	2.17	1,961	1.81	5.55	965	0.35	7.72	2,926	0.76

Source: Rhode Island Department of Environmental Management, Division of Air and Hazardous Materials.

3M, Guin, Alabama

Still another type of fuel switch, involving a trade between boilers and other sources, can be found at 3M's manufacturing facility in Guin, Alabama.[44] This bubble lowers the allowable emissions of particulates from three boilers able to burn fuel oil or natural gas. When natural gas is burned, particulate emissions are 50 percent below the former allowable levels. The boilers burn oil only when natural gas is unavailable; between 1979 and the bubble's approval two years later, they burned natural gas exclusively. In exchange for lowering the allowable emissions on the boilers, the allowable emissions on 3M's glass furnace line are raised fivefold, thereby eliminating the need for the company to place controls on the glass furnace line to comply with the previous allowable limit (figure 4.4).

This fuel-switch bubble produces no change in the Guin plant's actual emissions; it merely adjusts allowable emissions to reflect pre-existing levels of actual emissions. The plant is located in an area that has attained the national ambient standards for particulates, and modeling performed by the state showed that no air quality standards are endangered by the bubble. Critics of the bubble policy might argue that by forgoing controls on the glass furnace line, this bubble squanders an opportunity to reduce emissions. But it is also the case (a) that the bubble does nothing worse than preserve the status quo in this attainment area; and (b) that controls can be placed on the furnaces at a later date if necessary.

Emission Banks—General Electric and International Harvester, Louisville, Kentucky

A trade approved by EPA for General Electric Company (GE) and International Harvester Company in Louisville, Kentucky, is somewhat different from those described above. It involves an exchange of ERCs through one of the few formal emission banks in the country[45] and represents one of the few instances thus far in which those credits have been leased. It also demonstrates the usefulness of trading for addressing short-term compliance problems.

The circumstances of this particular lease were described by the Regulatory Reform Staff's Levin:

> In July 1981 General Electric's Louisville appliance plant discovered that it could not install a new plastic-parts line in time to meet Kentucky's October 1981 compliance deadline for emission control. The line's late arrival

Figure 4.4
Pre- and Post-Bubble Allowable Particulate Emissions—
3M Plant, Guin, Alabama

	Current allowable emissions (number per hour)	Proposed allowable emissions (number per hour)
Boilers		
Spencer	9.4	4.7
Cleaver Brooks	6.7	3.4
Power Master	8.2	4.1
Glass furnace line		
Furnace zone 1	2.85[1]	9.0
Furnace zone 2		1.2
Frit handling equipment		2.0
Raw materials moving equipment		2.8
Total	27.15	27.2

1. Total for operation.

Source: 46 Fed. Reg. 34817 (July 6, 1981).

meant that GE could either risk noncompliance (and substantial penalties) for two years, shut down its old metal-parts coating line with its heavy emissions (and with large production losses), or buy a $1.5 million emissions incinerator that would be worthless when the old line was replaced in 1983. Instead, GE leased several hundred tons per year of emission reductions that had previously been deposited by International Harvester in the Louisville "emissions" bank. GE paid $60,000 for its two-year lease, and used the leased emission reduction credits to meet regulatory requirements on the old line.[46]

In its status reports on bubbles, EPA cites this trade as producing 45 tons per year of reductions beyond conventional requirements, because the 445 tons of credits leased exceed by 45 tons the 400 tons per year of reductions that would have been required by imposing RACT requirements on GE.[47] EPA also maintains that the transaction sped GE's compliance with regulatory requirements.

This bubble provided an administrative fix to an awkward problem. The Jefferson County [Louisville] Air Pollution Control District has a policy of bringing prompt criminal enforcement actions against any discharger violating its regulations.[48] But it clearly made little sense to force GE to spend money to control emissions from a line that would soon be phased out. The leased reductions came from the shutdown by financially troubled International Harvester of some of its operations in Louisville. Harvester's shutdown had not been spurred by a desire to help Louisville combat pollution, but the availability of the resulting ERCs helped solve GE's interim compliance problem.

In Louisville, there appears to be no problem with double-counting of shutdowns, double-counting that EPA's Emissions Trading Policy Statement counsels states to avoid.[49] The Jefferson County Air Pollution Control District does not rely on shutdowns from specific sources or categories of sources in its implementation plan for attaining the ozone standard.[50] Moreover, the local regulators try to assure a net air quality benefit from trading transactions, by "discounting" ERCs when they are deposited in the bank.[51] In states and localities that ban the use of shutdown credits in trading, or that cannot account for them carefully, some more conventional administrative fix allowed by the Clean Air Act or state regulations might have been needed to accommodate GE's short-term noncompliance.*

Open Dust Bubbles
As chapter 3 noted, one particularly controversial type of emissions trade has involved bubbles that include control of fugitive dust sources of pollutants as part of their strategies. Three such bubbles together illustrate why there has been uncertainty over allowing such trades and how such uncertainty has been addressed through modeling and monitoring. Two of the bubbles have been approved. They demonstrate the type of discharger initiative that the bubble policy has been intended to encourage. They also show that open dust trades can produce considerable economic savings while reducing levels of particulate emissions, contributing to attainment of the existing ambient standard for particulates. While studying the three examples that follow, it is well to keep in mind two points. First, knowledge of the effectiveness of controls on open sources of particulates continues to accumulate. Second, the availability of open dust trades in the future will depend on the extent to which emissions of smaller particulates are reduced by road paving and other measures and on how those reductions compare to those achievable from controls on industrial processes.

---

*For example, the Clean Air Act provides for issuance of "delayed compliance orders" in some circumstances.[52]

Armco, Middletown, Ohio

The first and most important of these bubbles has been one developed by Armco Inc. for its Middletown, Ohio, steel mill. Under conventional regulatory approaches, Armco would have been obliged to control "process fugitive" particulate emissions from its blast furnace and basic oxygen furnaces.[53] Unlike those emissions usually directed to some stack, process fugitive emissions usually escape to the atmosphere through windows, doors and vents;[54] installing and operating controls for process fugitive emissions can be quite costly. Armco estimated both that the initial capital cost of conventional controls would have been $7.5 million, with those controls consuming substantial amounts of energy[55] and that this equipment would have removed 587 tons of process particulates, 92.4 percent of the estimated fugitive emissions from the sources.[56] The company expected the cost of control to be $11,905 per ton for particulates captured at the blast furnace cast house and $13,630 per ton for particulates captured at the basic oxygen-furnace charging and tapping operation.[57]*

In prodding EPA to approve its alternative of road paving, road sweeping, chemical treatment of unpaved roads, controls on storage piles, vegetation of bare areas, and reduction of in-plant traffic, Armco was able to cite several studies that suggested unpaved roads and other open dust sources contribute significant amounts of particulates to the air. For example, in "Fugitive Emissions from Integrated Iron and Steel Plants," a study published by EPA in March 1978, the Midwest Research Institute (MRI) estimated that emissions of fine particulates from road traffic and storage piles ranked second and fourth in terms of the magnitude of fugitive emissions emitted nationwide at iron and steel plants; electric arc furnaces ranked first, and basic oxygen furnaces third.[58]† MRI estimated that watering and oiling unpaved roads and sweeping paved roads were at least 20 times more cost effective in reducing particulate emissions than using canopy hoods in a typical electric arc furnace.[60] MRI conceded the difficulty of obtaining reliable information on the effectiveness of control

---

*If the bubble enabled Armco to avoid controlling fugitive emissions from its open hearth furnaces (a reduction of 64 tons at a cost per ton of $63,992), another $4 million in capital costs would be saved.

†The MRI analysis excluded coke ovens, charging of basic oxygen furnaces, and blast furnace cast houses, which were being examined under separate research contracts at the time.[59]

measures on open dust sources, but it concluded that controls of such sources should be included in fugitive-emission control programs.[61]

A survey of Armco's Middletown facilities estimated that 60 percent of all particulate emissions came from open dust sources.[62] Armco's cleanup plan proposed an 83 percent reduction in emissions from open dust sources, a total reduction of 3,965 tons per year. This reduction would be nearly seven times greater than the reduction of 587 tons expected from controls on process fugitive emissions from the blast furnace and basic oxygen furnaces and could be achieved at far less cost.[63] The cost per ton of particulates controlled by Armco's strategy would be significantly less than the thousands of dollars per ton estimated for the conventional strategy.

Armco began implementing its preferred option, with concomitant monitoring, even before receiving EPA approval. Armco had great confidence in its approach but had to overcome great skepticism at EPA. As MRI had indicated, there was great uncertainty over the estimated effectiveness of open dust controls. As a result, monitoring the actual effects of installed controls was necessary to test the effectiveness of Armco's alternative. EPA finally approved the Armco bubble in 1981, after reviewing monitoring data that indicated real reductions were occurring in ambient concentrations of particulates around the Armco plant.[64] Although that plant is in an area that had failed to project attainment of the national ambient standards for particulates, modeling insisted on by EPA indicated that the Armco bubble, together with fugitive dust control programs by neighboring sources, would bring the area into attainment.[65] Moreover, because EPA's policy at the time barred bubbles for facilities not in compliance or on a schedule to comply with existing regulations, Armco agreed to a consent order in response to a federal "notice of violation" regarding emissions from Middletown's coke ovens.[66]

EPA no longer designates the area as not attaining the primary standard for particulates, although it is still designated nonattainment for the more stringent secondary standards.[67]* Armco reports that, at the monitor site whose previous high readings were the principal reason for the area's designation of nonattainment, the average annual geometric mean concentrations of particulates since 1980 have

---

*It is the primary (health-based) standards for which the 1982 and 1987 deadlines are set; such firm deadlines have not been established for attaining the secondary (welfare-based) standards.

declined more than 50 percent from their levels in the five years preceding 1980.[68] Armco also reports that two monitors near the Middletown plant, one upwind and one downwind, indicate reductions in both larger and smaller particulates are occurring.[69] This is particularly important since environmentalists have long been suspicious of open dust trades, not only because of the inherent difficulty in assessing the effectiveness of controls on open dust, but also because of their concern that by-products of industrial processes can be finer and more toxic than particulates from open dust sources.[70]

In early 1984, EPA proposed revising its standard for particulates, so as to distinguish smaller, potentially more harmful particles from larger ones.[71] It is not clear what impact this proposal, if adopted, will have on past or future open dust trades. Regardless of how past trades are treated, in future trades EPA undoubtedly will take a close look at the sizes of the particles involved.

Shenango, Allegheny County, Pennsylvania

Armco's open dust bubble in Middletown has been the prototype for other such trades.* For example, Shenango, Inc., another steel company, sought a similar trade at its Neville Island Works in Allegheny County, Pennsylvania. Shenango had been negotiating with EPA and the county over the provisions of a consent decree for these facilities and, in 1980, sought regulators' approval of an open dust trade.[74] Controls on open dust sources would be substituted for more expensive controls on the cast house for Shenango's blast furnace. Shenango submitted a consultant's study from April 1979, calculating that emissions from ore storage and handling facilities were 3 times greater than emissions from the cast house and that emissions from roads in and approaching the plant were up to 10 times greater.[75] EPA initially told Shenango that its bubble could not be approved, because a SIP projecting attainment had not yet been developed by Allegheny County.[76] Shenango responded that, if the SIP ultimately approved required controls greater than those it proposed, it would implement them and that in the interim "there would seem to be no logical justification for saying the public is better served by having

---

*It should be noted, however, that the Armco bubble predated the proposed Emissions Trading Policy Statement. Air quality modeling requirements are now more specific, and RACT baseline levels for open dust sources have become controversial.[72] Also, EPA did not require RACT determinations to be made for all the sources under Armco's bubble, because modeling performed for the bubble projected that the area would attain the ambient standard as expeditiously as possible.[73]

the company spend more money while the public receives less emission reduction, such as would be the situation with Shenango casthouse controls."[77]

Like Armco, Shenango began implementing its program before receiving final regulatory approval.[78] EPA ultimately found Shenango's bubble proposal approvable when modeling demonstrated that the proposal would help bring the area into attainment.[79]* In approving the bubble, EPA estimated that the emission reduction from the open dust control would reduce emissions by 287 tons per year, while conventional controls on the cast house would have yielded only 90 tons per year of reductions.[80] Moreover, the open dust plan was projected to cost almost 90 percent less, saving the company an estimated $4 million in capital expenditures.[81]

Shenango reports that its initial experience with the control program has been quite positive.[82] Control efficiencies of 93 percent are being obtained, easily surpassing the original prediction of 80 percent. Monitoring indicates the primary national ambient standard (75 micrograms per cubic meter) was attained; recorded levels dropped from an annual geometric mean of 106 micrograms per cubic meter in 1977 down to 64 micrograms per cubic meter in 1982.[83] (Shenango notes that a portion of this reduction probably was a result of poor business conditions in 1982.[84]) The area immediately around the plant has been redesignated by EPA as attaining the particulate standards.[85]

Armco, Ashland, Kentucky

Armco tried to repeat its bubble efforts at its steel facility in Ashland, Kentucky, another nonattainment area.[86] Kentucky submitted a SIP revision for Armco's bubble in early 1983. But as of January 1986, EPA had not formally approved the bubble. Difficulty sorting out the impact of Armco's emissions from those of other sources, taking into account the area's hilly terrain, and selecting an appropriate baseline for calculations all confounded analysis of the proposal.[87]†

---

*As was the case for Armco's Middletown bubble, it was not necessary to make RACT determinations for the sources involved, because modeling projected that the 1982 attainment deadline would be met using the Shenango bubble.

†Armco has suggested that process emissions from its steel plants are insignificant contributors to nearby ambient concentrations, being far outweighed by other, fugitive sources. In 1982, even before Armco began implementing its open dust control plan, no violations of the ambient standards were recorded. However, this may have been the result of reduced industrial activity throughout the area.

Armco's environmental engineering manager, Bruce Steiner, review-ing the experience at Ashland, has noted that construction activities at the Armco plant and changes at other industrial sources in the area have made it far more difficult there than it was at Middletown to establish a cause-and-effect relationship between Armco's open dust control plan and ambient air quality.[88]

Bubbles Involving Baseline Controversies

As discussed in chapter 3, minimalists and expansionists have argued over whether the baseline for credits should be either the emission limits established by industry-wide RACT standards or "standard industry practice." The two groups have also argued over the appro-priateness of permitting emissions trading in areas where projections of attainment are lacking or suspect. The three case studies that follow graphically illustrate those disputes. They also suggest how great uncertainty can be as to whether an area is attainment or nonattain-ment and demonstrate why EPA is accused of giving dischargers "paper credits." The three bubbles have in common a representation by EPA that the trades in question would produce reductions in emis-sions. In all the cases, the reductions are in allowable emissions only and do not represent changes in actual emissions beyond those that were achieved previously.

Sohio, Trumbull County, Ohio

On June 1, 1984, EPA published its proposed approval of a bubble for VOC emissions from a gasoline loading rack and aviation fuel loading rack located at a Standard Oil Company (Sohio) fuel terminal in Trumbull County, Ohio.[89] Trumbull County is a nonattainment area for ozone. Its projection of attainment by December 31, 1982, based on sources' allowable emissions, had been approved by EPA in 1980 and 1982.[90] In early 1983, shortly before the state of Ohio proposed approving Sohio's plan, EPA declared that the county likely had attained the ozone standard as projected.[91]

Sohio's bubble would lower the allowable VOC emissions from the gasoline loading rack from 46.74 to 46.04 tons per year, or from 0.67 to 0.66 pounds of VOC per 1,000 gallons of gasoline.[92] At the same time, the bubble would raise the allowable VOC emissions from the aviation fuel loading rack from 0.08 to 0.38 tons per year. (See figure 4.5.)

EPA's notice of proposed approval stated that this trade would

**Figure 4.5
Pre- and Post-Bubble Allowable and Actual VOC Emissions—
Sohio Fuel Terminal, Trumbull County, Ohio**

Source	Allowable emissions (tons/year)			Actual emissions (tons/year)		
	Pre-bubble	Post-bubble	Change	Pre-bubble	Post-bubble	Change
Aviation fuel loading rack	0.08	0.38	+ 0.30	0.38	0.38	0.00
Gasoline loading rack	46.74	46.04	− 0.70	4.00	4.00	0.00
Totals	46.82	46.42	− 0.40	4.38	4.38	0.00

Source: Ohio Environmental Protection Agency, Fact Sheet, Draft Variance for Sohio Niles Terminal Sources J001 and J002, May 3, 1983; and U.S. Environmental Protection Agency, Internal Documents.

lead "to an overall decrease in VOC emissions of 0.4 tons per year," and, on paper, that would seem to be the case. In truth, however, there would be no change in actual emissions. The actual emission rate from the gasoline loading rack currently is 0.052 pounds of VOC per 1,000 gallons of gasoline, for an annual total of less than 4 tons per year. That is only one-twelfth of—or 43 tons per year less than—the existing and proposed allowable levels.[93] This low level is achieved by using vapor recovery equipment with a control efficiency of 97.3 percent.[94] Moreover, the 0.38-ton standard that would be established for the aviation fuel loading rack is equivalent to the current actual emissions level.

Sohio's bubble would enable the company to avoid spending an estimated $50,000 for vapor control equipment on its aviation gasoline rack.[95] Sohio claims the cost of $8.40 per pound to control VOCs at the aviation gasoline rack is cost-ineffective, when compared to EPA estimates of $0.03 to $0.06 per pound to control emissions at gasoline loading terminals.[96]

Because the claimed reduction of 0.4 tons per year of VOC emissions under this bubble would be quite small, one might not expect Sohio's proposal to be controversial. But it has become so for several reasons. The major reason is that the ERCs granted for controls on the gasoline loading rack are not the consequence of a new effort by Sohio to reduce emissions below required levels. Rather, they derive from administrative recognition of low levels of actual emissions that have been achieved since 1980 by Sohio's control equipment at the gasoline loading rack.

Expansionist critics of this bubble suggest that the baseline from which credits would be measured is too high. These critics argue that the baseline should be not the emissions allowed at the gasoline rack by Ohio regulations but rather the level of actual emissions Sohio has been achieving since 1980. They contend that the actual emissions, and not those allowed by Ohio, constitute the level achievable by application of "reasonably available control technology." If these actual emissions were to be considered the baseline from which credits were calculated, no credits would be available to Sohio from its controls on the gasoline rack, and the company would have to install the controls required on the aviation fuel rack.

The critics also observe that, while in early 1983 EPA expected Trumbull County to have attained the ozone standard on schedule, in mid-1984 EPA denied Ohio's request for redesignation of the area to "attainment."[97] EPA denied the request because, even though no air quality monitors are sited in the county, it is adjacent to three counties whose monitors continue to demonstrate nonattainment and is downwind from Youngstown, another urban nonattainment area.[98] NRDC, citing EPA's denial of Ohio's request to designate Trumbull County as "attainment," and characterizing the claimed reductions as "paper credits," opposed the proposed bubble.[99] NRDC was less concerned with the small amounts of pollution involved than with the use of allowable rather than actual emissions as the baseline in an area that might not have attained the ambient standards on schedule. NRDC was also upset that Sohio would be able to forgo clearly identified controls that could reduce actual emissions below current levels.

Finally, NRDC was irritated by EPA's representation that this bubble would produce a reduction in emissions, when, as has been noted, it would produce no reduction in actual emissions and would permit the aviation fuel racks to continue emitting VOCs at levels higher than otherwise would have been permitted.

The minimalists within EPA argue that reductions at the aviation fuel rack should not be insisted on simply because they were previously targeted by regulators. They argue that the nonattainment program seeks emission reductions not for their own sake but for the sake of attaining the national ambient standards, and they stress that at the time EPA proposed approving Sohio's bubble, the area had an EPA-approved projection of attainment.

As of January 1986, EPA had not published a final decision on Sohio's bubble.

Ashland Oil, Covington, Kentucky

A bubble proposed for the Covington, Kentucky, fuel terminal of Ashland Oil, Incorporated, is roughly analogous to the Sohio bubble.[100] Covington is located in Kenton County, whose SIP for attaining the ambient standard for ozone is based on allowable emissions. For air quality planning purposes, Kenton County is grouped with other Kentucky and Ohio counties in the Cincinnati area.

Kenton County's SIP has a convoluted administrative history.[101] The state of Kentucky first sought extension of the county's attainment deadline to 1987. As provided by the Clean Air Act and EPA rules, areas seeking extensions of the attainment deadline to 1987 must develop inspection and maintenance programs for automobiles.[102] Kenton County failed to develop such a program, and EPA imposed a ban on construction of new major stationary sources in the county.[103]

Kentucky then submitted a revised SIP, projecting attainment for the area by December 31, 1982. This would have eliminated the need for the inspection and maintenance program and the reason for the sanctions. In February 1983, after the December 31, 1982, attainment deadline, EPA proposed to approve the projection of attainment and indicated that the attainment deadline probably had been met.[104] In its *Federal Register* notice to this effect, EPA noted that the emission inventory for point sources in Kentucky was insufficiently documented. But, the agency added, point sources in Kentucky contribute so little to the Cincinnati area inventory that the uncertainty caused by the inventory inadequacy was likely to have only a negligible impact on emission reduction calculations.[105]

EPA had thought that Kenton County would meet the December 31, 1982, attainment deadline, but monitoring in mid-1983, undertaken after EPA proposed approving Ashland Oil's bubble, revealed violations of the ambient air quality standard for ozone.

In August 1984, EPA Regional Administrator Charles Jeter recommended approval of the Ashland Oil bubble.[106] He wrote that the county still had an attainment deadline of 1987 in effect, together with a ban on construction of major new sources of VOCs, but the stationary source rules on which the bubble was based remained acceptable.[107]*

Ashland Oil had proposed to lower the allowable emission rate from its gasoline truck loading facility from 90 milligrams of hydrocarbons per liter of gasoline loaded to 30 milligrams of hydrocarbons per liter of gasoline loaded.[108] This would reduce allowable annual emissions from 50.7 tons per year to 19.0 tons per year, yielding an emission credit of 31.7 tons per year. The actual emissions from the gasoline loading rack are 7.08 milligrams of hydrocarbons per liter of gasoline loaded, or 4.4 tons per year. (See figure 4.6.)

The ERC would be used to help Ashland Oil avoid placing secondary seals on seven storage tanks. The allowable emission limit on the storage tanks would be raised from the 9.3 tons per year allowed

---

*The 1987 deadline and the ban remained in effect even though EPA had proposed to approve a change in the deadline to 1982, because EPA had not issued a final, legally binding determination changing the deadline.

Figure 4.6
Pre- and Post-Bubble Allowable and Actual VOC Emissions— Ashland Oil Terminal, Covington, Kentucky

Source	Allowable emissions (tons/year)			Actual emissions (tons/year)		
	Pre-bubble	Post-bubble	Change	Pre-bubble	Post-bubble	Change
Gasoline loading facility	50.7	19	−31.7	4.4	4.4	0.0
Storage tanks	9.3	37.2	+27.9	37.2	37.2	0.0
Total	60.0	56.2	− 3.8	41.6	41.6	0.0

Source: May 18, 1982, state implementation plan revision submitted by Jackie Swigart, Secretary of Natural Resources and Environmental Protection, Commonwealth of Kentucky, to Charles Jeter, Regional Administrator, Region IV, U.S. Environmental Protection Agency.

by Kentucky regulations to 37.2 tons per year, the level of the tanks' actual emissions. On paper, the reduction from this transaction would be 3.8 tons per year of emissions, since allowable emissions would drop from 60.0 tons to 56.2 tons per year. In practice, the bubble would allow Ashland to forgo installing seals on its storage tanks; these seals would reduce actual emissions by an additional 27.9 tons.

As of January 1986, EPA had not taken final action on this proposal.

BFGoodrich, Avon Lake, Ohio

At its chemical plant in Avon Lake, Ohio, the BFGoodrich Company proposed increasing the allowable emissions from two boilers and decreasing the allowable emissions from three polyvinyl chloride resin storage silos.[109] Avon Lake is located in an area of Lorain County, Ohio, that was designated as not attaining the secondary ambient standard for particulates.* The area lacked an EPA-approved projection of attainment.

In February 1983, EPA proposed approving the bubble.[110] The agency stated that, consistent with the interim Emissions Trading Policy Statement, in this nonattainment area lacking a projection of attainment, regulations representing RACT should be used as a baseline for calculating ERCs. The agency decided that the Ohio regulations applicable to the BFGoodrich facilities were representative of RACT and, in its notice of proposed approval, declared that the net decrease in particulate emissions from the bubble would be 16.2 pounds per hour. The boilers, EPA argued, would be emitting 8.8 pounds per hour above previously allowable limits while the silos would be emitting 25 pounds per hour below previously allowable limits.[111] Allowable emissions from the boilers would increase by 37.2 tons per year, and allowable emissions from the silos would decrease 109.8 tons per year, yielding an annual reduction in allowable emissions of 72.6 tons (figure 4.7). In practice, however, there would be no change in actual emissions, and the emission reductions forgone by raising the allowable levels on the boilers would be 37.2 tons per year. By having the allowable limits on the boilers raised, BFGoodrich would be able to forgo controls on the boilers that otherwise would have been required.

*As noted previously, the secondary standard for particulates is more stringent than the primary standard, but the Clean Air Act does not set a firm deadline for attainment of the secondary standard.

NRDC and the state of New Jersey submitted comments opposing the bubble, arguing among other things that the baseline for calculating credits from the silos was far too loose.[112] NRDC, noting that the existing level of actual emissions from the silos was less than 0.6 percent of the allowable level, contended that the existing RACT baseline "could be achieved at these silos only by operating them with little or no emissions control equipment. Uncontrolled or poorly controlled operation does not represent RACT."[113] NRDC also asked EPA to lower the credit-calculation baseline to the level of control already accomplished by BFGoodrich at its silos.

In response to these complaints, EPA reversed its position and proposed instead to disapprove the BFGoodrich bubble. Accepting the critics' arguments, EPA redefined RACT for the silos from the previous allowable levels to their actual levels. This made BFGoodrich's actual emissions from the silos the baseline from which ERCs were to be calculated, effectively eliminating the credits that BFGoodrich hoped to use to permit it to forgo controls on its boilers.

In comments on EPA's public notice of the proposed disapproval, BFGoodrich argued, among other points, that EPA's characterization of the area as nonattainment did not reflect environmental conditions near the company's plant.[114] BFGoodrich cited data for 1982 and 1983 from the monitor closest to its plant, demonstrating compliance with the ambient standards for particulates. BFGoodrich also submitted modeling results for its bubble, suggesting that the bubble would benefit air quality, and contended that modeling done earlier for a boiler it never constructed demonstrated attainment of the national standards at emission rates even higher than the excess emissions from its existing boilers.[115]

BFGoodrich also took issue with NRDC's characterization of the existing RACT baseline as being too loose and representing virtually no control. The company noted that, though the pre-bubble baseline permitted 172 times the emissions actually coming from its silos, that limit was based on baghouse technology operating at a control efficiency of 99.86 percent.[116] BFGoodrich said that its baghouses, installed in 1980, were operating at an efficiency of 99.995 percent.[117] The company claimed that it deserved credit for improving on the technology on which the RACT baseline was based; it also asserted that its improved efficiencies, accomplished "by implementing measures involving such factors as the type of fabric in the bag, the air-to-cloth ratios, and the cleaning mechanism," were clearly "best

Figure 4.7
Pre- and Post-Bubble Allowable and Actual VOC Emissions—
BFGoodrich Avon Lake Plant, Ohio

Source	Allowable emissions (tons/year)			Actual emissions (tons/year)		
	Pre-bubble	Post-bubble	Change	Pre-bubble	Post-bubble	Change
Boilers (2)	112.8	150.0	+ 37.2	150.0	150.0	0.0
Silos (3)	113.1	3.3	− 109.8	0.7	0.7	0.0
Total	225.9	153.3	− 72.6	150.7	150.7	0.0

Source: Ohio Environmental Protection Agency, Fact Sheet for Draft Variances B006 and B007, May 4, 1982.

available control technology" and may even have represented "lowest achievable emission rate."[118]

In December 1984, EPA issued its final rule, disapproving BFGoodrich's proposed bubble.[119] The agency restated its view that BFGoodrich's baghouses represented RACT, since they fit the RACT definition of being "reasonably available" and "economically and technologically feasible." In addition, EPA disputed BFGoodrich's calculation of the efficiency of its baghouses; the agency contended that, because the company used an incorrect method for calculating efficiency, the actual efficiency of the baghouses was "significantly lower" than the claimed 99.995 percent. EPA also dismissed BFGoodrich's modeling results, claiming that the modeling failed to satisfy the agency's modeling guidelines and lacked some important elements. Finally, EPA rejected BFGoodrich's contentions based on monitoring data, arguing that the monitor site was not representative of the air quality in the area of the plant; for that and other reasons, the monitoring data could not be used as a basis for redesignating the area around the plant as being in attainment.

BFGoodrich believes that EPA's rejection of its bubble constituted "changing rules in the middle of the game."[120] The company maintains that, more often than not, it overcontrols its sources.[121] It might have used other sources for its bubble and might have submitted a different application had it known that the baseline for its calculations would be unacceptable.[122]

Shutdown Credits—Union Carbide, Texas City, Texas

In 1980, Union Carbide Corporation sought approval of a bubble for its Texas City, Texas, petrochemical plant. As compared to virtually all other bubbles approved or proposed for approval by EPA, the Union Carbide bubble is exceptional in its complete reliance on credits from a shutdown.

Texas City is in Galveston County, which EPA labels as a rural nonattainment area for ozone. EPA policy presumes that a substantial portion of the nonattainment problem for such rural areas (which have populations under 200,000) derives from nearby urban areas, so that even if all the sources within the rural areas were controlled, the areas would nevertheless be dependent on controls in the neighboring areas to reach attainment.[123] In such rural nonattainment areas, EPA simply insists on RACT controls on all major sources for which

EPA has issued RACT guidance.[124] In 1980, EPA conditionally approved Texas's SIP for Harris County (Houston), the urban area influencing ozone levels in Galveston County.[125] EPA granted Harris County an extension of the attainment deadline to 1987.[126]

In 1972, shortly after the 1970 amendments to the Clean Air Act were passed, Union Carbide received an exemption from controls on 29 storage tanks at its Texas City facilities, because emissions from the tanks were not regarded as contributors to the area's ozone problem.[127] Union Carbide also was operating a polyethylene plant in Texas City at the time but shut the plant in 1978 because it was technologically obsolete.[128] However, the 1,120 tons of emissions from that plant, including 243.3 tons from point sources, were included in the 1977 emissions inventory that was the basis for the revised Texas SIP that received conditional EPA approval.[129]

In 1979, the exemption for the storage tanks, which emitted 228.8 tons of pollutants, was lifted. Union Carbide estimated that future controls to be placed on the tanks would cost $3.5 million.[130] The company sought to avoid installing these controls by taking credit for the 243.3 tons of point-source emission reductions from the shuttered polyethylene facility.[131] Observing that, under the bubble, "emission reductions will [occur] well in advance of the compliance deadline for the storage tanks and loading facilities,"[132] EPA proposed to approve the bubble in 1981. When it published its final approval in 1982, the agency noted that the bubble would not interfere with reasonable further progress toward, and attainment of, the ambient standards.[133]

NRDC petitioned to have the bubble plan reconsidered.[134] NRDC argued that, even though Texas City is in a rural nonattainment area, opportunities should not be forgone to impose RACT on sources within that area, especially when the area is downwind from an urban nonattainment area whose attainment of the standards by the statutory deadline was in doubt.[135] NRDC maintained that approval of the credit would forgo 228.8 tons of real emission reductions and would keep emission levels from the storage tanks higher than they otherwise would be.[136] To give credit for the shutdown, NRDC argued, would postpone attainment of the standard, prolong public exposure to unhealthy air, and be in direct conflict with Texas's statutory obligation to meet the ambient standards as expeditiously as practicable.[137]

EPA's approval of this bubble predated the agency's mid-1983

Federal Register notice requesting public comments on alternative approaches to crediting shutdowns in emissions trading. EPA did not respond formally to NRDC's petition for reconsideration of the Union Carbide bubble, having promised to address shutdown issues in the final Emissions Trading Policy Statement.

Manipulated Assumptions and Shifting Judgments— National Steel, Wayne County, Michigan

The National Steel Corporation proposed an open dust bubble for its Great Lakes Steel subsidiary. The bubble initially was proposed for approval by EPA but then was disapproved after an analysis by NRDC demonstrated enormous errors in the modeling used to justify it. This bubble illustrates how manipulation of assumptions about emission rates can dramatically alter the outcome of modeling exercises and how shifting judgments about baselines can alter the conclusions about the environmental benefits of bubble proposals. This bubble also shows how bubble proposals can confound enforcement activity.

Many complex technical issues were disputed during consideration of this bubble. Perhaps the central issue was the level of control required by the use of RACT.* EPA, NRDC, state and local regulators, and National Steel disagreed over what constituted RACT. Consequently, disputes occurred over whether some of the controls proposed by National Steel were "better than RACT" and therefore could earn ERCs.

The Great Lakes Steel plant is located in Wayne County, Michigan, an area that had failed to attain the ambient standard for particulates by the original deadline set in the 1970 amendments to the Clean Air Act. At the time National Steel proposed its bubble, EPA's policy for particulate nonattainment areas insisted that revised SIPs prepared pursuant to the 1977 amendments required controls on industrial (or "traditional") sources. Where use of RACT on those sources was insufficient to project attainment by 1982 of the ambient standard for particulates, states were to assess the effectiveness of controls on urban fugitive dust, construction, and other "nontraditional" sources. States

---

*As noted earlier, RACT determinations were not an issue in the Armco-Middletown and Shenango open dust bubbles, because both of these bubbles projected attainment for their areas.

were also to submit a timetable for assessing and adopting controls on nontraditional sources.

Michigan and Wayne County regulators had not yet developed an EPA-approved projection of attainment before EPA began to consider and proposed approval of National Steel's bubble proposal in 1981 and 1982. Moreover, EPA, the county, the state, and the company were wrangling over the appropriate RACT requirements for iron and steel facilities.*

Under EPA's 1979 bubble policy, Wayne County's lack of an EPA-approved projection of attainment would have kept National Steel's bubble proposal from being considered. In the proposed revisions to the policy mentioned in EPA Administrator Douglas Costle's January 1981 press release (discussed in chapter 3), however, EPA indicated its willingness to consider bubbles in such areas.

The saga of the Great Lakes steel bubble began with EPA filing suit against National Steel in August 1979, alleging a host of violations of the Clean Air Act.[140] On October 31, 1980, EPA and National Steel agreed on a consent order outlining the actions the company would take to clean up its facilities at its Great Lakes Steel, Granite City (Illinois) Steel, and Weirton (West Virginia) Steel divisions.[141]†

The order obliged National Steel to place hoods and a baghouse on its No. 2 basic oxygen furnace shop and to clean up or close down other facilities at the Great Lakes site. The schedule for the basic oxygen furnace shop was quite tight, requiring demonstrated compliance by November 15, 1982 (later extended to December 31, 1982). The order provided for steep penalties if its various deadlines were not

---

*EPA had approved only some of the regulations submitted by state and local regulators. When it disapproved regulations that had been submitted, EPA substituted its own tougher RACT requirements. The wrangling over RACT requirements for iron and steel facilities in Michigan occurred against a backdrop of EPA concern that several states had proposed SIP revisions less strict than the tough abatement requirements the agency had succeeded in imposing on iron and steel producers through enforcement actions.[138] National Steel was unsuccessful in its legal challenge to EPA's RACT determinations for Michigan.[139]

†National Steel also sought bubbles for its facilities at Granite City and Weirton. EPA approved the Weirton bubble. But after proposing approval of the bubble for Granite City Steel, following comments by Citizens for a Better Environment and the Environmental Defense Fund criticizing the modeling for the Granite City facility, EPA disapproved the bubble there.[142] The Granite City Steel bubble was a "conditional" one, in that if attainment was not demonstrable by 1984, the company would have to install controls on its blast furnace.[143] The company is now providing added controls on road emissions and working to control its blast furnace.[144]

met. The order permitted National Steel to apply for a bubble at the Great Lakes facility but stipulated that such an application would not be grounds for delaying the order's requirements.[145] In other words, National Steel was obligated to spend money on a conventional control approach, to avoid violating the order, even though the money might prove to have been wasted if the bubble application ultimately was approved.

National Steel placed purchase orders for new control equipment as the consent order required.[146] But, after submitting its bubble proposal to EPA in September 1981, it cancelled the orders. National Steel calculated that the bubble would save it $16 million in capital costs and $2 million in annual operating costs.[147]

There was immediate disagreement within EPA as to the merits of the bubble application. The Regulatory Reform Staff, relying on a technical analysis prepared by EPA's Region V office, viewed it positively and recommended that the bubble be approved. They contended that approval could be granted by modifying the consent decree without requiring a formal SIP revision.[148] They characterized the proposal as producing a reduction in particulates of 5,325 tons per year from existing levels and a reduction of 350 tons per year beyond existing RACT requirements.[149] The 350-ton reduction beyond RACT was a result of increasing controls on National Steel's electric arc furnace and controlling road dust, while simultaneously easing or forgoing controls on the No. 2 basic oxygen furnace and blast furnace cast houses. The second and third columns in figure 4.8 show how the 350-ton reduction was calculated.

The Regulatory Reform Staff regarded the baselines selected by National Steel as consistent with existing requirements.[150] They recognized that some of the RACT requirements might be revised, especially since Wayne County had yet to project attainment, but noted that National Steel had acknowledged that it might later be obliged to implement further controls. Taking into account the company's willingness to add further controls, the Regulatory Reform Staff concluded that the bubble "would present no threat to future air quality in the area; would provide a rapid short term improvement in air quality, and would relieve National Steel of having to install very expensive controls when ultimate control requirements are uncertain."[151]

The view from EPA's air programs office in Washington was quite different. That calculation, which showed greater reductions from

Figure 4.8
Alternative Calculations of RACT Emissions and Bubble Emissions of Particulates—Great Lakes Steel Facilities

Source	Current	Emission rate (tons per year)			
		As presented		Corrected	
		RACT	Bubble	RACT	Bubble
Casthouses	681	170	681	57	681
No. 2 BOP secondary	643	227	428	38	535
EAF secondary	4,800	751	195	555	364
Steel mill roads	563	563	67	563	67
Total	6,686	1,711	1,361	1,213	1,647
		20% decrease		36% increase	

Source: Memorandum, U.S. Environmental Protection Agency, Office of Air, Noise, and Radiation, Mark Siegler to Michael Alushin, "National Steel Corporation Bubble Application for its Great Lakes Steel Division," September 29, 1981, pp. 2, 5.

RACT than from the bubble, are shown in the last two columns in figure 4.8. Without adjusting the figures for control of fugitive dust from roads, the air programs office concluded that RACT requirements would reduce allowable emissions to 1,213 tons per year and that emissions from under the bubble would be 1,647 tons. The office's analysis suggested that National Steel was claiming too many credits from sources it was "overcontrolling" and that it was understating the emissions at the undercontrolled cast houses. A memo from the office concluded, "National claims a 20 percent emissions benefit [350 tons] whereas on a stationary source basis alone it actually would permit at least 36 percent more emissions [424 tons]."[152]*

The air programs office's calculations were different from those of the bubble's proponents because the office disagreed with the proponents' assumptions about how effective certain control equipment would be, the amount of time certain manufacturing processes and their associated control equipment would operate during the year, and the degree of control required by EPA-approved state regulations defining RACT. Figure 4.8 shows, however, that, regardless of whose calculations were "correct," emissions from previous levels would have been reduced by thousands of tons.

After requiring National Steel's proposal to be submitted as a SIP revision by Michigan, EPA published a notice in December 1982 indicating that it proposed to approve the bubble, with slight revisions to take into account Michigan's evolving SIP and revised EPA policy governing bubbles.[153] In proposing the bubble for approval, EPA estimated that it would reduce emissions by 262 tons per year beyond RACT requirements.[154] As a result of the bubble, the control equipment specified in the consent order to reduce fugitive emissions from the No. 2 basic oxygen furnace would no longer be needed. Credit for controls on road dust were based on an assumption that a 50 percent reduction in emissions from unpaved roads would be required by RACT and that any controls beyond that level would be credited under the bubble.[155] That assumption was proposed by National Steel,

---

*The office also indicated that National Steel was claiming credit for reductions in road dust that ultimately would be required by the Michigan SIP. The office said that too many credits were being claimed from this source; however, it did not change the numbers in figure 4.8 to show the excessive credit, because the reductions in road dust to be required by the SIP had not yet been determined.

with the concurrence of the state of Michigan and EPA Region V.*

Air quality modeling demonstrated the bubble's ambient equivalency to conventional controls. Still, EPA's evolving policy on modeling for bubbles required supplemental modeling to demonstrate that the bubble would not result in a significant air quality impact on a short-term (24-hour) basis. EPA indicated that results of the additional modeling would be published during the period of public comment on the proposed bubble.

NRDC decided to examine the bubble proposal closely. The council's 60 pages of comments, supplemented by internal EPA memorandums, restated some of the group's general objections to bubbles in nonattainment areas without fully approved SIPs and then offered specific technical objections.[157] For example, NRDC alleged that the "credit" offered for controlling road dust was invalid since the controls proposed by National Steel were already required by portions of the SIP then in effect and by the general obligation to employ RACT.[158]

More important, NRDC contended that the supplemental modeling published during the public comment period failed to demonstrate that the bubble would not degrade air quality.[159] NRDC noted that the road segments in the model were one or more kilometers south of their actual locations.[160] Also, one road's length had been stretched from just under a quarter mile to just under a half mile, thereby reducing concentrations of emissions by spreading them over a larger area. NRDC maintained that these and other errors caused the model to misrepresent the bubble's ambient impact. In other words, the proposal failed to satisfy EPA's requirement that a bubble have an ambient impact equivalent to or better than the impact of conventional controls.

EPA did not agree with all of NRDC's criticisms, but, after correcting National Steel's analysis for the errors, the agency concluded that emissions from under the bubble would produce a "significant" increase in ambient concentrations of particulates. Consistent with

---

*EPA was aware when it proposed approval of the bubble that the agency's baselines for calculating credits for reductions of road dust made the proposal's legal basis shaky. The 50 percent level of control was based on using water to reduce road dust, although chemical dust suppressants, such as those used by Armco and Shenango, could have achieved much higher levels of control. In an October 1982 meeting, EPA air programs office personnel and Region V staff agreed that, in future bubbles, the RACT baseline for calculating credits for controls on road dust would be 75 percent.[156]

its Emissions Trading Policy Statement and subsequent technical guidance, EPA reversed itself (with the concurrence of its Regulatory Reform Staff) and declared that the bubble could not be approved, for it lacked a demonstration that it would not contribute significantly to violations of the ambient standard for particulates.[161]

EPA also indicated that it had reconsidered how RACT should be defined for several emission points. For example, for controlling road dust, EPA defined RACT as those techniques proposed by National Steel for use under the bubble. Because they were no longer judged as improvements beyond RACT requirements, National Steel would no longer be able to claim any credits from its dust control operations.

Following EPA's rejection of the bubble, the federal government returned to court, asking that National Steel be penalized for violating the consent order's requirement that the company control emissions from its basic oxygen furnace. National Steel's attorneys replied that their company should not have to pay the penalties because, among other reasons, EPA had not been diligent in reviewing the bubble proposal, had repeatedly changed its mind on technical matters, and had failed to adhere to statements made in Costle's press release and elsewhere to the effect that bubbles would be encouraged and would be processed in expedited fashion.[162]

Federal District Judge Anna Diggs Taylor was unimpressed by National Steel's arguments. She commented that National had gambled "that either EPA would approve the alternative plan it had in mind, or that it could force EPA to do so by eliciting a set of confused and mixed signals from the EPA throughout this period."[163]

National Steel appealed the $5 million fine to the Sixth Circuit U.S. Court of Appeals. The Sixth Circuit upheld the lower court's imposition of a fine but lowered the penalty by several million dollars.[164] The appeals court, observed that there was "plenty [of blame] available to both sides," that EPA's policy staff and technical staff were "not in harmony" regarding the bubble's propriety, that EPA did give mixed signals, and that National Steel "sought to bypass the technical staff to obtain relief directly from the policymakers."[165]*

LESSONS FROM THE BUBBLE POLICY IN PRACTICE

Experience with the bubble policy in practice has been both positive and discomforting. Some of the principal lessons are discussed below.

---

*Prior to the court's decision on National Steel's appeal, the company brought itself into compliance with the emission limits on the No. 2 basic oxygen furnace.[166]

Actual versus On-Paper Reductions

By stressing in its statements about bubbles the reductions achieved in allowable emissions, EPA has made itself vulnerable to allegations that the credits being claimed exist only on paper. Some bubbles (for example, 3M-Bristol and du Pont Chambers Works) yield both substantial reductions in actual emissions from previous levels and reductions below levels that would be achieved by conventional controls. But other bubbles (for example, du Pont-Kinston, 3M-Guin, and Sohio) simply reflect administrative recognition of past emission reductions and do not result in additional reductions in emissions. Additional reductions do not have the importance in attainment areas that they have in nonattainment areas. However, uncertainty about the reductions required to attain national ambient standards in areas where attainment has been in doubt has intensified conflict over specific bubble proposals (for example, Sohio and Ashland).

Some administrative accounting changes enable companies to forgo reductions that otherwise would be required. Regulatory reformers generally regard these adjustments as unobjectionable if they are shown not to jeopardize statutory goals of attaining national ambient standards and protecting PSD increments. They reflect a more cost-effective approach to attaining clean-air goals and use companies' superior knowledge of their own facilities to encourage better control methods and to improve the inventories on which state implementation plans are based.*

To critics, forgone controls represent squandered opportunities to minimize emissions, because companies are able to avoid previously established abatement requirements. One of the harshest characterizations of industry actions can be found in a letter from NRDC soliciting funds for a project to monitor emissions trading. Citing the Great Lakes bubble, a bubble proposed by the Monsanto Corporation that relied partly on shutdowns, and an emissions trade involving mobile sources,† NRDC wrote:

---

*The changes in inventories resulting from bubbles described in this chapter are only a sample of bubbles' informational impact. EPA's Regulatory Reform Staff, trying to document information impacts, has reported that one bubble proposal disclosed a plant that had been left out of a state's emission inventory. A second proposal, for a plant in a nonattainment area, revealed the plant's permit to be 30 times less demanding than the area's projection of attainment assumed.[167]

†The mobile source trade did not occur pursuant to policies established in the Emissions Trading Policy Statement. Rather, it was an effort by General Motors

NRDC has discovered that for the past several years you and I have been victims of pollution scams run by some of America's most reputable corporations! These companies have used [trading] scams to avoid installing air pollution controls *that are required by federal law.*[169]

Development of Attainment Projections and Actual Reductions Beyond RACT Requirements

Two bubbles in areas that previously had failed to project attainment (Armco-Middletown and Shenango) helped such projections to be developed. One bubble in an area that had yet to develop a detailed projection (du Pont Chambers Works) provided reductions beyond those otherwise required by "reasonably available control technology," at reduced cost. Preliminary, incomplete, non-peer-reviewed results of an air programs office study of 37 bubbles, conducted in mid-1985, suggest there have been several more such bubbles, producing improvements beyond RACT.

Cost Savings

Bubbles produce significant cost savings. Even if one were to discount claims of savings by a 20 to 50 percent "skepticism factor," the savings from many bubbles (for example, Armco-Middletown, Shenango, and miscellaneous fuel switches) remain considerable. Regulatory reformers see these savings as one of the prime purposes of the bubble policy—achieving emission reductions at reduced cost. But this "cost-rationalizing" element of bubbling is vulnerable to criticism where costs are saved by forgoing previously identified control opportunities in areas whose ability to attain ambient standards is in doubt. In such circumstances, cost-saving approaches are not necessarily more cost-effective ways of meeting a goal; instead, they may be ways to avoid costs that may be necessary to meet the goal. Suspicions multiply if a recalcitrant polluter is involved. But, even if additional reductions ultimately will be needed, it makes sense to schedule the most inexpensive reductions first.

Corporation to avoid recalling autos violating auto emission standards. General Motors promised instead to produce new cars that would emit pollutants at levels below those required by federal law. EPA agreed to the proposal, but a federal court reversed the EPA action, holding that recalls were the only remedy provided by the Clean Air Act for cars violating emission standards.[168]

Technological Innovation

Sometimes bubble opportunities facilitate technological innovations. A prime example is 3M-Bristol. Similar operations involving low-solvent and solventless coatings likely have been approved under state generic rules. However, most innovations under bubbles merely are rearrangements of conventional technologies, better accounting for conventional technologies, or fuel switches. Yet, as one advocate of bubbles has argued, emissions trading "has promoted more pollution control for less money and that is the only kind of innovation that matters."[170]

Accelerated Compliance

Bubbles speed compliance in two ways. One way is by bringing levels of actual emissions down to or below the levels required by existing regulations and by doing so in a speedier fashion than through use of conventional control strategies. This has been done, for example, with the du Pont Chambers Works. A second way (used by du Pont-Kinston, Sohio, Ashland Oil, and BFGoodrich) is by adjusting regulatory requirements so that allowable emissions are raised to levels of actual emissions at points whose actual emissions previously exceeded allowable emissions. Where this second method has been used in attainment areas, it happens to be less problematic than in nonattainment areas. This second method appears to occur frequently. In those instances where regulators have invested considerable resources in initiating an enforcement action against a noncomplying source, company efforts to "bubble into compliance" may well cause considerable frustration for enforcement personnel.

Added Flexibility

Bubble opportunities add useful flexibility to administration of the Clean Air Act, as demonstrated by the General Electric-International Harvester trade. They supplement the existing repertoire of delayed compliance orders, variances, conventional SIP revisions, and other traditional approaches designed to adjust previously adopted requirements. Delayed compliance orders provide flexibility for sources encountering difficulty in meeting emission reduction deadlines. Conventional SIP revisions have been used to allow sources to increase their emissions legally. To the extent that all these techniques involve extensions of deadlines, increases in actual emissions, and other apparent backsliding from the goals established in the Clean Air Act, they have been criticized by environmentalists on grounds that the goals of that act are being threatened. Bubbles have a significantly higher profile, however, than many of those other administrative techniques, so they draw an especially intense level of criticism.

Public and Administrative Scrutiny

Careful public and administrative scrutiny of bubble proposals is vitally important. NRDC's views of how bubble decisions should be made have not always been adopted by EPA, but NRDC's monitoring activities have helped reveal questionable calculations by industries proposing bubbles and have raised important policy questions deserving further attention by EPA. In some instances, NRDC has identified shortcomings in data that had escaped regulators' attention.

More Varied Involvement of Industries

The steel industry, which earned a reputation for environmental recalcitrance in the mid-1970s, was an early beneficiary of the bubble policy. During the bubble policy's earliest years, the steel industry's proposed or approved bubbles outnumbered those of any other industry whose bubbles were approved or considered for approval by EPA. The industry benefited from increased knowledge about the contribution of unpaved roads and storage piles to ambient concentrations of pollutants, enabling it to use open dust trades for compliance purposes. The industry also benefited from opportunities to trade sulfur dioxide emissions. However, most bubbles approved or proposed for approval under state generic rules and many more pending at EPA involve coating industries and other sources of volatile organic compounds, so the predominant role of the steel industry in bubble activity has been declining rapidly.

Judging "Standard Industry Practice"

The Sohio and Ashland Oil bubbles demonstrate how substantially better than state emissions standards for RACT the technologies at overcontrolled points can perform. If these companies' technologies represent what the command expansionists characterize as "standard industry practice" for complying with RACT requirements, then many industries may already be reducing emissions by substantially more than RACT. The command minimalists are correct, however, that making administrative judgments about what is standard practice for a given industry would be a difficult, time-consuming process, one that would create considerable uncertainty for those wishing to bubble.

The Role of Shutdowns

As noted in the preceding chapter, state attitudes vary regarding use of bubbles in shutdowns. Jefferson County, Kentucky, found credits from International Harvester's closing useful for accommodating General Electric's compliance problems. Union Carbide is using shutdowns to avoid controls in an area where critics have argued that additional reductions will be needed for attainment. In New Jersey, where credits from shutdowns are not used in bubbles, 26 bubbles have been approved, and 10 are under review. New Jersey's experience suggests that, in states where no shutdowns are permitted for bubbling, bubble opportunities may still be plentiful, yielding reductions beyond those accomplished merely by shutting old facilities.

Determining Crucial Standards

Determinations of emission rates, RACT and other baselines, modeling requirements, and attainment status are critical elements of bubble decisions, and for these reasons have been the focus of tugs-of-war between the command minimalists and expansionists. At first glance, the disputes over these determinations have an other-worldly character, because the arguments often are over assumptions and estimates as much as they are over actual conditions. These theoretical disputes sometimes appear to have little or no relationship to actual environmental conditions. But, in fact, the arguments are quite important, because such determinations govern the degree of difficulty industries have adjusting regulatory requirements through emissions trading.

Disputes over bubbles have highlighted some of the difficulties in making important judgments about standards, baselines, and related matters and have underscored some of the many uncertainties associated with the Clean Air Act's implementation. The closing chapter

of this report offers recommendations on how administrative practices might be changed, and the final Emissions Trading Policy Statement drafted, to eliminate or reduce some of the worst fears critics
have of emissions trading while enhancing its environmental benefits.
But before offering those conclusions, this report turns to trading
for new and modified sources.

Chapter 5

Bubbles and Netting for New and Modified Sources

Emissions trading for new and modified sources of pollutants has evolved amid great uncertainty, as it has for existing sources. Its progress has often seemed slow, largely because of tugs-of-war within the U.S. Environmental Protection Agency (EPA) and because of judicial scrutiny of EPA proposals.

Emissions trading ideas for new and modified sources have evolved over the past dozen years, primarily through three EPA programs— New Source Performance Standards, the Prevention of Significant Deterioration program, and special requirements for siting new and modified major sources in nonattainment areas. Each of these programs is considered in this chapter.

BUBBLES IN THE NEW SOURCE PERFORMANCE STANDARD PROGRAM

New Source Performance Standard (NSPS) provisions are a major technology-forcing feature of the Clean Air Act. They reflect Congress's judgment that new and modified sources should use new, high-quality technologies to abate emissions. The standards "reflect the degree of emission limitation . . . achievable through application of the best . . . technological system of continuous emission reduction which . . . has been adequately demonstrated."[1] The standards are set on an industry-by-industry basis by the EPA administrator, who can take costs, energy requirements, and other factors into account when setting them. (See box, "Sources Subject to New Source Performance Standards".) In theory, NSPSs create a guaranteed market for new technologies developed by vendors of pollution control equipment, reduce the need for costly retrofits to increase control at a later date, and permit continued economic growth without threatening environmental quality.

EPA has attempted to use NSPSs to allow two general types of bubbles for new or modified sources. The first, "applicability bubbles," would have allowed modified points in a plant to avoid NSPS requirements if their emission increases were balanced by equal decreases elsewhere. Applicability bubbles, however, were ruled illegal by a federal court in 1978. Their history demonstrates the important role that the specific terms of the Clean Air Act, and their interpretation by the courts, have played in the evolution of emissions trading. With the second type, "compliance bubbles," EPA can simply use its discretion in writing an NSPS for an entire industry and choose to group several new points within a plant together, set an emission limit for all of them jointly, and leave it to the dischargers to formulate the most cost-effective abatement strategy. New and modified source bubbles of this sort are conceptually no different than bubbles for existing sources and are apparently legal, although the legality of some variant compliance bubbles still under discussion remains untested.*

Economic and Environmental Rationales for New Source Bubbles

NSPS bubbles, especially those providing for trades between new or modified points and existing points, are promoted for both economic and environmental reasons. As emission standards are tightened, it becomes increasingly expensive to remove each additional amount of a pollutant.[2] For example, in one hypothetical situation it might cost $500,000, or $5,000 per ton, to remove the last 100 tons of a pollutant from a point subject to a strict NSPS. In that

---

*These variant compliance bubbles might include, for example, trades between industry sources subject to different NSPSs (such as a new power plant and a new cement plant) or between new sources and existing sources, with emission reductions otherwise required at the new sources by applicable NSPSs being obtained instead from the existing sources.

Sources Subject to New Source Performance Standards

Fossil-fuel-fired steam generators
Incinerators
Portland cement plants
Nitric acid plants
Sulfuric acid plants
Asphalt concrete plants
Petroleum refineries
Storage vessels for petroleum liquids
Secondary lead smelters
Secondary brass and bronze ingot production plants
Iron and steel plants
Sewage treatment plants
Primary copper smelters
Primary zinc smelters
Primary lead smelters
Primary aluminum reduction plants
Phosphate fertilizer industry
   Wet-process phosphoric acid plants
   Superphosphoric acid plants
   Diammonium phosphate plants
   Triple superphosphate plants
   Granular triple superphosphate storage facilities
Coal preparation plants
Ferroalloy production facilities
Steel plants—Electric arc furnaces

Kraft pulp mills
Glass manufacturing plants
Grain elevators
Surface coating of metal furniture
Stationary gas turbines
Lime manufacturing plants
Lead-acid battery manufacturing plants
Metallic mineral processing plants
Automobile and light-duty truck surface coating operations
Phosphate rock plants
Ammonium sulfate manufacture
Graphic arts industry—Publication rotogravure printing
Pressure-sensitive-tape and -label surface coating operations
Industrial surface coating—Large appliances
Metal coil surface coating
Asphalt processing and asphalt roofing manufacture
Equipment leaks of VOC in the synthetic organic chemicals manufacturing industry
Beverage can surface coating industry

Source: 40 CFR Part 60 (1984).

case, it might be wiser to allow the point's owner to spend only $250,000 to eliminate 100 tons of the pollutant from another point where the cost per ton controlled would be only $2,500. This approach could be taken not only within a particular plant but also by shifting control obligations between different plants in a geographical area.

A Congressional Budget Office (CBO) study estimates that, if the emission reductions expected from the existing NSPS for power plants were obtained from a combination of new and old sources via trading, rather than exclusively from new sources, the incremental cost per ton of sulfur dioxide removed would drop from $2,411 to $500.[3] These cost comparisons should not be taken at face value, however. As the CBO acknowledges, certain costs have been excluded from its pricing of the trading alternative.[4] Moreover, any future trading opportunities undoubtedly will be limited by local ambient air quality conditions. Nevertheless, the substantial difference in the costs of the two approaches is noteworthy.

Senator Pete Domenici (R.-N.M.) cites another example of savings. He notes that bubbles involving trades between existing copper smelters and new power plants in the West could be a way to fund pollution controls for the smelters, which often are financially pressed.[5] According to Domenici, the cleanup costs would be between $100 and $500 per ton of sulfur at smelters compared with $1,600 per ton with new power plants.[6] Such trading might be environmentally beneficial in the short run, not only because the smelters hitherto have been able to carve major relief for themselves from Clean Air Act requirements but also because smelters are a major cause of impaired visibility throughout the southwestern United States.[7]

Trading advocates suggest further that new-point-by-new-point application of NSPSs may be environmentally detrimental rather than beneficial because the cost of meeting the standards can be so great that companies continue operating older, more polluting facilities rather than investing in cleaner new plants. Such an outcome was suggested by studies conducted for EPA when the agency was revising the NSPS for coal-fired utility boilers in the late 1970s. One model, which assumed that utilities strive to minimize their costs, projected that there would be more emissions of sulfur dioxide in 1995 if the new NSPS required 90 percent removal of sulfur dioxide emissions by full "wet" scrubbing than if utilities were offered a less costly option of using low-sulfur coal and only 70 percent removal by partial "dry" scrubbing.[8]

The case that NSPSs are environmentally detrimental is far from proved, however. Pollution control costs are only one part of investment decisions.[9] Even if it is true that the marginal cost of pollution abatement to meet NSPSs is relatively high, this does not necessarily deter investment in new facilities or, where new and old facilities coexist, encourage greater use of poorly controlled older facilities. Pollution control costs may be either a major or a minor factor, and, even if they are a major expense, nonenvironmental factors may be the overriding element in decisions.

A recent study of several utilities showed that those companies will not necessarily choose to use older, dirtier plants rather than newer plants that rely on scrubbers to meet the 1971 and 1978 NSPSs for coal-fired utility boilers.[10] Newer plants can be more efficient than older ones, thereby compensating for the newer facilities' greater pollution control expenses. Moreover, because of transportation costs, expensive long-term coal supply contracts, and other considerations, the costs of coal may be higher at some of the older, less controlled units.[11] In sum, while the marginal cost of abating pollution from new facilities may be greater than that from older facilities, those costs, by themselves, do not necessarily encourage the prolonged use of older, dirtier facilities.

Applicability Bubbles

EPA's earliest effort to allow a bubble for modified sources demonstrates the important role administrative and judicial interpretations of statutory language play in emissions trading.

The NSPS section of the Clean Air Act defines a "stationary source" as "any building, structure, facility or installation" emitting an air pollutant.[12] A "modification" is defined as any change in a stationary source that increases the emissions of air pollutants from it.[13] EPA, in its initial NSPS regulations published in 1971, remained faithful to the statute, defining narrowly the points subject to the performance standards.[14] In December 1972, however, the smelting industry and the U.S. Department of Commerce proposed that a stationary source be defined as an entire plant. No modification of a source would be deemed to have occurred unless a pollutant's total emissions from an entire plant had increased. Increases at one point could be offset by decreases at another, so NSPS requirements would not be triggered.[15]

EPA initially resisted this broadened definition of a stationary source.[16] But in December 1975, "in response to industry proposals and demands from the Department of Commerce," the agency changed its regulations.[17] EPA noted that, generally speaking, "sources" were entire plants[18] and ruled that a stationary source could be defined as including a "combination . . . of . . . facilities."[19] The agency declared that, if an existing facility at a plant was changed so that its emissions increased but emissions elsewhere at that plant were decreased enough to offset those increases, the altered facility would not be required to meet an NSPS.

EPA did, however, place limits on this netting, fearing it would undercut some of the major objectives of the NSPS program. The agency ruled that, when a completely new facility was constructed at an existing source, to add new capacity or to replace old capacity, the new facility would be required to meet any NSPSs, regardless of offsetting reductions elsewhere in the source.[20] If the bubble were to be allowed for such "reconstruction," the agency explained, it would produce the anomalous situation of having NSPSs required for new facilities at new sites but not for new facilities at existing sites.[21] Existing sources would be able to avoid indefinitely the application of NSPSs by replacing facilities in kind as they wore out or by adding new capacity at existing sites. That would fly in the face of the NSPSs' basic purpose—gaining substantial control of pollution from new sources at the time of their construction.

This new approach to applying NSPSs was challenged in *ASARCO, Inc* v. *Environmental Protection Agency*, a lawsuit involving ASARCO, a smelting company, on one side, the Sierra Club on the other, and EPA in the middle. ASARCO wanted EPA to extend netting to cover new construction at existing plants, while the Sierra Club contended that even the more limited netting permitted by EPA was contrary to the Clean Air Act's definition of a stationary source as a single facility.

On January 27, 1978, a divided three-judge panel of the D.C. Circuit Court of Appeals overturned EPA's regulations.[22] In the principal opinion in the case, Judge Skelly Wright suggested that those regulations were nothing more than an attempted compromise between the 1971 regulations permitting no netting and the netting for completely new facilities at existing plants sought by the smelting industry and the Commerce Department.[23]

Judge Wright sharply criticized the concept of netting.* He contended that the arguments EPA had offered against the netting proposed by ASARCO were equally valid against the agency's own netting proposal.[25] Moreover, he said, EPA's regulations were clearly contrary to the plain language of the Clean Air Act.[26]†

Compliance Bubbles

Because Judge Wright's ruling applied only to applicability bubbles, EPA has felt free to propose other bubbles in its NSPS program.

---

*It appears that Judge Wright came down hard on EPA because he thought the agency was buckling under to political pressure rather than acting on the basis of a well-reasoned administrative record.[24]

†The conflict was between the Clean Air Act's definition of *source* as a "facility" and EPA's definition of *source* as a "combination . . . of . . . facilities."[27]

These emissions trading efforts, known as compliance bubbles, do not enable sources to avoid NSPSs completely but do permit them greater flexibility in meeting limits established in those performance standards.

A good example of a compliance bubble policy is that developed by EPA for the pressure-sensitive-tape and -label coating industry. This policy, which has not been challenged in court, appears to be within EPA's legal authority. It demonstrates why compliance bubbles might be beneficial environmentally, technologically, and economically.

When EPA first suggested an NSPS for the tape and label coating industry in 1980, the agency defined an "affected facility" as any individual coating head and drying oven combination along a coating line. That definition meant that each such combination would have to comply individually with an applicable NSPS.[28] The industry responded by arguing that, by requiring factories to add new controls to each point along their coating lines, the new rules might perpetuate existing solvent-based coating formulations and technologies.[29] The coating companies also insisted that, if an affected facility were instead defined as an entire coating line (encompassing several coating head and drying oven combinations), EPA could promote development and use of low-solvent and solventless technologies, resulting in lower emissions at reduced cost.

Persuaded by the industry comments and the data on new solvents that accompanied those comments, EPA accepted the broader definition in October 1983 and established NSPSs for entire lines.[30] If these revised rules do, in fact, stimulate emissions-reducing innovation, they will demonstrate that placing advanced technology on each piece of equipment, when its emissions increase, may be more detrimental to air quality and innovation than trading strategies adopting a broader approach.*

A significantly more controversial compliance bubble is one that EPA custom-tailored and proposed in January 1985 in response to a request from the Central Illinois Public Service Company. Even though this bubble is under attack by environmentalists and many state regulators, it demonstrates why it might be both economically

---

*EPA has also provided a compliance bubble for the rotogravure printing industry, and plans to indicate its receptiveness to future bubble proposals in forthcoming NSPSs for manufacturers of rubber tires.[31]

and environmentally beneficial to permit compliance bubbles for new sources. It also shows what safeguards EPA believes are necessary to ensure that real environmental benefits are produced.

If eventually adopted, this compliance bubble would be unusual in two respects. First, unlike other NSPSs, which apply to the broad categories of industry sources listed in the box on NSPSs, the performance standard for this bubble would apply solely to the two 600-megawatt boilers of a coal-fired power plant operated by Central Illinois in Newton, Illinois. Second, this new NSPS would alter a previously existing NSPS that was already being met at the plant. Unit I began operation in 1977, with Unit II beginning in 1982. Each of the two boilers has been subject to the performance standard set in 1971 for new utility boilers, which requires that individual boilers emit no more than 1.2 pounds of sulfur dioxide per million British thermal units of heat generated (abbreviated as 1.2 lbs./MBtu) (figure 5.1).[32] Unit I has been meeting the limit by employing a dual-alkali scrubber so that its actual emissions average about 1.0 to 1.1 lbs./MBtu. Unit II has been meeting the limit by burning low-sulfur coal that does not need scrubbing; its actual emissions average about 1.0 lb./MBtu.[33]

In a petition to EPA in 1982, submitted before Unit II commenced operation, Central Illinois sought to change the emission limits applicable to the plant. Under the company's request, the new allowable level of emissions for both units taken together would be 1.1 lbs./MBtu. Central Illinois would overcontrol Unit I to an emissions level of 0.6 lbs./MBtu by running its scrubber at an increased level of efficiency. In exchange for the emission reduction credits (ERCs) it earned from this overcontrol, the company would undercontrol emissions at Unit II by raising them to a level of about 1.6 lbs./MBtu.* Under the bubble, Unit II would burn medium-sulfur coal, which normally would have to be scrubbed. Central Illinois proposed, however, not to undertake this scrubbing, saving the company an estimated $22 million annually.[35]†

---

*EPA's notice of proposed rule making placed the undercontrolled level at 1.8 lbs./MBtu, but Central Illinois has claimed that the level should be 1.6 lbs./MBtu.[34] The 1.1 lbs./MBtu average emission rate for the two facilities evidently is derived from adding the rates for each stack (0.6 + 1.6 = 2.2), then dividing the sum by 2.

†In its notice of proposed rule making, EPA incorrectly attributed the savings of $22 million to the difference in cost between low- and medium-sulfur coals. In comments on the rule making, Central Illinois noted that these savings would derive exclusively from not using a scrubber.[36]

Figure 5.1
Pre- and Post-Bubble Allowable
and Actual Sulfur Dioxide Emissions—
Central Illinois Public Service Company, Newton, Illinois

| | Emission rate (pounds of sulfur dioxide per million Btu heat input) | | | |
| | Allowable emissions | | Actual emissions | |
	Current	Bubble	Current	Bubble (anticipated)
Unit I	1.2	(1.1	1.0–1.1	(0.95
Unit II	1.2	combined)	1.0	combined)

Source: 50 Fed. Reg. 3688 (January 25, 1985), and internal U.S. Environmental Protection Agency documents.

Through its development of the Central Illinois bubble, EPA is trying to generate general principles that could govern all similar compliance bubbles. These principles address a host of issues (for example, baselines and enforceability) customarily associated with bubbles for existing sources. The state regulators and environmentalists who criticize this bubble question EPA's calculations and assumptions, believe the bubble does not satisfy EPA's own general criteria, and think it establishes a precedent for undercutting the interstate uniformity intended for the NSPS program.

On its face, Central Illinois's bubble has great appeal, since it seemingly provides a way not just for industry to spend only as much money as is necessary to meet NSPS requirements but also for companies actually to improve their environmental performance beyond those NSPSs while still saving money. This bubble proposal, however, is far more complex than it first appears.

EPA's first general principle for compliance bubbles is that dischargers will not be permitted to use credits based on the difference between the emissions rate allowed for a compliance technology and the emissions rate expected from the technology. Because of the methods used by EPA to establish performance standards, a difference between allowable and actual emissions already is expected. NSPSs are set at levels that reflect the performance of the routine compliance

technology under "the worst, reasonably-to-be expected situation."[37]*
In addition, the allowable limits of emissions specified in NSPSs are
set higher than the average long-term performances of the compliance
technologies on which the NSPSs are based, so that routine variations in operations do not result in the standards being exceeded.[39]
If ERCs were allowed for the difference between actual and allowable
emissions, a bubble could cause actual emissions to increase. For example, if an NSPS permitted a point to emit 115 tons per year of
a pollutant, yet the standard technology on which the NSPS was
based typically emitted only 100 tons per year, a second new point
controlled by the discharger might be allowed under a bubble to emit
15 tons more per year than it would otherwise be allowed.

In some industries, the size of the difference between actual and
allowable emissions can be quite substantial. For example, EPA cites
the case of the portland cement industry, where the average actual
emissions of new sources subject to an NSPS are 50 percent below
allowable emissions.[40] By contrast, according to EPA, within the utility industry actual emissions tend to be close to allowable emissions,
so windfall gains in ERCs are less likely to occur.

EPA believes that the Central Illinois bubble would be consistent
with its principle, but critics disagree. As already noted, Central
Illinois's dual-alkali scrubber for Unit I has been operated so that
it emits just under the level of allowable emissions—at between 1.0
and 1.1 lbs./MBtu. Because Central Illinois previously could have
had lower emissions of 0.6 lbs./MBtu, the rate that the power company proposes to achieve, by using its scrubber at full capacity, critics
of this bubble argue that the company should not receive credit for
the difference between its current actual emissions and the lower
proposed rate.

Among those critics, the Jefferson County [Louisville, Kentucky]
Air Pollution Control District notes that dual-alkali scrubbers installed
between 1977 and 1983 at seven units of the Louisville Gas and Electric
system emit sulfur dioxide at rates between 0.35 and 0.94 lbs./MBtu,[41]
levels much lower than Central Illinois's current levels from its scrubber. If some average of the Louisville emissions were regarded as
the average expected rate of actual emissions from dual-alkali scrubbers, EPA seemingly would be giving credit for emission reductions
that exceed the average expected rate. Moreover, because some of

*This is done so that the standards can be achieved consistently, as required
by the Clean Air Act.[38]

the Louisville scrubbers have been retrofitted onto existing sources, it appears that EPA would be giving special credit to Central Illinois for reducing emissions at a new source to levels already reached at existing sources.

EPA tries to be true to its principle by noting that, in the Central Illinois case, the agency does not have to make judgments about what prospective actual emissions from Unit I might be, when compared to emissions it is allowed under the applicable NSPS. In this case, because Unit I already operates, it has been clearly established that its actual emissions are quite close to its allowable emissions. Accordingly, EPA can argue that the additional reductions from Unit I under the bubble are beyond what otherwise would be achieved. EPA also argues that the dual-alkali scrubber used by Central Illinois should not be compared to other dual-alkali scrubbers but should instead be compared to the lime- and limestone-based scrubber technologies on which the 1971 NSPS was based. These scrubbers tend to emit higher levels of pollutants than do dual-alkali scrubbers.[42]

A second general principle that EPA has developed for compliance bubbles is that an extra margin of safety, in the form of additional emission reductions, may be required from a source.[43] Such a reduction may be necessary, for example, where the level of emissions under a bubble is difficult to predict. In an attempt to build a margin of safety into the Central Illinois bubble to assure that actual emissions are reduced from their existing levels, EPA is taking two steps. First, by lowering the average allowable emission level from the current 1.2 lbs./MBtu to 1.1 lbs./MBtu, it would be requiring a concomitant decrease in Central Illinois's actual emissions. The agency estimates that total emissions from the plant would have to average 0.95 lbs./MBtu for the 1.1 lbs./MBtu limit to be met. It is because of this that EPA expects a 2,500-ton-per-year drop in total emissions from the plant.

Critics, however, question that calculation of reductions in actual emissions.[44] Moreover, the Natural Resources Defense Council (NRDC) believes that reductions in current emissions from the Newton plant should be forthcoming even in the bubble's absence. NRDC maintains that existing EPA regulations require Central Illinois to operate its dual-alkali scrubber on Unit I at its highest efficiency. NRDC also maintains that requirements of the Prevention of Significant Deterioration program were not, and should have been, applied to Unit II and contends that Central Illinois's permit from the State of Illinois requires it to install a scrubber on Unit II if the bubble is not approved.

If EPA grants final approval to Central Illinois's bubble, NRDC is likely to challenge that approval in court, so, probably, the judges presiding over that lawsuit will determine the correctness of NRDC's reading of the statute and regulations. If NRDC's view is upheld, Central Illinois's coming forward with its bubble application will have revealed that requirements of the command-and-control system have not been implemented properly. Were it not for the bubble, these discrepancies might never have surfaced. However, if NRDC's legal arguments are incorrect and EPA's calculations are valid, then the Central Illinois bubble may yield reductions in actual emissions that otherwise could not be required.

In a further effort to assure additional reductions, EPA is altering its method for defining compliance. The agency says that its new method, had it been applied previously, would have reduced emissions (by 600 tons per year) from Central Illinois's plant in the past.[45] Critics of the bubble question the adequacy of this safeguard, but the validity of those criticisms requires too much technical description to be evaluated here.

A third general principle EPA has developed is that any bubble should be as enforceable as conventional control strategies.[46] In theory, bubbles can be quite difficult to enforce if, for example, it is necessary to obtain simultaneous measurements from several points under each bubble. Under the Central Illinois bubble, the emissions from each stack would have to be monitored continuously. Already, a computer constantly computes the emission rate from Unit I, and Central Illinois has pledged to use another computer for Unit II. Those two computers would not only keep track of the individual emission rates from each unit but also constantly compute the combined rate from both units. Despite the good record of the continuous emissions monitor operating on Unit I and Central Illinois's willingness to add a second monitor, critics have expressed skepticism about this bubble's enforceability.*

Moreover, critics have voiced complaints about the Central Illinois bubble that reflect larger issues.[48] For example, they argue that Central Illinois should not be allowed to burn medium-sulfur coal without

---

*For example, NRDC asserts that EPA proposes requiring monitoring for only 65 percent of the facility's operating time.[47]

a scrubber when many believe that emissions of sulfur dioxide from the Midwest should be curtailed to reduce acid rain falling in the northeastern United States. Aside from noting that the bubble would reduce existing emissions from the power plant, EPA responds to this criticism by pointing out that Unit II could be retrofitted with a scrubber should additional emission reductions be necessary.[49]

As of January 1986, EPA had not published a final decision on the Central Illinois bubble. Even though critics have expressed doubts about the validity of EPA's estimates of reductions in actual emissions and about the adequacy of EPA's strategy for monitoring compliance, final EPA approval of this particular bubble could proceed as an experiment. If the courts affirm the approval, the validity of EPA's estimates could be assessed in the future. Reductions in actual emissions, if they occurred, would be consistent with the general objectives of the NSPS program. The monitoring protocol would provide useful information about the feasibility of simultaneous continuous emission monitoring for bubble applications. In case the reductions did not occur, or the bubble proved to be less enforceable than anticipated, EPA could still require Central Illinois to take further steps to reduce emissions at Unit II.

NETTING AND BEST AVAILABLE CONTROL TECHNOLOGY REQUIREMENTS

Debate over trading in the Prevention of Significant Deterioration (PSD) program has differed substantially from that involving the NSPS program. The difference is illustrated, for example, in the roles that statutory language has played in determining emissions trading's legality. In the NSPS program, EPA has been constrained by congressionally established definitions of regulated points. In the PSD program, definitions conducive to trading were first developed by EPA and then adopted by Congress in amendments to the Clean Air Act, effectually giving EPA much greater freedom to allow trading. Moreover, trading related to the PSD program has not had to confront the technology-forcing concerns raised in NSPS-related proposals. Even though major new and modified sources in PSD areas must meet a "best available control technology" (BACT) standard at least as stringent as an applicable NSPS, technology forcing *per se* is not one of the statutory objectives of the PSD program.

EPA Proposals

The 1970 amendments to the Clean Air Act lacked detailed PSD provisions,* so, in response to a Sierra Club lawsuit, EPA administratively established a PSD program in 1974.[51] The regulations for that program set limits (called increments) on permissible increases in ambient concentrations of sulfur dioxide and particulate matter. Those increments applied to those areas where national ambient standards for those pollutants were already being attained. In the absence of a program to prevent significant deterioration, the air in those areas could be polluted up to the limits established by the national ambient standards, causing fears that a "greying of America" might result.[52]

Under the PSD program, all proposed new or modified sources were to be reviewed prior to their construction to assure that they would cause no exceeding of the increments for the area in which they were located. To assure that ample room existed within those increments for many new and modified sources to be constructed, each new or modified source was to minimize its pollution by complying with a BACT standard. Initially, industry-wide BACT standards would be equal to any NSPSs that had been established for those industries. In cases where there were no NSPSs, BACTs would be determined source by source so that increments would not be violated.

The regulations specifically named 18 types of new and modified sources for which preconstruction review would be required. Significantly, many of these sources were entire plants (for example, coal cleaning plants, portland cement plants, sulfuric acid plants, and petroleum refineries).[53] EPA had greater legal freedom to define *source* in the PSD program than it had in the NSPS program because the term had not been defined for the PSD program by the 1970 amendments.

The EPA regulations permitted netting for modifications, except in instances of reconstruction.[54] Substantive and administrative requirements of the PSD program (including use of BACT and analysis of the impact of emissions on ambient air quality) could be avoided if modifications to existing sources did not constitute reconstruction

---

*Law professor William H. Rodgers, Jr. has summed up the statutory background well: "The legislative history must be read as endorsing vaguely a view that state plans should not allow good air to go bad."[50]

and if increases in emissions at one point within a plant were offset by decreases at another point. EPA's definitions of *modification* and *reconstruction* were the same as those the agency used in its then-pending revisions to NSPS regulations.

In this context, since the PSD program's primary concern was the avoidance of increased emissions that could cause air quality to deteriorate, allowing netting seemed to be a logical policy. A reasonable case could be made that, when emission decreases equaled emission increases, such deterioration would not occur. Further, although the PSD program required BACT on new sources and modifications, diffusion of advanced technology did not seem to be its major purpose.

After being challenged in court by both environmentalists and industry, EPA's initial PSD regulations were upheld in 1976 by a three-judge panel of the D.C. Circuit Court.[55] Netting was not addressed in the court's decision, however, and does not appear to have then been a major concern to environmentalists.[56]

The 1977 amendments to the Clean Air Act included, with modifications, EPA's increment and BACT concepts to establish a firm, expanded PSD program.[57] (See box, "Industrial Operations Subject to Permit Requirements of the PSD Program.") The amendments' PSD provisions defined three categories of attainment areas—Class I (most restrictive), Class II (less restrictive), and Class III (least restrictive)—to determine how strict the limits on increases in ambient concentrations of individual pollutants should be. For example, large national parks and wilderness areas were classified as Class I and were subject to very strict limits.

The amendments expanded on the list of sources in EPA's 1974 regulations, enumerating 28 categories of "major emitting facilities." Again, many of those categories consisted of entire plants.[58] Preconstruction reviews of new and modified major emitting facilities were to use modeling of the ambient impacts of emissions to determine whether those proposed facilities' emissions would violate any PSD increments. Affected plants were to employ BACT, which would be at least as demanding as any applicable NSPS.[59] As was the case in EPA's earlier PSD program, sources subject to the new requirements were to control their emissions as stringently as necessary to avoid violating the increments.

In its final rules published in June 1978, EPA continued to allow modifications yielding no net increases in emissions to be exempt from BACT and ambient impact analysis.[60] This policy did not, however, leave facilities totally free from the agency's oversight; they still had to undergo a somewhat less-demanding regulatory review, so that authorities would be assured that increases were in fact equaled by decreases.[61] Moreover, reconstruction remained subject to both the BACT and ambient review requirements.[62]

The *Alabama Power* Litigation

As they often had done with earlier EPA proposals, industry and environmental groups filed suit against the agency's 1978 rules. Netting was just a small part of the litigation. Environmentalists generally disliked various exemptions from the regulations, while industry contended that EPA was casting its regulatory net unduly wide.[63]

In a December 1979 decision, *Alabama Power Co.* v. *Costle*, a three-judge panel of the D.C. Circuit Court not only upheld the use of netting in the PSD program but expanded it. The judges declared that netting could be used by modified sources to avoid the remaining regulatory review procedures to which the EPA regulations had left them subject.

The judges stated that the definition of *source* that EPA had used in developing the PSD program was consistent with the intent of the Clean Air Act.[64] They also declared that EPA had discretion to define the component terms of *source* and, when developing definitions, could consider differences among the purposes and structure of the PSD, NSPS, and other programs of the Clean Air Act.[65] The judges contended that, in the PSD program, Congress was interested in technological improvement primarily in regard to construction of new sources, not in regard to existing sources whose changes produced no increase in emissions. Thus, netting was an appropriate element in determining whether modifications subject to PSD requirements had occurred.

By distinguishing the purposes of the PSD and NSPS programs, the judges were able to justify netting in the PSD context. This was important as a matter of law, because Judge Wright's earlier, precedent-setting opinion in the ASARCO case had decried netting. Most legal commentators, however, regard as weak the judges' effort to distinguish their holding from Judge Wright's.[66] Uncertainties over the meaning of these two court decisions contributed to subsequent disputes over whether netting could be allowed for major modified sources seeking to site in nonattainment areas.

Industrial Operations Subject to Permit Requirements of the PSD Program*

Fossil-fuel-fired steam electric plants (>250 million Btu/hr. heat input)
Coal cleaning plants (with thermal dryers)
Kraft pulp mills
Portland cement plants
Primary zinc smelters
Iron and steel mill plants
Primary aluminum ore reduction plants
Primary copper smelters
Municipal incinerators (charging >250 tons refuse/day)
Hydrofluoric, sulfuric, and nitric acid plants
Petroleum refineries
Lime plants
Phosphate rock processing plants
Coke oven batteries
Sulfur recovery plants
Carbon black plants (furnace process)
Primary lead smelters

Fuel conversion plants
Sintering plants
Secondary metal production plants
Chemical process plants
Fossil-fuel boilers (or combinations thereof) totaling >250 million Btu/hr. heat input
Petroleum storage and transfer units (with total storage capacity >300,000 barrels)
Taconite ore processing plants
Glass fiber processing plants
Charcoal production plants

*The PSD provisions apply to new sources in these categories only if they emit or have the potential to emit 100 tons per year or more of any pollutant subject to regulation under the Clean Air Act. The PSD provisions also apply to a number of other sources not listed above.

Source: Section 169 of the Clean Air Act, 42 U.S.C. 7479.

A Squandered Opportunity?

Critics of netting for modified sources in attainment areas argue that netting, by allowing industries to avoid installing BACT, squanders the opportunity provided by the PSD program to capture large amounts of pollutants when major modifications occur.[67] If those emission reductions were maximized, so the argument goes, more room would be left within an attainment area's increment to site additional sources. Those who defend netting argue that it may not make that much of a difference environmentally, since many modifications avoiding BACT would nevertheless be subject to NSPS requirements.

The magnitude of the squandered opportunity problem may be assessed by determining how many PSD permits are issued for modifications, how many modifications are subject to NSPS and how many are not, and how much stricter in practice BACT requirements are compared with NSPS.

Recent studies of the PSD program indicate that most PSD permits have been issued to modifications rather than new sources. This is not surprising, because the threshold for review of modifications is much lower than the threshold for review of new sources. The ratio of permits for modifications to permits for new sources has been approximately two to one.[68]

No good data exist on how many modifications have managed to net out of review under the PSD program yet have remained subject to NSPS requirements. Some inferences, however, might be drawn about the relationship between NSPS and BACT requirements from those sources that have remained subject to PSD review. The proportion of emissions subject to NSPS as well as BACT review appears to depend on the number of utilities seeking permits. More than 90 percent of utility emissions subject to PSD review also have been subject to NSPS, while only about 30 percent of nonutility emissions have been subject to NSPS.[69] Therefore, the proportion of total (utility and nonutility) emissions under the PSD program also subject to NSPS requirements has been influenced heavily by the proportion of utility emissions permitted. One study found that, in a sample of 285 permits issued between 1977 and 1981, 71 percent of the permitted emissions came from utilities, and 73 percent of total permitted emissions were covered by NSPS.[70] But, for a later period, through mid-1984, covering 397 permits, utility emissions comprised only 43 percent of the emissions, and only 57 percent of all the permitted emissions were also covered by the NSPS program. In sum, more than half of the emissions subject to BACT have been subject to NSPS. As for the emissions not subject to NSPS, they likely were subjected to some other control requirements.

Where both BACT and NSPS have been applicable to emissions, little difference apparently has existed between the reductions required by the two standards. The studies indicate that some reductions beyond those resulting from NSPSs have been required for a small portion of the permits, but those reductions have tended *not* to be the result of applying a BACT standard instead of an NSPS. Rather, they more often have been a consequence of the need to assure that a PSD increment or a national ambient air quality standard would not be violated in an area.[71]

Summing up, it appears that, on a nationwide basis, the squandered opportunity from netting permitted in attainment areas might not be substantial. Still, because of unique circumstances in particular attainment areas, substantial adverse effects might be possible in those regions.

NETTING AND LOWEST ACHIEVABLE EMISSION RATE REQUIREMENTS

Incongruities between the *ASARCO* and *Alabama Power* decisions left unclear the legality of netting in yet another EPA program— attaining the national ambient air quality standards in nonattainment areas. The place of netting in attaining the standards was an especially sensitive issue because concentrations of pollutants in nonattainment areas are, by definition, a risk to human health. Hot debates occurred over the role that netting for modifications should play in EPA's offset policy for nonattainment areas and over the agency's related regulations banning permits for major new and modified sources in areas with inadequate state implementation plans (SIPs). Critics feared that netting would slow attainment by reducing pressure on states to develop satisfactory SIPs and on industries to reduce emissions.

As in earlier controversies, EPA's position shifted from time to time, a consequence of uncertainty within the agency over netting's legality and desirability. The intra-agency dispute pitted those with great confidence in the command-and-control system against those who viewed some of its requirements for new and modified sources as environmentally counterproductive. EPA's shifting positions on netting in nonattainment areas reflected, at different times, a victory for the reformers, a win for the traditionalists, or a compromise between the two.*

As they have been on bubble policy issues for existing sources (see chapter 3), the principal EPA proponents of regulatory reform related to modified sources were organized in the Office of Planning and Management. In pushing emissions trading for modified sources, these regulatory reformers found allies in EPA's Office of General Counsel but had to overcome great skepticism from the agency's air programs office and from EPA enforcement officials who had been fighting

---

*The two groups were largely identical to those labeled command minimalists and expansionists in the dispute over bubbles for existing sources.

lengthy battles with recalcitrant industrial polluters. The competing groups disagreed over three primary issues:

- whether air quality would benefit or suffer from allowing industries to use netting to avoid either certain permit requirements in some nonattainment areas or bans on permits for major modifications in others;
- how much flexibility states should have in planning their pollution abatement strategies, particularly how states should define *source* in their SIPs; and
- how much confidence should be placed in the plans that states had already developed for meeting ambient air quality standards and that EPA had approved.

Battles over these issues were fought, within and outside EPA, when the agency issued regulations in 1979, 1980, and 1981 governing review of major new and modified sources in nonattainment areas. State regulators participated in these controversies, but they rarely spoke with one voice; some state regulators approved of netting while others viewed it as a threat to ambient air quality.

EPA's shifting actions landed it in court, sued first by industry and then by environmentalists. The Supreme Court ultimately upheld a liberal view of netting adopted by EPA, on the basis that the courts should defer to agencies' reasonable interpretations of ambiguous statutory language.

Birth of the Offset Policy

As noted in chapter 2, EPA promulgated its offset policy in 1976 in response to the failure of many areas to meet the Clean Air Act's initial deadlines for attaining national ambient air quality standards. The policy permitted major new stationary sources and major modifications to site in nonattainment areas, by requiring offsets for the pollutants that these new sources and modifications would add to a region's air.[72]*

The offset policy had several components. In addition to offsetting added emissions, a major new source or a modified major source had to satisfy a "lowest achievable emission rate" (LAER) standard. All other major sources in the area owned or controlled by the applicant also had to be in compliance, and the applicant had to

---

*The offset policy was EPA's pragmatic effort to avoid a potential political backlash stemming from a ban on construction of new sources in nonattainment areas.

demonstrate that the proposed new or modified source would produce a positive net air quality benefit in the affected area. These conditions were intended to make a new or modified source a vehicle
for moving an area toward attainment and to give enforcement personnel in regulatory agencies additional leverage in negotiations with
multiple-source owners (especially steel companies) that wished to
change their operations.

The 1977 Clean Air Act Amendments

When Congress amended the Clean Air Act in 1977, it adopted EPA's
offset policy in modified form and revised the deadline for attaining
the national ambient air quality standards.[73] As noted earlier, states
were obliged to revise their SIPs by January 1979 to demonstrate
how they would attain the standards no later than December 31,
1982.[74] (For the automobile-related pollutants—ozone and carbon
monoxide—some areas could qualify for extension of the deadline
to December 31, 1987.[75]) On a year-to-year basis, the state plans
would have to demonstrate "reasonable further progress" in attaining the standards.[76] Existing sources would be obliged to employ
"reasonably available control technology" (RACT).[77]

Congress permitted the states to choose between two options for
accommodating new growth in their nonattainment areas. They could
require offsets from new sources, or, alternatively, they could control existing sources beyond the levels necessary merely to attain the
national standards.[78] Extra control on existing sources would create
a margin for growth into which major new sources could be fitted
without their obtaining offsets. In either case, the LAER and statewide
compliance requirements would still apply.* Once revised SIPs were
in place, an offset policy administered by EPA itself would no longer
apply, except in narrow circumstances.[79]

If states failed to submit revised SIPs in a timely manner, or
submitted SIPs that were found inadequate, they faced several sanctions, including a ban on permits for construction of major new
sources and major modifications.[80] The sanctions were a stick to per-
suade the states to do the job right and on time, but they could also
be defended as a means for keeping new pollutants from being added

---

*The enlarged requirement for an applicants' sources to be in compliance—state-
wide rather than just in the nonattainment area—was one of the changes in the
offset policy enacted by Congress in the Clean Air Act Amendments of 1977.

in those areas that still had not figured out how to eliminate sufficient amounts of existing pollutants.

EPA's Revised Nonattainment Rules

In the aftermath of the 1977 amendments, EPA had to revise its offset policy for those circumstances where it would still apply and had to develop rules governing revised SIPs and the sanctions. The agency issued its first revised offset policy and related changes in other nonattainment rules in January 1979.[81]

The revised rules outlawed netting both where EPA's own offset policy applied and where the ban on construction applied, but it allowed netting where a state had an approved SIP.* This reflected a compromise between the competing factions within EPA.[82] The traditionalists had wanted to outlaw netting altogether, while the reformers contended that the agency should allow netting just as it had in its PSD regulations.[83] The reformers argued, in part, that netting would give industry an incentive to achieve controls that might not be identified by regulators revising a SIP and that modified facilities would still be required to satisfy NSPSs.

The January 1979 version of the offset policy allowed netting under approved SIPs, as sought by EPA's regulatory reformers, and outlawed netting where EPA's own offset rules and the construction ban applied, as traditionalists had wanted.[84] The agency adopted the proposition that, where SIPs could project attainment, states had discretion to permit netting, because modifications yielding no net increase in emissions could be tolerated. However, prior to the SIPs' approval —when EPA's offset policy applied, or when a construction ban was in effect—netting would not be permitted because attainment of the standards by the statutory deadline could not be assured.[85]

Another set of revised nonattainment rules followed in 1980. The nonattainment provisions of the 1977 amendments to the Clean Air Act had not defined the term *source*, so, when EPA revised its PSD regulations in September 1980 in response to the *Alabama Power* decision, it also reevaluated the definition of *source* it had used in its nonattainment program.[86] In its decision, the D.C. Circuit Court had granted the agency the discretion to define the component terms

---

*Netting, in this context, would allow a modified source to avoid either the construction ban or the LAER and related requirements if emission increases at one point in the source were compensated for by emission reductions at another point in the source.

of *source* and had ruled that netting was permissible if it comported with the general purposes of a particular program under the Clean Air Act.

In what was a victory for the traditionalists within EPA, the agency decided to restrict netting even further than it had in 1979.[87] It did so by modifying its definition of *source* in nonattainment areas and by reversing its stand on the desirability of netting in approved SIPs. Although it used a single plantwide definition—one equating "source" with "plant"—in its revised PSD rules,[88] it discouraged states from using such a single definition within their revised SIPs.[89] For non-attainment purposes, *source* was defined as (*a*) an individual piece of equipment *and* (*b*) a grouping of activities, including a grouping as large as a plant. This dual definition was expected to maximize regulatory review. Ostensibly, it was superior to the single definition for encouraging revisions of SIPs and promoting attainment of the ambient standards. The dual definition would subject to review increases at individual points that could not be offset by decreases elsewhere in a source. It also would make sure that an entire plant could not escape review if several points within it increased their emissions, but each at a level just below the threshold for regulatory review. In both circumstances, a major modification that increased emissions would be subject to LAER, offset, and statewide compliance requirements. This was to be the case both under EPA's offset policy, where it would still apply, and in approved revised SIPs.

The dual definition was adopted by EPA over the protest of the agency's regulatory reformers. They had argued that the requirement for offsets was, in practice, not very important, so very little would be lost by allowing individual pieces of equipment to net out from it.[90] The reformers also downplayed the importance of the requirement for statewide compliance and suggested that the ban on permits for major modifications of individual pieces of equipment was not likely to be a major factor in prodding states to adopt necessary SIP revisions.[91]

When the notice of the dual definition was published in the *Federal Register*, it dismissed the arguments of those both within and outside EPA who supported a single definition. It simply asserted that the dual definition would "bring more units in for review in areas with unhealthy air and thereby result in reducing emissions from the status quo."[92]

Commenters on EPA's proposed rules had suggested that EPA,

by defining *source* as a plant in PSD areas, and by defining *source* as both a plant and a piece of equipment in nonattainment areas, would simply be making the regulatory system complex, while getting little abatement in return. EPA replied that the additional complexity was outweighed by the need for a more inclusive definition "in order to assure attainment of standards."[93] EPA did not indicate why this was so, even though commenters on the proposed rule, echoing EPA's own regulatory reformers, had suggested that industry investment in cleaner new facilities would be discouraged by the expensive LAER requirement. In addition, in areas lacking approved SIPs, the commenters had contended that potentially beneficial modifications could not be issued permits.

Ronald Reagan's election as president in 1980 gave the advocates of the single definition a second chance to advance their case. Although some reform-minded Carter appointees were gone, like-minded career staff pushed the single definition ahead. They found a receptive audience among those in the Reagan administration who were anxious to show that the new president meant business when it came to regulatory reform.[94] The reformers dropped in the Reagan team's lap a proposal for "regulatory relief" for which it was more than happy to take credit.

In March 1981, EPA proposed to eliminate the double definition in nonattainment areas, both in those with approved SIPs and those subject to a construction ban.[95] EPA proposed to define a *source* only as a plant, thereby conforming the nonattainment definition with the PSD definition. The agency concluded that the change would substantially reduce regulatory burdens without significantly interfering with timely achievement of the goals of the Clean Air Act.[96]

EPA, adopting the rationale it had earlier rejected, said that the dual definition could actually "retard progress in air pollution control by discouraging replacement of older dirtier processes or pieces of equipment with newer cleaner ones."[97] EPA added that broadening the definition should not interfere with the fundamental purpose of the nonattainment provisions—attainment of ambient standards—because states with approved SIPs would remain obliged to show reasonable further progress toward the standards regardless of the scope of review of new sources. Moreover, sources netting out of the construction ban would not worsen an area's pollution significantly. EPA simply "reconsidered" the concerns it had expressed when issuing its August 1980 regulations and decided that the dual definition was excessively and unnecessarily burdensome.[98]

NRDC challenged EPA's position in comments on the proposed rule, taking issue with all of EPA's reasons for promulgating the single definition.[99] Among other points, NRDC argued that EPA had not advanced any data to support the agency's contention that the dual definition was a disincentive to new investment and modernization. Moreover, NRDC argued that the disincentive likely was small, because so many factors contribute to the cost of a new industrial investment.[100]

Only nine state and local governments commented on the changed definition, but nearly all supported it. Their letters usually were brief, less than a page in length, merely asserting with little evidence that the single definition either would be a useful standardization of practice or would permit modernization.[101] A major exception to the state responses was a lengthy commentary by the head of Pennsylvania's air quality program, who questioned EPA's reliance on SIPs' assurances of reasonable further progress toward attainment.[102] NRDC had also questioned those assurances in its comments.*

EPA responded to its critics when it published its single definition in final form in October 1981.[103] The agency seemingly had little patience with critics who stressed the inadequacy of states' projections of attainment. The agency emphasized that Congress intended states to retain "the maximum possible flexibility to balance environmental and economic concerns in designing plans to clean up nonattainment areas" and stressed further that it was the states' obligation to demonstrate that the national standards would be met by the statutory deadline.

Replying to complaints about data inadequacy, EPA expressed the belief that examples provided by commenters on its proposed regulation supported its view that the dual definition impeded legitimate efforts to modernize existing plants.[104] The agency's reference to commenters notwithstanding, an independent consulting firm examining the comments concluded that there was a "puzzling . . . dearth" of empirical evidence surfaced in support of the change.[105]

*These concerns about the quality of approved SIPs echoed those voiced in disputes over the bubble policy for existing sources. See chapters 3 and 4.

The *NRDC* v. *Gorsuch* Decision

In November 1981, NRDC filed suit in D.C. Circuit Court to challenge EPA's single definition. In its August 1982 decision, yet another three-judge panel of the court wrestled with the questions of statutory meaning and agency discretion.[106] The judges relied heavily on the two earlier court decisions on netting. Stating that it was not writing "on a clean slate," the panel felt "impelled by the force of our precedent in *Alabama Power* and *ASARCO* to hold [the single definition] impermissible."[107] The panel claimed to find in these opinions what it labeled "a bright line" test:

> The bubble [netting] concept, *Alabama Power* declares, is mandatory for Clean Air Act programs designed merely to maintain existing air quality; it is inappropriate, both *ASARCO* and *Alabama Power* plainly signal, in programs enacted to improve the quality of the ambient air.[108]

The judges noted EPA's failure to develop an adequate administrative record to support its altered definition. The change therefore, could not be characterized as well reasoned:

> [I]n abandoning its earlier position, EPA did not cite, nor have we found . . . in the record, any study, survey, or support for the . . . position . . . that the dual definition would indeed retard improvement of air quality *in the aggregate.*[109]

The panel, in making this observation, failed to note that even though the record for the single definition was not very good, the record supporting the dual definition had not been very good either.

The panel's discovery of the "bright line" test was quite striking, especially considering the remarkable difficulty many legal commentators had found in their earlier attempts to reconcile the *ASARCO* and *Alabama Power* decisions. The judges' declaration of the test was likened by one commentator to Alexander the Great's undoing of the Gordian knot with a single dramatic stroke.[110] Said another, "The panel had little difficulty in making quite simple [two] rulings that appear to many to be of mind-bending complexity and ambiguity."[111] The panel's striking conclusion was perhaps best explained in the words of a third commentator: "Among the welter of words used in the *ASARCO* and *Alabama Power* opinions the court's new test can be found, but many other ideas are disregarded in the process."[112]

The *Chevron v. NRDC* Decision

EPA, joined by industry, sought review of the D.C. Circuit's ruling by the U.S. Supreme Court. EPA and its industry allies argued that EPA's single definition was consistent with the Clean Air Act's policies, was a reasonable exercise of administrative discretion, and should not have been overturned by a reviewing appellate court that had substituted judges' own version of good policy for the agency's.[113] NRDC replied in its brief that the single definition was contrary to the provisions, legislative history, and purposes of the Clean Air Act and was a sharp, unjustified break with long-standing EPA regulations.[114] The attorneys-general of eight states filed a "friend of the court" brief defending the dual definition. They argued that netting would reduce the scope of review of new sources in some jurisdictions, thereby increasing economic pressure on other jurisdictions to adopt it.[115] Appended to the states' brief were letters defending the dual definition, forwarded to EPA in July 1983 by the State and Territorial Air Pollution Program Administrators and the Association of Local Air Pollution Control Officials.

The Supreme Court's 6-0 decision supporting EPA's position focused more on the role of the courts in reviewing agency actions than on the policy arguments for the competing definitions of *source*.[116] In very strong language, the Court told the D.C. Circuit to back away from its close scrutiny of EPA policy decisions. The Court contended that, since the Clean Air Act's legislative history regarding the definition of *source* was ambiguous, and since Congress had not specifically addressed the netting question, the role of a reviewing court was limited to determining whether EPA's interpretation of the statute was a reasonable one.[117] The Court decided that EPA's action was reasonable and supported by the public record.[118]

Does Netting in Nonattainment Areas Make a Significant Environmental Difference?

As with netting in attainment areas, the most important question concerning netting in nonattainment areas is "Does it make a significant environmental difference?" As chapter 2 noted, many nonattainment areas remain. Millions of Americans live in those areas, which encompass the nation's major urban centers.

Ozone nonattainment areas are the focus of the discussion here, because they far outnumber other nonattainment areas.* How much of a difference netting will make in these areas may depend in part on how many of the areas' nonattainment problems are due to stationary sources and how many are due to mobile sources. Where the nonattainment problem for ozone is largely attributable to automobiles, as it is in the Washington, D.C., metropolitan area, netting is an insignificant concern.[119] But even where stationary sources are major contributors to the ozone nonattainment problem, netting may still matter only slightly, because the problem is due principally to dirty existing sources. This is suggested in data cited by the Procter and Gamble Company for eight cities in Ohio. The emissions growth from new projects in those cities ranged from 0.17 percent to 0.72 percent between 1975 and 1980, an average yearly increase of only 0.3 percent.[120]† Procter and Gamble found that, even if offset requirements were waived in most of those cities, attainment would be delayed by only a few months.[121]

Recent permitting experience in Illinois reinforces the conclusions from Ohio. Research on permitting in Illinois reveals that, if netting continues at its present level in the state, by 1987 it will add only 0.16 percent to the level of volatile organic compound emissions in the state's 1982 inventory.[122] The research also disclosed that nearly all netting was the result of shutting down equipment; state regulators believe that the shutdowns would have taken place with or without netting.[123] This suggests that netting was not causing dischargers to reduce their pollution any more than they would have anyway.

Experience in additional areas confirms the insignificant role of new sources.[124] Further, since LAER standards are likely to be

---

*The next most numerous are nonattainment areas for particulates, but the particulate standard is being reconsidered and the magnitude of the nonattainment problem for particulates is difficult to foresee. The third most numerous nonattainment areas are for carbon monoxide. Carbon monoxide is largely a mobile source problem that will not be affected by netting for stationary sources.

†The annual emission increases of approximately 0.3 percent can, of course, increase in significance as time passes. Over five years, for example, the average 0.3 percent increase may add up to an increase of about 1.5 percent. However, even in such circumstances, allowing netting would not make a significant difference in the total emission inventory, since industries would still have to find ERCs for netting. If netting were not permitted, these same credits would be used instead to satisfy most of the requirement for offsets.

equivalent to NSPSs in practice,[125] just as were BACT standards, those sources that remain subject to NSPSs after netting probably are not emitting significantly more pollution than they would emit if they had not netted.

One may reasonably conclude from the foregoing data that there is little to be gained from insisting on a dual definition of *source*. Even if more sources come under regulatory review, the resulting change in emissions in nonattainment areas is likely to be relatively minor.[126]

Still, three countervailing considerations must be weighed in deciding whether netting in nonattainment areas is good policy. First, and most important, the Clean Air Act requires reasonable further progress toward attainment, with attainment to take place no later than 1982 or 1987. By definition, even if new sources that net out of review in nonattainment areas constitute but a small portion of the inventory, and by netting out simply maintain the status quo, they will still contribute to the exceeding of a standard toward whose attainment reasonable further progress must be made.

Second, some sources may be able to net out not by reducing their net emissions to zero but by keeping their emissions below thresholds of regulatory review.* In such instances, they will be adding emissions to areas that are required by law to reduce their aggregate emissions. Such netting out, even though it may affect a small portion of areas' emission inventories, will redistribute the burden of reducing emissions. Because aggregate emissions in those areas will still have to be reduced, some other sources in the areas will be called on to reduce their emissions.

Third, the LAER requirement is only one of several conditions attached to review of new sources in nonattainment areas. Statewide compliance is another. Even if the latter requirement is not applied often, in those instances where it could help, netting may preclude its use by regulators; a modified source might net out of it.

Since the amount of emissions involved in netting is so slight, these countervailing arguments do not seem to deserve much weight.

---

*For example, unless states have established lower thresholds, increases of less than 40 tons per year of sulfur dioxide and 25 tons per year of particulates will not trigger regulatory review. But even in netting's absence, such increases would not trigger regulatory review and would contribute to continuing nonattainment.

However, some policy analysts may disagree, believing that air quality problems are a composite of many small increments of pollution, making it important to control even the smallest contributors. These analysts may be correct in their assessment of the causes of air pollution problems, and some of the negative consequences of permitting netting, but these analyses do not make a compelling case for outlawing netting.

CONCLUDING OBSERVATIONS

Emissions trading involving new and modified sources has followed a somewhat more convoluted path than has the bubble policy for existing sources. To some extent, arguments over both new and modified sources, on one hand, and existing sources, on the other, are similar. For example, are industries' actual emissions often routinely lower than allowable emissions, and should credit be given for the difference? And, in nonattainment areas, should some flexibility be provided through trading, on the assumption that on balance it will help rather than hinder attainment, even though some identifiable control opportunities on specific emission points might be forgone?

More important, emissions trading for new and modified sources attacks some conventional wisdom of command and control regulation—the idea that it is important to regulate new and modified sources quite stringently, on the assumption that this will promote attainment and maintenance of healthful air quality both in the short- and long-term. This conventional wisdom deserves continued close scrutiny.

Chapter 6

Where Should Emissions Trading Go from Here?

The bubbles described in the preceding chapters illustrate empirically some of the major points of contention between emissions trading's proponents, the command minimalists, and its critics, the command expansionists. Because of these two groups' sharply contrasting attitudes regarding the role that bubbles should play in remedying the shortfalls of the conventional regulatory system, the U.S. Environmental Protection Agency (EPA) has had difficulty developing a final Emissions Trading Policy Statement (ETPS), as chapter 3 noted.

Trading advocate John Palmisano, formerly of EPA's Regulatory Reform Staff, expresses views typical of the minimalists, writing that emissions trading focuses attention on the "invalid assumptions" on which the "crazy-quilt" of existing programs for controlling air pollution sometimes are based.[1] Emissions trading has been the "message bearer" and has borne "the stigma of the message." Expressing concern that emissions trades have been discouraged because they have been forced to bear the burden of correcting the command-and-control system's defects, Palmisano complains, "Some officials apparently felt that doing away with the message bearer was easier than remedying [a] system which swept its problems 'under the rug' and away from the view of an unknowing public."

Countering the minimalists' arguments are expansionists such as Al Shehadi, who worked in EPA's air programs office in Washington:

> In order to fully understand why emission trading is so prone to abuse, it is important to have an understanding of the highly speculative and imperfect nature of most SIPs [state implementation plans]. . . . The perverse incentive that results from overlaying [a theoretically neat bubble] policy on such a messy foundation is for sources to line up the "neat" policy against the "messy" reality of SIPs, identify the "loopholes," and "jump" through them. . . .
>
> As [the Natural Resources Defense Council] emphasizes, what is needed is either to adapt the bubble policy to account for the messy SIPs that underpin it, or to expend the resources necessary to clean up all SIPs, state inventories, RACT ["reasonably available control technology"] determinations, and monitoring data, etc., before implementing the bubble policy. Either way, to understand this choice, it is necessary to understand how tenuous—how "fictional"—SIPs currently are.[2]

Consultant William Foskett, an observer of emissions trading's development, is sympathetic to selected arguments of both the minimalists and the expansionists. He comments that there are still "basic pieces of the [command-and-control] system that should be in place but are not."[3] He adds, "People are trying to develop procedural and administrative safeguards to provide information that they're somehow uncertain about, and this increases burdens on those trying to trade."

To gain some of its benefits while avoiding some abuses stemming from its awkward fit with the existing regulatory system, a middle-ground approach to emissions trading would be EPA's best policy. As the agency develops its final ETPS, it should simultaneously (a) undertake specific steps to ensure that emissions trading can continue to help correct the command-and-control system's shortcomings and (b) act to correct the weaknesses that have been evident in trading thus far. EPA should tighten emissions trading rules, clarify the risks of emissions trading, systematically monitor and evaluate state trading activity, adopt a "truth-in-trading" policy, explore the potential for trading's use with new and modified sources, and pay greater attention to monitoring emissions and ambient conditions. In addition, Congress should move to clean up the Clean Air Act.

RULE TIGHTENING

Emissions trading could deliver real environmental progress at less cost than the command-and-control system, but a strong backlash against its abuse might eliminate any benefits it could produce. It is better to tighten rules and reduce the number of trades than to have the entire program's credibility threatened.

As noted at the end of chapter 3, EPA is moving toward tightening trading rules in nonattainment areas lacking projections of attainment. EPA Administrator Lee Thomas is considering three options for such areas. The first is a total ban on bubbles for existing sources. Such a ban certainly would reduce the administrative burden bubble applications place on state and federal regulators. The potential magnitude of this burden is unclear, but it is reasonable for state regulators to be concerned about this demand, especially given other demands on their time and the downward trend in federal support (in real dollars) for state air programs during the 1980s.[4] For similar resource reasons, the regions' and air programs office's dislike of bubbles in areas lacking projections of attainment is understandable, especially since the environmental benefits of bubbles under existing rules have not been overwhelmingly positive.

More desirable than a total ban is a second option, the tightening of trading rules suggested by the Regulatory Reform Staff. These proposed rules would be likely to increase the proportion of environmentally beneficial bubbles, decrease the proportion of nonmeritorious bubble applications, and eliminate the worst abuses of the existing bubble rules. Use for baselines of the lowest of (a) SIP-allowable,* (b) RACT-allowable, or (c) actual emissions; insistence on a reduction of at least 20 percent beyond the baseline; elimination of unused capacity as a basis for credit; and restrictions on the uses of shutdowns for credits—all would increase the likelihood of better bubble applications being submitted. The resource demands of bubble applications must be acknowledged, but resource demands alone are not sufficient to bar bubbles, especially since the new rules might produce real environmental improvement and the other benefits that trading promises.†

Those who would bar bubbles in nonattainment areas without projections suggest, among other things, that bubbles should not be permissible because they would reduce the incentive for industries to support development of fully approvable plans or they would encour-

---

*"SIP-allowable" refers to those SIP provisions that, for reasons not important in this context, have not formally been defined as RACT.

†As a practical matter, NRDC probably will challenge any bubble EPA approves under the new rules, thereby delaying any impact the rules could have.

age industries to argue for lax RACT requirements. But it is not likely that the absence of bubble opportunities significantly influences industry attitudes toward SIP development or RACT requirements; industry certainly has sufficient incentives already to argue for lax RACT requirements.

Those who would bar bubbles in nonattainment areas without fully approved plans also argue that it is not possible to define emission reductions that are surplus and would therefore qualify for emission reduction credit in bubbles. But there are two definitions of "surplus"—(a) reductions that regulators do not or are not likely to require and (b) reductions that are not needed for attainment. If an area has been unable to find sufficient reductions to project attainment, regulators are unlikely to revisit sources for which regulations previously have been developed. Regulators are more likely to find additional sources to control, either large sources in additional categories or smaller sources in existing categories, or to try to tighten controls on mobile sources. It is reasonable, therefore, to treat reductions below the baselines proposed by the Regulatory Reform Staff as surplus for the purpose of bubbling. Even though regulators in areas lacking approved projections will not have figured out where to get all the reductions they need to attain ambient standards, they will at least satisfy some of their need from the bubbles approved under the Regulatory Reform Staff's proposed rules.

A third option for nonattainment areas lacking projections is use of a "standard industry practice" baseline for calculating emission reduction credits. Adopting such an ill-defined term would be tantamount to banning bubbles, because no industry is likely to attempt to bubble when the baseline is so unclear.

Different rules might be appropriate for attainment areas and for nonattainment areas with approved projections. Of course, the problem of approved projections lacking credibility is widely recognized, although a good response remains to be developed. Trading in areas with approved projections will continue to be tainted by the projections' credibility problems. It would be most desirable to quickly and publicly identify the tainted projections and then apply the "nonprojection" trading rules in those areas. Assuming this approach is legal, it would protect the credibility of emissions trading.

To the fullest extent legally permissible and practicable, both in nonattainment areas with approved projections and in attainment areas, credits should not be given for unused capacity and other reductions of nonexistent emissions. Again, credibility is the key; it is more important than the savings industries can achieve from trading phantom reductions.

The exact environmental effects of tightening the rules in the manner described above are difficult to predict. The tightening endorsed here is not as restrictive as some of trading's critics would like it to be, but it should have the salubrious effect of winnowing out those bubble proposals of the type most vulnerable to criticism.

RISK CLARIFICATION

This report has noted repeatedly that the uncertainties of existing SIPs are a major basis for conflicts over emissions trading. But many of the adjustments allowed thus far by bubbles, and likely to be allowed by most bubbles in the future, may be so small as to be insignificant when compared to the statistical uncertainties of the myriad assumptions on which SIPs are built. It might be useful to develop a better estimate than is now readily available of how successful or unsuccessful existing SIPs have been or are likely to be in attaining ambient standards. More detailed data would be helpful because, in their absence, proponents and opponents of trading are apt simply to argue past one another on the basis of conflicting and unverified assumptions. More data probably will not end disputes, because of the philosophical differences between opponents and proponents, but they should help distinguish important issues from unimportant ones and major problems from minor ones.

EPA is now processing SIP revisions for those states that were supposed, but failed, to attain the ambient standards by December 31, 1982. As part of its final Emissions Trading Policy Statement, EPA ought to publish data that display clearly how many areas of the country attained those standards as scheduled, how many areas failed to attain them and the probable reasons for failure, by what amount those areas failed to attain, and to what extent stationary sources are contributing to continued failure. Some of these data already have been published, others may exist only in internal agency documents, and others may not yet have been developed. They need to be brought together in the emissions trading context so that the public can have a better sense of the progress produced by SIPs and how much of an impact on future progress emissions trading might have.

Similarly, data should be brought together on progress being made in those areas whose deadline for attaining the ozone standard is

December 31, 1987. Based on progress thus far, how many areas are likely to miss the deadline, by how much, and why?* It seemingly would be in EPA's own interest to have this information publicly available to defend the choices it makes about trading rules.†

SYSTEMATIC MONITORING AND EVALUATION

Significant emissions trading activity is shifting to the states, pursuant to adoption by states of generic trading rules. EPA should continue to monitor developments in states for clues to the administrative demands made by emissions trading, innovative approaches to crediting shutdowns, and compliance monitoring. States have demonstrated, and in all likelihood will continue to demonstrate, considerable ingenuity in managing emissions trading.

The Regulatory Reform Staff has commissioned two studies that are important initial steps. The first is a compilation by the Environmental Law Institute of state emissions trading regulations.[5] A thorough combing of state emissions trading regulations, and the supplemental policy guidance accompanying them, should identify general patterns of state responses to shutdowns and other irksome matters. The review should also identify innovative state approaches that may merit further attention.

The Regulatory Reform Staff in 1984 also commissioned a frank report on state and regional experience with and attitudes toward emissions trading.[6] Based on interviews in eight states and three EPA regions, the report highlighted the ways that problems in implementing emissions trading are intertwined with problems of data deficiencies, unclear definitions of regulatory requirements, and other central elements of the conventional command-and-control regulatory strategy.[7] Those interviewed generally believed that emissions trading had not harmed air quality and had produced information useful in revising SIPs. The interviewees also expressed great frustration

---

*As noted in chapter 2, in October 1985 EPA was estimating that up to 32 metropolitan areas might not attain the ozone standard by the December 31, 1987, deadline.

†EPA ought to be pulling this information together independent of the emissions trading rules, so it can explain to the public why standards are or are not being attained, and what additional strategies are needed.

over long delays in resolving trading issues, stressed the importance of strengthening the emissions data base used for SIPs, and supported development of generic state rules that would minimize EPA's project-by-project review.[8]

These two studies are a good start for evaluation, but more systematic analysis is needed. Some auditing is occurring now as part of routine annual EPA reviews of state air programs. But a more detailed, quantitative analysis of such questions as how many bubbles are being approved, what types of emissions are involved, and whether reductions in actual emissions as well as allowable emissions are being achieved could be developed if states routinely filed with EPA the types of data that are now being entered into the Regulatory Reform Staff's data base for bubbles EPA approved as SIP revisions. Monitoring of bubble activity under state generic rules must be done with some sensitivity, since states are understandably uneasy about being second-guessed by EPA in their judgments about specific bubbles. To accommodate such state concerns, these data could be filed on a quarterly, biannual, or annual basis, long after specific bubbles have been approved. The data from bubbles not only could be entered into the emissions trading data base for analysis but also could be available for use in developing RACT guidelines, "best available control technology" (BACT) and "lowest achievable emission rate" (LAER) determinations, and EPA regulations for New Source Performance Standards (NSPSs).

Some trading proponents fear that using voluntarily developed stringent control techniques developed under bubbles to tighten future regulations could have a chilling effect on trading activity. However, if the savings from bubbles are as substantial in individual cases as they appear to be, and if there is a substantial lag between the initial use of a specific stringent control technique and its adoption as a uniform regulatory requirement, then the chilling effect should be minimal.

"TRUTH IN TRADING"

As should be evident after reading chapters 2-5, emissions trading has had a credibility problem. The time has come to institute a program of "truth in trading," to provide a clearer picture of what trades actually accomplish.

First, EPA's information summaries should distinguish more clearly changes in allowable emissions from changes in actual emissions. In its *Federal Register* notices for bubble proposals, EPA should routinely publish tables showing pre- and post-bubble levels of actual and allowable emissions; the format could be that used for the tables in chapter 4 describing the Sohio, Ashland Oil, and BFGoodrich bubbles. Second, when it makes statements about bubbles promoting compliance, EPA should make clear how compliance has been accomplished—either by reducing actual emissions at specific points to satisfy or do better than previously established regulatory requirements *or* by raising allowable emission levels to actual levels so that previous instances of noncompliance at particular points have been accommodated. Third, in the summary reports it periodically prepares on progress in emissions trading, the Regulatory Reform Staff should incorporate the distinctions noted here between actual and allowable emissions, and between the two different forms of compliance, or it should refrain altogether from statements about the environmental and compliance benefits of trading.

EPA has begun to recognize the need for clearer statements about emission reductions from bubbles. In its report for calendar year 1984, dated May 31, 1985, the Regulatory Reform Staff recited the number of bubbles approved or proposed for approval by EPA, but it made no claims about emission reductions from them. Rather, it stated that "previous figures on . . . environmental benefits from individual emissions trades should be viewed with caution" and that emission reductions "may vary in either direction" from original estimates.[9] The Regulatory Reform Staff adopted a similarly cautious approach to estimated savings from bubbles. While noting that total estimated savings exceeded $800 million, the staff stated that initial estimates for individual bubbles were based on circumstances or data, such as comparative fuel prices, that may since have changed.[10]

The Regulatory Reform Staff has substantially improved its data management system for emissions trading activity. In the future, it must get the cooperation of the states and EPA regional offices that process bubble proposals. Assuming that happens, this data management system should be a useful device for generating summary information on actual and allowable emissions, compliance status of points being bubbled, attainment status of areas in which bubbles are proposed, and other information essential to understanding the use and impact of trading.

TRADING FOR NEW AND MODIFIED SOURCES

Technology-forcing has been a major tenet of the Clean Air Act, particularly of the act's provisions governing review of new and modified sources. The various new source provisions of the act, including those requiring NSPS, BACT, and LAER technologies, have been successful in minimizing emissions from new and modified sources. The NSPS provisions in particular have provided a uniform floor of emission requirements, thereby providing for industry planners concrete guidance as to the technologies required for new sources. The NSPSs also place a floor on the negotiated weakening of new source abatement requirements in interstate competition for new industry. NSPS requirements operate independently of the ambient standards of the Clean Air Act, although Congress presumed that NSPSs would encourage the ambient standards' long- and short-term attainment. Likewise, the LAER requirements were presumed by Congress to encourage the standards' short- and long-term attainment, and the BACT requirements were presumed to be important means for protecting increments in Prevention of Significant Deterioration (PSD) areas.

EPA has been successful in gaining court approval of netting for modified sources in both the PSD and nonattainment program, and it is not readily evident that this netting has a significant adverse environmental effect. EPA ought to continue its exploration of trading in the context of the NSPS program, particularly the grouping of emission points in newly developed or revised NSPSs. While netting out of LAER and BACT requirements might reduce administrative burdens, EPA still must pay careful attention to any such burdens that federal and state regulators might have to bear under broadened rules for bubbling of new sources.

FOCUSING ON THE BASICS

Although emissions trading is an effort to overcome some of the Clean Air Act's faults, it has stumbled over the harsh reality that, after all these years, regulators still are unable to answer some basic questions about air pollution in the United States today. They have only a rough sense of how much pollution dischargers are emitting and of how much progress is being made in cleaning the air. As one commentator has observed, "If we're going to spend that much money to control pollution, you'd think [we would] put a little more money toward knowing whether we're making progress, how fast, where we're not and why we're not."[11]

EPA and the states must make a major effort to improve the inventories and monitoring systems that are required for both the conventional command-and-control system and emissions trading to work. Emissions trading offers potentially large economic and environmental benefits, but its turbulent history reflects deeply felt fears that, if it is not carefully structured, it will encourage environmentally unproductive gamesmanship based on manipulating weaknesses of the current system.

The Natural Resources Defense Council's David Doniger has equated emissions trading with "The Force" in the *Star Wars* trilogy—though it has "capacity for good," one should beware of being seduced by its "dark side."[12] Improved accounting systems would reduce the need for emissions trading rules to be burdened with so many safeguards designed to compensate for widely acknowledged weaknesses in the existing regulatory system. In this way emission trading's capacity for good could be more fully realized, and its feared abuses generally avoided.

CLEANING UP THE CLEAN AIR ACT

Difficulties encountered in implementing emissions trading should provide a sobering lesson to reform theorists who advocate more market-oriented approaches to environmental management. It is relatively easy to show how cost-inefficient the existing system of regulation is, but it is quite hard to refine procedures for implementing a market approach. Since it has taken so long to implement the command-and-control approach of the Clean Air Act Amendments of 1970 and 1977, and since this approach continues to be so problematic, it is not surprising that efforts to implement emissions trading have been so difficult. The rules for both the command-and-control approach and for emissions trading both have required considerable fine-tuning.

The most ardent defenders of the command-and-control approach might derive great satisfaction from the harsh encounters the theory of emissions trading has had with the reality of the Clean Air Act. But the practical difficulty of implementing such a market approach is only one of the major lessons from trading's experience. Another major lesson is that the implementation of the Clean Air Act is terribly flawed.

The Clean Air Act is long overdue for serious reevaluation. Congress needs to take a searching look at the validity of the assumptions underlying the existing command-and-control system. Unfortunately, the Reagan administration's frontal assault on environmental institutions has given a very bad name to regulatory reform, because its efforts appear to be as much an assault on the goals of environmental protection as on the techniques of regulation. This is a shame, because intelligent regulatory reform can produce environmental improvement at less cost.

If it reauthorizes the Clean Air Act anytime soon, Congress should allow EPA to continue its experiments with emissions trading. Even though emissions trading has not yet produced some of the wonderful results that its most enthusiastic promoters once expected, it continues to hold promise as a device for promoting more cost-effective pollution control. For Congress to kill emissions trading, after all these years of trying to make it work, and with evidence that it sometimes does produce results not attainable by conventional controls, would send the wrong signal to would-be innovators in the public and private sector.

Trading has been the victim of unduly high expectations. Fine-tuning the rules governing it has been extremely difficult. But it has produced some noteworthy benefits, and further benefits will be lost if it is abandoned.

Postscript

In a May 1986 memorandum, U.S. Environmental Protection Agency (EPA) Administrator Lee Thomas decided major issues disputed by his agency's air programs office and Regulatory Reform Staff, as a prelude to publication of a "final" Emissions Trading Policy Statement in the *Federal Register*. As this report was going to press, publication of the final statement was planned for July 1986.

Thomas's memo focused mainly on rules governing bubbles in nonattainment areas lacking EPA-approved projections of attainment. These rules are tighter than were those in the interim policy statement published in 1982. In Thomas's view, "These and other tightenings will prevent any recurrence of alleged problems with some past bubbles, while strengthening the bubble's ability to help get us where we need to go."

Tightenings in the rules for areas lacking projections include changes alluded to in chapters 4 and 6 of this report: limitation on use of past shutdowns, use of the lower of RACT-allowable or actual emissions as the baseline for calculating credits, and a minimum 20 percent reduction in emissions. In nonattainment areas with approved projections of attainment, the baseline would be the emissions allowed in a state implementation plan and assumed by the plan to provide for attainment. In attainment areas, bubbles would have to be "neutral" in effect, meaning that "bubble trades which produce ambient effects equivalent to pre-trade emission limits will generally be approved."

Commenting on the interplay between bubbles and the existing command-and-control system, Thomas observed:

> The bubble is a creative way to supplement and enhance the air management scheme embodied in the statute. While it cannot solve—and should not be asked to solve—all the problems of that scheme, it makes an important contribution in terms of needed flexibility, ability to respond to changing circumstances, and stronger incentives for environmental progress.

In addition, recognizing that his decisions would be criticized as being either too stringent or too lenient, Thomas stated: "I am convinced that taken together [the revisions] are a responsibly balanced package which will strengthen bubbles' ability to advance environmental progress as well as regulatory flexibility."

References

CHAPTER 1. UNDERSTANDING THE BASICS

1. The current and most comprehensive statement of EPA's emissions trading policy is found at 47 Fed. Reg. 15076, April 7, 1982. This is an "interim" policy that took effect immediately on publication. See also EPA's supplemental discussion and request for further public comment, 48 Fed. Reg. 39580, August 31, 1983. EPA expects to publish a final version of the policy in mid-1986.

2. David Doniger, "The Dark Side of the Bubble," *The Environmental Forum* 4 (July 1985):33.

3. For an excellent overview of the theory of transferable discharge permits, see Thomas H. Tietenberg, *Emissions Trading: An Exercise in Reforming Pollution Policy* (Washington, D.C.: Resources for the Future, 1985), and the sources cited there.

4. The brief review in the text of the theory of transferable permits paraphrases Tietenberg, *Emissions Trading*, pp. 14-16.

5. See Tietenberg, *Emissions Trading*, chapter 6, for discussion of "market power" in emission reduction credits. See also Richard A. Liroff, *Air Pollution Offsets: Trading, Selling, and Banking* (Washington, D.C.: The Conservation Foundation, 1980), pp. 26-28.

6. See 47 Fed. Reg. 49322, October 29, 1982; 49 Fed. Reg. 31032, August 2, 1984; and 50 Fed. Reg. 718, January 4, 1985. See also "EPA Data Show Most Large Refiners Meet New Lead Standards With Trading," *Inside EPA*, August 12, 1983, p. 4.

7. See, for example, EPA's trading proposal for particulate emissions from heavy duty diesel trucks, 49 Fed. Reg. 40258, October 15, 1984.

8. For discussion of the costs associated with alternative trading proposals, see "Excerpts from Acid Rain Briefing Document Prepared for Ruckelshaus by EPA's Acid Rain Deposition Task Force, Including Policy Options," *BNA Environment*

150   RICHARD A. LIROFF

Reporter—Current Developments, September 2, 1983, pp. 775-85. For a discussion of some obstacles to implementation, see Roger Raufer and Stephen Feldman, "Emissions Trading and What it May Mean for Acid Deposition Control," *Public Utilities Fortnightly,* August 16, 1984, pp. 17-25.

9. See 50 Fed. Reg. 52418, December 23, 1985.

10. Brian J. Cook, "The Politics of Regulatory Form: An Analysis of Policy Choice in Environmental Regulation" (Unpublished doctoral dissertation, Department of Government and Politics, University of Maryland, 1984), pp. 165-67. See also Stephen L. Elkin and Brian J. Cook, "The Public Life of Economic Incentives," *Policy Studies Journal* 13 (1985):797-813.

11. The stopping point argument is presented in Michael H. Levin, "Building a Better Bubble at EPA," *Regulation* 9 (March/April 1985):33-42.

12. The best published sources of proponents' views are ibid. and Michael H. Levin, "Getting There: Implementing the 'Bubble Policy,' " in Eugene Bardach and Robert Kagan, eds., *Social Regulation: Strategies for Reform* (San Francisco: Institute for Contemporary Studies, 1982). See also Laurens H. Rhinelander, "The Proper Place for the Bubble Concept under the Clean Air Act," *Environmental Law Reporter* 13 (1983):10406-10417.

13. The principal cases are discussed later in this report. They are: *ASARCO, Inc* v. *Environmental Protection Agency,* 578 F. 2d 319, 8 ELR 20164, 20277 (D.C. Cir., 1978); *Alabama Power Co.* v. *Costle,* 636 F. 2d 323, 10 ELR 20001 (D.C. Cir., 1979); and *Natural Resources Defense Council, Inc* v. *Gorsuch,* 685 F. 2d 718, 12 ELR 20942 (D.C. Cir., 1982) reversed sub nom. *Chevron U.S.A. Inc* v. *Natural Resources Defense Council, Inc,* 104 S. Ct. 2778, 14 ELR 20507 (U.S., 1984) (hereafter cited as *Chevron* v. *NRDC*).

14. *Chevron* v. *NRDC.*

15. David Doniger, "Comments on the Environmental Protection Agency's Emissions Trading Policy Statement," submission to the U.S. Environmental Protection Agency, July 6, 1982, p. 3.

16. This definition of modeling derives from Environmental Research and Technology, Inc., "ERT Handbook on Requirements for Industrial Facilities under the Clean Air Act," 7th ed. (Concord, Mass.: ERT, Inc., 1984), p. 24.

CHAPTER 2. THE CLEAN AIR ACT: IMPLEMENTATION PROBLEMS AND THE RISE OF EMISSIONS TRADING

1. The Clean Air Act is codified at 42 U.S.C. §§7401 et seq.

2. See the Clean Air Act, Sections 160-169, 42 U.S.C. §§7470-7479, for description of the program for preventing significant deterioration.

3. Clean Air Act, Section 110, 42 U.S.C. §7410, and Section 172, 42 U.S.C. §7502.

4. Clean Air Act, Sections 110(a)(2)(I) and 176, 42 U.S.C. §§7410(a)(2)(I) and 7506.

5. Clean Air Act, Section 111, 42 U.S.C. §7411.

6. 40 CFR Part 50 (1985).

7. Marc J. Roberts and Susan O. Farrell, "The Political Economy of Implementation: The Clean Air Act and Stationary Sources," in Ann F. Friedlaender, ed., *Approaches to Controlling Air Pollution* (Cambridge, Mass.: MIT Press, 1978), p. 156.

8. Ibid., pp. 156-157.

9. For a table summarizing much of the litigation, see "Principal Litigation Under the Clean Air Act," *Environmental Law Reporter* 3 (1973):10022-10030.

10. The fight over the "applicability bubble" for new sources is described in detail in chapter 5.

11. *ASARCO, Inc* v. *Environmental Protection Agency*, 578 F. 2d 319, 8 ELR 20164, 20277 (D.C. Cir., 1978).

12. See Richard A. Liroff, *Air Pollution Offsets: Trading, Selling and Banking* (Washington, D.C.: The Conservation Foundation, 1980), pp. 6-11.

13. See Senator Edmund S. Muskie's statement on the report of the U.S. Senate Committee on Environment and Public Works on S. 252, reprinted in U.S. Senate, Committee on Environment and Public Works, *A Legislative History of the Clean Air Act Amendments of 1977*, 95th Cong., 2d Sess., 1978, Serial No. 95-16, vol. 3, p. 717.

14. The Clean Air Act Amendments of 1977 were Public Law 95-95, supplemented by the Clean Air Act Technical Amendments, Public Law 95-190, §14.

15. Clean Air Act, Section 172(a)(2), 42 U.S.C. §7502(a)(2).

16. This definition is recited at 45 Fed. Reg. 59331, September 9, 1980.

17. Clean Air Act, Section 110(a)(2)(I), 42 U.S.C. §7410(a)(2)(I).

18. For discussion of state staffing problems, see U.S. Comptroller General, *Federal-State Environmental Programs—The State Perspective* (Washington, D.C.: U.S. General Accounting Office, 1980), pp. 60-67.

19. National Commission on Air Quality, *To Breathe Clean Air* (Washington, D.C.: U.S. Government Printing Office, 1981), p. 117.

20. Pacific Environmental Services, "Study of the 1979 State Implementation Plan Submittals," prepared for U.S. National Commission on Air Quality (Elmhurst, Ill.: Pacific Environmental Services, 1980), p. 8-2.

21. Clean Air Act, Sections 160-169, 42 U.S.C. §§7470-7479.

22. *Alabama Power Co.* v. *Costle*, 636 F. 2d 323, 10 ELR 20001 (D.C. Cir., 1979).

23. EPA data are cited in The Conservation Foundation, *State of the Environment: An Assessment at Mid-Decade* (Washington, D.C.: The Conservation Foundation, 1984), pp. 86-90.

24. For a fuller discussion of these matters, see ibid.; The Conservation Foundation, *State of the Environment 1982* (Washington, D.C.: The Conservation Foundation, 1982), pp. 47-59; and Robert W. Crandall, *Controlling Industrial Pollution* (Washington, D.C.: The Brookings Institution, 1983), pp. 16-31.

25. Letter from Darryl D. Tyler, Director, Control Programs Development Division, to Richard A. Liroff, October 25, 1985.

26. EPA's proposal for revising the standard is published at 49 Fed. Reg. 10408, March 20, 1984.

27. For some intercity comparisons, see The Conservation Foundation, *State of the Environment 1982*, p. 48.

CHAPTER 3. THE EVOLUTION OF THE BUBBLE POLICY FOR EXISTING SOURCES

1. The Office of Planning and Resource Management is now the Office of Policy, Planning, and Evaluation.

2. U.S. Senate, Committee on Environment and Public Works, *Progress in the Prevention and Control of Air Pollution, 1977, Annual Report of the Administrator of the Environmental Protection Agency to the Congress of the United States*, 95th Cong., 2d Sess., 1978, S. Doc. No. 95-100, p. 88.

3. Ibid., p. 90.

4. "Steel's Cleanup Dilemma," *Business Week*, May 7, 1979, p. 166. Much the same thing was said by the *Wall Street Journal* in an article published in 1980; the *Journal* noted that U.S. Steel was softening its "bitter resistance to environmental regulations." See "Some Analysts Believe Red Ink at U.S. Steel Is a Good Sign for Firm," *Wall Street Journal*, January 31, 1980. The industry's resistance aside, its compliance expenditures have been considerable. See U.S. Department of Commerce figures cited in U.S. Congress, Office of Technology Assessment, *Technology and Steel Industry Competitiveness* (Washington, D.C.: U.S. Government Printing Office, 1980), p. 342.

5. *BNA Environment Reporter—Current Developments*, December 9, 1977, p. 1172.

6. Armco's reputation is noted in Michael H. Levin, "Getting There: Implementing the 'Bubble Policy,' " in Eugene Bordach and Robert Kagan, eds., *Social Regulation: Strategies for Reform* (San Francisco: Institute for Contemporary Studies, 1982), p. 71.

7. Letter from Richard Ayres and Frances Dubrowski to Honorable Douglas Costle, May 25, 1978, p. 1; copy in author's files.

8. Memo accompanying ibid., p. 5.

9. U.S. Environmental Protection Agency, "Report of the Bubble Concept Task Force" (Washington, D.C.: U.S. Environmental Protection Agency, September 18, 1978, processed).

10. Ibid., p. 4.

11. Ibid., p. 6.

12. Letter from Richard Ayres and Frances Dubrowski to James Kamihachi, September 22, 1978; copy in author's files.

13. Ibid., p. 3.

14. Memo from David Hawkins to EPA General Counsel Jodie Bernstein, July 24, 1978, captioned "Steel Talks Memo (Memo of July 20, 1978)." See also memo from the EPA Assistant Administrator for Enforcement to the EPA Administrator re "Discussions with Iron and Steel Industry Representatives," July 7, 1978, and memorandum from Chuck Warren to EPA Administrator Douglas Costle re "Steel Issues," September 5, 1978. Copies in author's files.

15. Ibid.

16. Levin, "Getting There," p. 61. Levin's views in the article are personal, not the official views of EPA.

17. 44 Fed. Reg. 3740, January 18, 1979.

18. 44 Fed. Reg. 3740, 3741, 3742, January 18, 1979.

19. 44 Fed. Feg. 3740, 3742, January 18, 1979.

20. 44 Fed. Reg. 3740, 3743, January 18, 1979.

21. Natural Resources Defense Council and Sierra Club Legal Defense Fund, "Comments on EPA's Proposed Bubble Policy," March 19, 1979; copy in author's files.

22. Letter from Harry D. Williams to Honorable Douglas Costle, December 15, 1978, p. 1; copy in author's files.

23. "Testimony on behalf of STAPPA before EPA, on proposed Policy for Alternative Emission Reduction Option, March 15, 1979"; copy in author's files.

24. Levin, "Getting There," p. 75.

25. "Recommendation for Alternative Emission Reduction Options within State Implementation Plans," 44 Fed. Reg. 71780, December 11, 1979.

26. As noted below in the text, EPA's altered position on fugitive dust reflected recognition of studies submitted during the comment process.

27. 44 Fed. Reg. 71780, 71783, 71788, December 11, 1979.

28. 44 Fed. Reg. 71780, 71783, December 11, 1979.

29. Ibid.

30. 44 Fed. Reg. 71780, 71786, December 11, 1979.

31. Levin, "Getting There," p. 77.

32. U.S. Environmental Protection Agency, "Progress in the Prevention and Control of Air Pollution in 1980 and 1981" (undated, processed), p. V-3.

33. 45 Fed. Reg. 15531, 15540, March 11, 1980.

34. The author of this report attended the conference.

35. 45 Fed. Reg. 77459, 77460, November 24, 1980. See also, Levin, "Getting There," p. 82, for discussion of the New Jersey regulation.

36. EPA also took the opportunity to lift a restriction that it had previously placed on trades between certain types of VOC sources. In technical parlance, EPA lifted the restriction on trades between the sources for which different control technology guidance (CTG) documents had been issued. EPA's reason for banning such trades had not been well articulated in past Federal Register notices on the bubble policy.

37. 46 Fed. Reg. 20551, April 6, 1981.

38. See "EPA Announces Major Changes in Bubble Policy," press release, January 16, 1981; copy in author's files.

39. Levin, "Getting There," p. 81.

40. Ibid.

41. Ibid., p. 82.

42. Ibid., pp. 67-79.

43. These activities are described ibid., pp. 83-84.

44. Ibid.

45. See memorandum from Roy Gamse, Deputy Associate Administrator for Policy and Resource Management, "Request for Informal Comment on Draft Proposed Controlled Trading Policy Statement," August 28, 1981; copy in author's files.

46. 47 Fed. Reg. 15076, April 7, 1982.

47. 47 Fed. Reg. 15076-15077, April 7, 1982.

48. 47 Fed. Reg. 15077, April 7, 1982.

49. EPA's offset and banking project produced numerous publications on trading emission reduction credits. See, for example, U.S. Environmental Protection Agency, Office of Planning and Resource Management, *Emission Reduction Banking Manual* (Washington, D.C.: U.S. Environmental Protection Agency, 1980).

50. 47 Fed. Reg. 15076, 15077, April 7, 1982.

51. 47 Fed. Reg. 15077, April 7, 1982.

52. See memorandum from Roger Strelow, Assistant Administrator for Air and Radiation, to Regional Administrators, Regions I-X, "Guidance for Determining Acceptability of SIP Regulations in Non-attainment Areas," December 9, 1976; reprinted in *BNA Environment Reporter—Current Developments*, December 17, 1976, p. 1210. See also U.S. Environmental Protection Agency, "Workshop on Requirements for Nonattainment Area Plans" (Washington, D.C.: U.S. Environmental Protection Agency, 1978), pp. 154-56.

53. Ibid.

54. Ibid.

55. U.S. Environmental Protection Agency, "Workshop on Requirements for Nonattainment Area Plans," p. 287.

56. 47 Fed. Reg. 15076, 15080, April 7, 1982.

57. 47 Fed. Reg. 15076, 15081, April 7, 1982.

58. 48 Fed. Reg. 39580, August 31, 1983.

59. 48 Fed. Reg. 39580, 39582, August 31, 1983.

60. 48 Fed. Reg. 39580, 39583, August 31, 1983.

61. 48 Fed. Reg. 39580, 39584, August 31, 1984.

62. See Leslie Sue Ritts, "Summary of Comments: August 31, 1983 Shutdown Notice, 48 Fed. Reg. 39579," report to the U.S. Environmental Protection Agency (Washington, D.C.: Environmental Law Institute Report, 1984), pp. 7-10.

63. "Comments on the Emissions Trading Policy Statement, Request for Further Comments on Shutdown and Other Issues," submission to the U.S. Environmental Protection Agency, October 31, 1983.

64. See David Doniger, "The Dark Side of the Bubble," *The Environmental Forum* 4 (July 1985):34, a published adaptation of the speech.

65. This conclusion is based on the author's review of the state and local letters received by EPA.

66. Ritts, "Summary of Comments," p. 11.

67. Letter from Herbert Wortreich, Assistant Director, Air and Noise Quality, New Jersey Department of Environmental Protection, to EPA's Ivan Tether, September 29, 1983, p. 2.

68. Ibid., p. 3.

69. Letter from Thomas F. Heinsheimer, Chairman, South Coast Air Quality Management District, to EPA's Central Docket Section, October 5, 1983, pp. 1-2.

70. *BNA Environment Reporter—Current Developments,* October 5, 1984, pp. 886-87.

71. Ibid.

72. Undated memorandum produced by Indur Goklany, Regulatory Reform Staff; copy in author's files.

73. Ibid.

74. See memorandum (with attachment) from Darryl D. Tyler, Control Programs Development Division, to Mike Levin, Chief, Regulatory Reform Staff, "Comments on Your Note, 'Why Bubbles Will Produce Progress in NA Areas Without Fully-Approved Plans,' " November 1, 1985, attachment p. 3, copy in author's files.

75. See Michael H. Levin, "Building a Better Bubble at EPA," *Regulation* 9 (March/April 1985):42, and *BNA Environment Reporter—Current Developments,* January 11, 1985, p. 1471.

CHAPTER 4. THE BUBBLE POLICY FOR EXISTING SOURCES IN PRACTICE

1. "Emissions Trading Status Report," January 10, 1985. This two-page status report, published periodically by EPA, summarizes key developments in emissions trading.

2. Ibid., p. 1.

3. Ibid.

4. Ibid.

5. Ibid.

6. Ibid.

7. Ibid., pp. 1-2.

8. Ibid., p. 2.

9. U.S. Environmental Protection Agency, Regulatory Reform Staff, "Annual Report—CY 84" (May 1985, processed).

10. Ibid., appendix A, "Bubble Information Available as of December 1984," and chart, "EPA Approved and Proposed Bubbles by Industrial Category."

11. The New Jersey figures are from "New Jersey Generic Bubble Rules," February 4, 1986, a one-page summary prepared by the state for a meeting with EPA Administrator Lee Thomas in February 1986. U.S. Environmental Protection Agency, Regulatory Reform Staff, "Annual Report—CY 84," appendix A, p. 11, lists the VOC bubbles approved by New Jersey.

12. U.S. Environmental Protection Agency, Regulatory Reform Staff, "Annual Report—CY 84," figure—"EPA Approved and Proposed Bubbles by Pollutant."

13. "Area Status of EPA Approved Bubbles" (Draft Chart, September 24, 1984), and note from Barry Elman, Regulatory Reform Staff, to Richard A. Liroff, July 15, 1985.

14. "Emissions Trading Status Report," January 10, 1985, p. 1; "Emissions Trading Status Report," October 1, 1984, p. 1.

15. Memo to the EPA Administrator from Joseph A. Cannon, Associate Administrator for Policy and Resource Management re "Emissions Trading—End of Year Status Report," April 5, 1983, p. 1; copy in author's files.

156 RICHARD A. LIROFF

16. Michael H. Levin, "The Supreme Court's 'Bubble' Decision: What It Means," *EPA Journal* 10 (September 1984):11.

17. 46 Fed. Reg. 53408, October 29, 1981. The description of this bubble in the text is based entirely on this *Federal Register* notice.

18. "Emissions Trading Status Report," May 7, 1984, appendix I; copy in author's files.

19. 48 Fed. Reg. 52055, November 16, 1983.

20. The specific emission reductions at each point are summarized in "Compliance Plan for 3M Bristol Plant, Bristol, Pennsylvania, submitted [by 3M] to the Pennsylvania Department of Environmental Resources, October 9, 1979"; copy in author's files.

21. Ibid., pp. 7, 9.

22. Ibid., p. 10.

23. See letter from Jeffrey Muffat, 3M, to Glen Hanson, EPA Region III, Philadelphia, December 12, 1979; copy in author's files.

24. See EPA's approval notice in 46 Fed. Reg. 41779, August 18, 1981.

25. Author's conversation with Jeffrey Muffat, 3M, February 26, 1985.

26. As noted in the text, RACT required a 74 percent reduction in emissions.

27. 46 Fed. Reg. 41779, August 18, 1981.

28. This is suggested in a draft report, TCS Management Group, Inc., "Evaluation of the Impacts of Emission Bubbles," prepared for U.S. Environmental Protection Agency, Regulatory Reform Staff (Nashville, Tenn.: TCS Management Group, 1984), p. 18. This draft was not relied on heavily for the text's description of the 3M bubble, for it was never produced in final form.

29. See 42 U.S.C. §7413.

30. This description of the plant is drawn from "Du Pont Experience, Chambers Works 'Bubble' for Control of Volatile Organic Substances (VOS) under New Jersey Administrative Code 7:27-16.1 et seq.," remarks delivered by William H. Elliott, Jr., Senior Supervisor of the Chambers Works Air Quality Control Group, at a Joint EPA-Armco Conference on the Bubble Policy, Philadelphia, Pennsylvania, December 3, 1981; copy in author's files. It also draws on an undated paper describing the characteristics of the revised bubble: William H. Elliott, Jr., "The Chambers Works Generic VOC Bubble."

31. Elliott, "The Chambers Works Generic VOC Bubble," p. 2.

32. Letter from William H. Elliott, Jr. to Richard A. Liroff, February 11, 1985.

33. This appears to be the major difference in the controls described in Elliott, "Du Pont Experience," and Elliott, "The Chambers Works Generic VOC Bubble."

34. Elliott, "The Chambers Works Generic VOC Bubble," table II, p. 8.

35. Ibid., p. 4.

36. Ibid.

37. Elliott, "Du Pont Experience," figure III.

38. Elliott, "The Chambers Works Generic VOC Bubble," table III, p. 9. If reductions under the bubble are calculated on an hourly rather than annual basis, the reductions from the bubble are approximately 30 percent below the RACT level. Regardless of whether sets of annual or hourly assumptions are employed, the reductions are substantial.

39. See "Description of Representative Bubbles," distributed by U.S. Environmental Protection Agency, Regulatory Reform Staff, at the EPA-Armco Conference.

40. See 40 CFR §52.1572(a)(1985).

41. See §129(c) of the Clean Air Act, codified as a note to 42 U.S.C §7502.

42. 46 Fed. Reg. 5980, January 12, 1981. See also the bubbles approved in Pennsylvania for Scott Paper Company, Arbogast and Bastian, Inc., and J.H. Thompson, Inc., 47 Fed. Reg. 42760, September 29, 1982, and 48 Fed. Reg. 21326, May 12, 1983.

43. Details of the conditions can be found in EPA's notice approving the bubble, 47 Fed. Reg. 28097, June 29, 1982. See also John B. Ramil and William N. Cantrell, "Application of the 'Bubble Concept' to a Utility Coal Conversion" (Paper delivered at the 1981 annual meeting, Air Pollution Control Association, Philadelphia).

44. See EPA's notices of proposed and final rule making, 46 Fed. Reg. 34817, July 6, 1981, and 46 Fed. Reg. 46130, September 17, 1981.

45. For descriptions of the bank's operations, see Richard A. Liroff, *Air Pollution Offsets: Trading, Selling, and Banking* (Washington, D.C.: The Conservation Foundation, 1980), pp. 34-37, and Michael T. DeBusschere, "Integrating Emissions Banking and Emissions Source Review Processes" (Paper delivered at 1984 annual meeting, Air Pollution Control Association, San Francisco).

46. Michael H. Levin, "Getting There: Implementing the 'Bubble Policy,' " in Eugene Bardach and Robert Kagan, eds., *Social Regulation: Strategies for Reform* (San Francisco: Institute for Contemporary Studies, 1982), p. 60.

47. See, for example, "Emissions Trading Status Report," May 7, 1984, and "Description of Representative Bubbles."

48. Conversation between Michael T. DeBusschere, Jefferson County Air Pollution Control Officer, and the author, March 22, 1985.

49. See discussion in chapter 3 of double counting.

50. See letter from Michael T. DeBusschere to U.S. Environmental Protection Agency, September 14, 1983, page 1, commenting on EPA's August 31, 1983, request for comments on alternative approaches to calculating emission reduction credits.

51. Liroff, *Air Pollution Offsets*, p. 34.

52. See 42 U.S.C. §7413.

53. See EPA's notice of proposed rule making, 46 Fed. Reg. 8583, January 27, 1981.

54. See Pedco Environmental, Inc., "Technical Guidance for Control of Industrial Process Fugitive Particulate Emissions" (Research Triangle Park, N.C.: U.S. Environmental Protection Agency, Office of Air Quality Planning and Standards, 1977), p. 1-2.

55. The cost estimates are from "The Armco Middletown Works Fugitive Dust (Bubble Concept) Control Program," undated Armco document, probably from 1979, p. 2. The basis for the cost estimates are found in another Armco document, "Supplementary Information for Armco's Bubble Concept Presentation, July 6, 1979." Both documents were submitted to EPA. The energy consumption estimates are found in a November 9, 1979, letter from Armco's John Barker to

EPA's David Hawkins. Copies of these documents are in the author's files.

56. See "The Armco . . . Control Program," p. 2.

57. Ibid.

58. Russel Bohn et al., "Fugitive Emissions from Integrated Iron and Steel Plants" (Research Triangle Park, N.C.: U.S. Environmental Protection Agency, Office of Research and Development, Industrial Environmental Research Laboratory, 1978), pp. xvi-xviii.

59. Ibid., pp. 1-2.

60. Ibid., pp. xvii-xviii.

61. Ibid., pp. xv, xviii.

62. "The Armco . . . Control Program," p. 1.

63. Armco invested $5.2 million in 1979 and committed another $1.8 million to the project in 1980. Ibid., p. 8.

64. See EPA's notice of proposed rule making, 46 Fed. Reg. 8585, January 27, 1981.

65. See EPA's notice of approval of the bubble, 46 Fed. Reg. 19469, March 31, 1981.

66. These emissions were not involved in the bubble. Notice of the consent agreement is published at 45 Fed. Reg. 75803, November 17, 1980. The consent agreement's linkage to the bubble plan is referred to in "Plain Dust Is the Key to Pollution 'Bubble' at Armco Steelworks," *Wall Street Journal*, October 1, 1980, and in "EPA Accepts Armco Bubble Proposal to Control Emissions at Ohio Plant," *BNA Environment Reporter—Current Developments*, October 24, 1980, p. 921.

67. 40 CFR §81.336 (1985).

68. See Bruce Steiner, "Fugitive Dust Control in Iron and Steel Plants" (Paper presented at the 31st Ontario Industrial Waste Conference, June 1984, Toronto, Canada), p. 3. Steiner notes that production at this plant varied over this 10-year period. Maximum annual production occurred in 1978, the minimum production in 1980 was 71 percent of the 1978 maximum, and production in 1983 was 91 percent of the 1978 level. Ibid., p. 3. One might infer from Steiner's data that the reductions in monitored concentrations are not attributable primarily to production cutbacks.

69. Steiner, "Fugitive Dust Control," table II.

70. See, for example, NRDC's petition to the EPA Administrator, requesting establishment of ambient air quality criteria, standards, and control programs for fine particulates, May 29, 1980; copy in author's files.

71. EPA's proposal is published at 49 Fed. Reg. 10408, March 20, 1984.

72. See discussion of the National Steel bubble in the text below.

73. 46 Fed. Reg. 19468, 19470, March 31, 1981.

74. See letter from Shenango President W.P. Snyder III to EPA Administrator Douglas Costle, February 15, 1980, copy in author's files.

75. Ibid., p. 6.

76. Ibid., p. 7.

77. Ibid.

78. See George Manown, "Experience of a Coke and Iron Production Facility with Non-Traditional Dust Control" (Paper presented at 1983 annual meeting, Air Pollution Control Association, Atlanta), June 1983, p. 1. See also James R.

Zwikl et al., "An Alternative Emission Control Plan for Industrial Plants—Birth of a Concept and Its Regulatory Implications" (Paper delivered at 1981 annual meeting, Air Pollution Control Association, Philadelphia).

79. See EPA's notice of approval of the bubble, 46 Fed. Reg. 62849, December 29, 1981.

80. Ibid. Zwikl et al., *Birth of a Concept*, p. 7, report that Shenango would reduce emissions from unpaved roads by 70 percent and from paved roads by 80 percent.

81. See "EPA Approves Bubble Plan for Shenango," *Journal of the Air Pollution Control Association* 32 (1982):284.

82. Manown, *Experience of a Coke and Iron Production Facility*, p. 5.

83. Ibid., p. 7.

84. Ibid.

85. 40 CFR §81.339 (1985).

86. The details of Armco's proposal are found in the February 4, 1983, SIP revision package submitted by Kentucky to EPA's region IV office in Atlanta; copy in author's files.

87. The disagreements are documented in a host of internal EPA documents in the author's files.

88. Steiner, "Fugitive Dust Control," p. 4.

89. 49 Fed. Reg. 25009, June 19, 1984.

90. 49 Fed. Reg. 25008, 25009, June 19, 1984.

91. Ibid.

92. Ohio Environmental Protection Agency Fact Sheet for Draft Variance, May 3, 1983, section 7; copy in author's files.

93. Letter from Sohio to Ohio Environmental Protection Agency, October 30, 1980, appendix J, in Ohio Environmental Protection Agency technical support information for Sohio bubble; copy in author's files.

94. Ibid.

95. Letter from Sohio to Ohio Environmental Protection Agency, November 30, 1979, attachment, in Ohio Environmental Protection Agency technical support information for Sohio bubble.

96. This estimate is contained in a letter from Sohio's Patricia Kiraly to Ohio Environmental Protection Agency, March 15, 1983; copy in author's files.

97. 49 Feb. Reg. 24124, June 12, 1984.

98. See EPA's notice regarding the designations, 48 Fed. Reg. 32677, August 10, 1983.

99. Letter from David Doniger to EPA's Gary Gulezian, August 7, 1984; copy in author's files.

100. See EPA's notice of proposed rule making, 48 Fed. Reg. 16683, April 19, 1983.

101. For a more detailed summary than that provided in this and the following paragraph, see *Dressman* v. *Castle*, 759 F.2d 548, 15 ELR 20434 (6th Cir., 1985), upholding EPA's construction ban.

102. Clean Air Act, §172(b)(11)(B), 42 USC §7502(b)(11)(B).

103. 45 Fed. Reg. 62810, September 22, 1980.

104. 48 Fed. Reg. 5022, 5122, February 3, 1983.

105. 48 Fed. Reg. 5022, 5120, February 3, 1983.

106. Memorandum from EPA Region IV Administrator Charles Jeter to EPA Administrator William Ruckelshaus, August 16, 1984; copy in author's files.

107. Ibid.

108. These and other figures in this paragraph are from EPA's *Federal Register* notice and from the SIP revision package submitted to EPA by the Commonwealth of Kentucky.

109. See EPA's notice of proposed rule making, 48 Fed. Reg. 7211, February 18, 1983.

110. Ibid.

111. Ibid.

112. These comments are cited in EPA's notice proposing to disapprove the bubble, 49 Fed. Reg. 14145, April 10, 1984.

113. Letter from NRDC's David Doniger to EPA's Delores Sieja, May 5, 1983, p. 5; copy in author's files.

114. Letter from BFGoodrich's W.C. Holbrook to EPA's Gary Gulezian, May 9, 1984; copy in author's files.

115. Ibid., pp. 2-3.

116. Ibid., p. 6.

117. Ibid.

118. Ibid., p. 7.

119. 49 Fed. Reg. 48542, December 13, 1984. The balance of the paragraph in the text is based on this notice.

120. Telephone conversation between BFGoodrich's W. C. Holbrook and the author, February 6, 1985.

121. Ibid.

122. Ibid.

123. For discussion of rural nonattainment areas, see the sources cited in EPA's notice of proposed rule making for the Union Carbide bubble, 46 Fed. Reg. 40774, August 12, 1981.

124. See U.S. Environmental Protection Agency, "Workshop Requirements for Nonattainment Area Plans" (Washington, D.C.: U.S. Environmental Protection Agency, 1978), p. 287.

125. 45 Fed. Reg. 19209, March 25, 1980.

126. Ibid.

127. 46 Fed. Reg. 40774, August 12, 1981.

128. See p. 3 of Union Carbide's bubble proposal to the Texas Air Control Board; copy in author's files.

129. See "EPA Review of the Union Carbide Corporation Alternative Emission Reduction Proposal," February 1981, table II; copy in author's files.

130. See EPA's notice of proposed rule making, 46 Fed. Reg. 40774, 40775, August 12, 1981, and "Air Bubble—First Use of Revised Pollution Rule Granted," *Washington Post*, June 29, 1982.

131. EPA final rule making, 47 Fed. Reg. 21533, May 19, 1982.

132. 46 Fed. Reg. 40774, 40775, August 12, 1981.

133. 47 Fed. Reg. 21533, 21534, May 19, 1982.

134. David D. Doniger and Stephen M. Smith, "Petition for Reconsideration of Proposed Revisions to the Texas State Implementation Plan for the Alternative Emission Reduction Plan of Union Carbide Corporation," July 13, 1982; copy in author's files.

135. Ibid., pp. 5-6.

136. Ibid.. p. 10.

137. Ibid., p. 11.

138. See, for example, undated memo (circa 1979) from Richard Wilson, Deputy Assistant Administrator for General Enforcement, to David Hawkins, Assistant Administrator, Office of Air and Waste Management re "The 1979 SIP Revisions and the Steel Industry"; copy in author's files.

139. See *National Steel* v. *Gorsuch*, 18 ERC 1794 (6th Cir., 1983).

140. Except where otherwise indicated, the chronology in this and the next paragraph is drawn from the United States' brief, p. 3., in *United States* v. *National Steel Corp.*, 767 F.2d 1176, 15 ELR 20678 (6th Cir., 1985).

141. See "EPA, National Steel Reach Agreement on Pollution Control at Several Plants," *BNA Environment Reporter—Current Developments*, November 7, 1980, p. 991.

142. See 49 Fed. Reg. 1903, January 16, 1984.

143. See Christopher P. Romaine, "Bubbles or Alternative Control Strategies in Illinois" (Paper delivered at 1984 annual meeting, Air Pollution Control Association, San Francisco), p. 8.

144. Ibid.

145. United States' brief in *U.S.* v. *National Steel Corp.*, p. 6.

146. Statement of National Steel's Ralph Purdy, paragraph 14, cited in ibid., p. 21.

147. See *U.S.* v. *National Steel Corp.*

148. See memorandum from Ivan Tether to Michael Alushin, September 23, 1981, p. 1; copy in author's files.

149. Ibid.

150. Ibid., pp. 1-2.

151. Ibid., p. 4.

152. See EPA memo from Mark S. Siegler to Michael Alushin, September 29, 1981, p. 5; copy in author's files.

153. 47 Fed. Reg. 56518, 56519, December 12, 1982.

154. Ibid.

155. Ibid.

156. See "Comments of Natural Resources Defense Council, Inc. and Dennis Piper on Proposed Revision of the Michigan Steel Implementation Plan ('Great Lakes Steel Bubble')," March 7, 1983, pp. 28-29. See also memo from EPA General Counsel Robert Perry to EPA Assistant Administrator for Air, Noise, and Radiation Kathleen Bennett, December 7, 1980; copy in author's files.

157. "Comments of NRDC and Dennis Piper."

158. Ibid., p. 2.

159. Ibid., pp. 2-3.

160. Ibid., p. 52.

161. See 49 Fed. Reg. 11832, March 28, 1984, and September 28, 1983 EPA Technical Support document; copy in author's files.

162. See transcript, *U.S.* v. *National Steel Corp.*, May 23, 1983 proceedings (E.D. Mich., No. 79-73214).

163. Ibid., p. 56.

164. See *Inside EPA*, August 2, 1985, p. 6, and *U.S.* v. *National Steel Corp.* (6th Cir., 1985).

165. *U.S.* v. *National Steel Corp.*, 15 ELR 20678, 20680 (6th Cir., 1985).

166. Ibid., at 20679.

167. These and other examples are found in footnote 20 of the July 15, 1985, draft preamble for the final Emissions Trading Policy Statement, and in a memorandum from the Regulatory Reform Staff's Barry Elman to Michael Levin, August 28, 1984; copies in author's files.

168. For discussion of the EPA proposal and the court decision, see "EPA's G.M. 'Mobile Bubble' Held Unlawful," *The Environmental Forum* 3 (January 1985):45.

169. Undated letter to NRDC members from NRDC Executive Director John Adams.

170. John Palmisano, "An Evaluation of Emissions Trading" (Paper delivered at 1983 annual meeting, Air Pollution Control Association, Atlanta), p. 19.

CHAPTER 5. BUBBLES AND NETTING FOR NEW AND MODIFIED SOURCES

1. Section 111(a)(1) of the Clean Air Act, 42 U.S.C. §7411(a)(1).

2. See Robert W. Crandall, *Controlling Industrial Pollution* (Washington, D.C.: The Brookings Institution, 1983), pp. 34-39, for comparisons and discussion of incremental costs.

3. Congressional Budget Office, *The Clean Air Act, the Electric Utilities, and the Coal Market* (Washington, D.C.: U.S. Government Printing Office, 1982), pp. xviii-xix.

4. Ibid., p. 58.

5. "Emissions Trading: The Subtle Heresy," *The Environmental Forum* 1 (December 1982):23.

6. Ibid., p. 24.

7. Clean Air Act, Section 119, 42 U.S.C. §7419. See also D.H. Nochumson and M.D. Williams, "Copper Smelters and Atmospheric Visibility in the Southwest, Seasonal Analysis," *Journal of the Air Pollution Control Association* 34 (1984):750-52.

8. EPA studies cited in Crandall, *Controlling Industrial Pollution*, pp. 122-24.

9. Ibid., p. 43, citing an EPA study concluding that pollution control costs do not have a major impact on investment decisions.

10. ICF, Inc., "Memorandum Discussing Preliminary Analysis of Selected Topics Regarding New Source Emphasis in the Electric Utility Industry," prepared for U.S. Environmental Protection Agency, Economic Analysis Division, (Washington, D.C.: ICF, Inc., 1984).

11. Ibid., memo 1, p. 14.

12. Clean Air Act, Section 111(a)(2), 42 U.S.C. §7411(a)(2).

13. Clean Air Act, Section 111(a)(3), 42 U.S.C. §7411(a)(3).

14. 36 Fed. Reg. 24876, 24877, December 23, 1971.

15. See *ASARCO, Inc* v. *Environmental Protection Agency*, 578 F. 2d 319, 8 ELR 20164, 20277 (D.C. Cir., 1978), 8 ELR 20164 at 20166.

16. Ibid.

17. Ibid.

18. 40 Fed. Reg. 58416, December 16, 1975.

19. 40 Fed. Reg. 58416, 58418, December 16, 1975.

20. 40 Fed. Reg. 58416, 58417, December 16, 1975.

21. Ibid.

22. *ASARCO, Inc* v. *EPA*, at 20164.

23. Ibid., at 20169.

24. The judge's suspicions seem well-founded. In a draft letter to William Nordhaus, a member of the President's Council of Economic Advisors, EPA General Counsel Jodie Bernstein wrote that the record of the ASARCO case "is crystal clear that EPA adopted the 'bubble' only in response to pressure from the smelter industry and the Department of Commerce," and that "there is nothing in the record beyond the most general statements to support the proposition that a 'bubble' is desirable on the merits." Copy in author's files.

25. *ASARCO, Inc* v. *EPA*, at 20170, note 40.

26. Ibid., at 20169-70.

27. Compare the Clean Air Act, Section 111(a)(2), 42 U.S.C. §7411(a)(2), with EPA's regulations, 40 Fed. Reg. 58416, 58418, December 16, 1975.

28. 45 Fed. Reg. 86278, December 30, 1980.

29. 48 Fed. Reg. 48368, October 18, 1983. See also U.S. Environmental Protection Agency, Office of Air Quality Planning and Standards, "Pressure Sensitive Tape and Label Surface Coating Industry-Background Information for Promulgated Standards" (Research Triangle Park, N.C.: U.S. Environmental Protection Agency, September 1983), pp. 1-2, 1-3. See also "3M Company Seeks Broader NSPS Definition to Open More Bubbling Opportunities," *Inside EPA*, April 3, 1981, p. 13.

30. 48 Fed. Reg. 48368, October 18, 1983.

31. For background on the NSPS for tire manufacturing and the compliance bubble for it, see EPA's notice of proposed rule making, 48 Fed. Reg. 2676, January 20, 1983, and Rubber Manufacturers Association, "Advantages Accruing from Application of an NSPS Bubble to the Tire-Manufacturing Category" (February 15, 1982, processed); copy in author's files. The NSPS for the rotogravure printing industry is found at 40 CFR §60.430 (1985).

32. The NSPS to which these units are subject was superceded by an even tougher NSPS in 1978. See 40 CFR §60.40(a)(1985).

33. For Unit II's emission rates, see EPA's notice of proposed approval of the Central Illinois bubble, 50 Fed. Reg. 3688, 3689, January 25, 1985. The current emission rates for Unit I are found at 50 Fed. Reg. 3690, January 25, 1985.

34. See Central Illinois memorandum, appendix E to its comments on EPA's proposed approval of its bubble. The utility's comments are document number IV-D-113 in EPA's rule-making docket for this bubble, docket number A84-01.

35. 50 Fed. Reg. 3688, 3689, January 25, 1985.

36. See appendix E of Central Illinois's comments, document number IV-D-113 in docket number A84-01, referencing Section 4D of Central Illinois's original rule-making petition to EPA, document number II-D-7.

37. 50 Fed. Reg. 3688, 3689, January 25, 1985.

38. Ibid.

39. Ibid.

40. Ibid.

41. Letter from Michael DeBusschere, Air Pollution Control District of Jefferson County, to EPA Central Docket Section, February 28, 1985, re Docket number A-84-01.

42. These EPA arguments are found in an "Action Memorandum" from EPA's Assistant Administrator for Air and Radiation to the EPA Administrator, March 19, 1984, p. 4; copy in author's files.

43. 50 Fed. Reg. 3688, 3689, January 25, 1985.

44. See NRDC's comments on the proposed bubble, April 24, 1985. NRDC even alleges that actual emissions will increase.

45. 50 Fed. Reg. 3688, 3691, January 25, 1981.

46. 50 Fed. Reg. 3688, 3689, January 25, 1981.

47. NRDC comments, April 24, 1985, p. 34.

48. Ibid., pp. 37-38.

49. See EPA "Action Memorandum," March 19, 1984, p. 5.

50. *Environmental Law* (St. Paul, Minn.: West Publishing Company, 1977), p. 280.

51. *Sierra Club* v. *Ruckelshaus*, 344 F. Supp. 253, 2 ELR 20262 (D.D.C., 1972), aff'd per curiam, 2 ELR 20656 (D.C. Circ. 1972), aff'd by an evenly divided court sub nom. *Fri* v. *Sierra Club*, 412 U.S. 541, 3 ELR 20684 (U.S. 1973). For the EPA regulations, see 39 Fed. Reg. 42510, December 5, 1974.

52. For a more detailed history of the PSD program, see Jacquelyn Branagan, "Nondegradation and the Clean Air Act Amendments of 1977: Preventing the Graying of America," *Urban Law Annual* 14 (1977):203-32.

53. 39 Fed. Reg. 42516, December 5, 1974.

54. 39 Fed. Reg. 42513, December 5, 1974.

55. *Sierra Club* v. *Environmental Protection Agency*, 540 F.2d 1114 (D.C. Cir., 1976).

56. Two environmentally oriented critiques of the regulations do not mention netting. See Thomas M. Disselhorst, "Sierra Club v. Ruckelshaus—On a Clear Day," *Ecology Law Quarterly* 4 (1975):739-80, and Thomas G.P. Guilbert, "Up in Smoke: EPA's Significant Deterioration Regulations Deteriorate Significantly," *Environmental Law Reporter* 4 (1974):50033.

57. Clean Air Act, Sections 162 and 165, 42 U.S.C. §§7472 and 7475.

58. Clean Air Act, Section 169(1), 42 U.S.C. §7479(1).

59. Clean Air Act, Section 169(3), 42 U.S.C. §7479(3).

60. 43 Fed. Reg. 26383, 26394, June 19, 1978.

61. Ibid.

62. Ibid.

63. *Alabama Power Co.* v. *Costle*, 636 F.2d 323, 10 ELR 20001 (D.C. Cir., 1979).

64. Ibid., at 20033.

65. Ibid.

66. The interested reader can find a detailed critique of the *Alabama Power* ruling in Jack L. Landau, "Economic Dream or Environmental Nightmare? The Legality of the Bubble Concept in Air and Water Pollution Control," *Boston College Environmental Affairs Law Review* 8 (1980):741-81, and in Laurens H. Rhinelander, "The Bubble Concept: A Pragmatic Approach to Regulation Under the Clean Air Act," *Virginia Journal of Natural Resources* 1 (1980):178-228. Landau, p. 761, has suggested that the two cases "simply do not add up," that the conflict between the two rulings should have been acknowledged, and that the *Alabama Power* panel should have explicitly overruled Judge Wright's opinion.

67. The "squandered opportunity" phrase was used in the Sierra Club/Environmental Defense Fund intervention brief in the *Alabama Power* case and is cited in Rhinelander, "The Bubble Concept," p. 214.

68. This figure derives from the two most recent and comprehensive analyses of PSD permitting. See U.S. Environmental Protection Agency, Office of Planning and Management, "Analysis of New Source Review (NSR) Permitting Experience" (Washington, D.C.: U.S. Environmental Protection Agency, 1982); and Radian Corporation, "Analysis of New Source Review (NSR) Permitting Experience," draft final report to the U.S. Environmental Protection Agency (Research Triangle Park, N.C.: Radian Corporation, May 1985). The principal researcher for both reports was Leigh Hayes. (The two reports are hereafter cited as New Source Review I and New Source Review II, respectively.) For figures on modifications, see New Source Review I, p. 5, and New Source Review II, p. 16.

69. See New Source Review I, p. 23, and New Source Review II, p. 37.

70. Ibid.

71. New Source Review I, pp. 140-141, and New Source Review II, pp. 88-90.

72. 41 Fed. Reg. 55524, December 21, 1976.

73. Clean Air Act, Sections 172(a), 129(a), and 173, 42 U.S.C. §§7502(a), 7502 (note), and 7503.

74. Clean Air Act, Section 172(a), 42 U.S.C. §7502(a).

75. Clean Air Act, §172(a)(2), 172(b), 42 U.S.C. §§7502(a)(2), 7502(b).

76. Clean Air Act, Sections 171(1) and 172(b)(3), 42 U.S.C. §§7501(1) and 7502(b)(3).

77. Clean Air Act, Section 172(b)(3), 42 U.S.C. §7502(b)(3).

78. Clean Air Act, §173, 42 U.S.C. §7503.

79. EPA's policy would apply, for example, to sources in one state contributing to a violation of ambient standards in others. See EPA's 1979 emission offset rules, 44 Fed. Reg. 3274, 3275, January 16, 1979.

80. Clean Air Act, Section 110(a)(2)(I), 42 U.S.C. §7410(a)(2)(I).

81. 44 Fed. Reg. 3274, January 16, 1979. Although its published ruling focused primarily on the offset policy, EPA offered comments as well on requirements for SIPs and on the definition of "source." See 44 Fed. Reg. 3274, 3276, January 16, 1979.

82. "EPA Issues Final Offset Policy; 'Bubble' Concept Remains Unresolved," *BNA Environment Reporter—Current Developments*, January 15, 1979, p. 1643.

83. "EPA General Counsel Challenges Disallowing 'Bubble Concept' in Offsets," *BNA Environment Reporter—Current Developments*, September 29, 1978, p. 1045.

84. 44 Fed. Reg. 3274, January 16, 1979.

85. 44 Fed. Reg. 3274, 3277, January 16, 1979.

86. 45 Fed. Reg. 52676, 52694-95, August 7, 1980.

87. See "EPA Policy, Air Offices Clash on Defining 'Source' in Non-Attainment Areas," *Inside EPA*, May 16, 1980, p. 1.

88. 45 Fed. Reg. 52676, 52694-95, 52731, August 7, 1980.

89. 45 Fed. Reg. 52676, 52697, August 7, 1980.

90. The arguments of the two sides are summarized in an undated memorandum from William Drayton, Jr., Assistant Administrator for Planning and Management to EPA Administrator Douglas Costle, "Definition of 'Source' in Nonattainment Areas"; copy in author's files. Drayton and his allies contended that few states were requiring greater than 1:1 offsets.

91. Drayton's views on the insignificance of the statewide compliance requirements were at odds with the views of the EPA Office of Enforcement, which regarded the requirement as important in obtaining consent decrees from the recalcitrant steel industry. Ibid., pp. 4-5.

92. 45 Fed. Reg. 52676, 52697, August 7, 1980.

93. 45 Fed. Reg. 52676, 52697, August 7, 1980.

94. "Reagan Reformers Seek to Ease Air Permitting with Carter-Era Bubble Policy," *Inside EPA*, March 13, 1981, pp. 1, 5.

95. 46 Fed. Reg. 16280, March 12, 1981.

96. 46 Fed. Reg. 16280, 16281, March 12, 1981.

97. Ibid.

98. Ibid.

99. David D. Doniger, "Comments on the Proposed Change in the Definition of 'Source' in Nonattainment Areas and the Proposed Deletion of the 'Reconstruction' Rule in Nonattainment Areas," April 13, 1981; copy in author's files. Comments were also submitted by the Environmental Defense Fund and Citizens for a Better Environment.

100. Ibid., p. 10.

101. The commenters, other than Pennsylvania, were Missouri, Maryland, Erie County (New York), Ohio, California, New York State, Arizona, and the Dayton (Ohio) Regional Air Pollution Control Agency. Only Maryland's Department of Health and Mental Hygiene opposed the dual definition. The California Air Resources Board expressed the view that local air pollution control agencies could be more stringent than EPA if they chose to be. Copies of the states' letters are in the author's files.

102. Letter from James K. Hambright, Director, Pennsylvania Bureau of Air Quality Control, to Michael Trutna, Standards Implementation Branch, EPA Office of Air Quality Planning and Standards, April 3, 1981; copy in author's files.

103. 46 Fed. Reg. 50766, October 17, 1981.

104. 46 Fed. Reg. 50766, 50768, October 17, 1981.

105. Performance Development Institute study cited in *Inside EPA*, December 18, 1981, p. 12. Indeed, while many industries applauded EPA's action very few

provided concrete examples of its beneficial effects. For a specific example, see the comments of the Louisiana-Pacific Corporation; copy in author's files.

106. *Natural Resources Defense Council, Inc* v. *Gorsuch*, 685 F.2d 718, 12 ELR 20942 (D.C. Cir., 1982) (hereafter cited as *NRDC* v. *Gorsuch*) reversed sub nom. *Chevron U.S.A. Inc* v. *Natural Resources Defense Council, Inc*, 104 S.Ct. 2778, 14 ELR 20507 (U.S., 1984) (hereafter cited as *Chevron* v. *NRDC*). NRDC's co-plaintiffs were Citizens for a Better Environment and the Northwestern Ohio Lung Association.

107. *NRDC* v. *Gorsuch*, at 20943.

108. Ibid., at 20947, footnote omitted.

109. Ibid., at 20947-48, note 41. Italics in the original, footnote omitted.

110. Phillip D. Reed, "*NRDC v. Gorsuch*: D.C. Circuit Bursts EPA's Nonattainment Bubble," *Environmental Law Reporter* 12 (1982):10093.

111. Bud Ward, "EPA Overturned on Scrapping 'Dual Definition' of Nonattainment 'Source,' " *The Environmental Forum* 1 (November 1982):41.

112. Laurens H. Rhinelander, "The Proper Place for the Bubble Concept Under the Clean Air Act," *Environmental Law Reporter* 13 (1983):10414, footnotes omitted.

113. See Brief for the Administrator of the Environmental Protection Agency, *Chevron* v. *NRDC*.

114. See Brief for Respondents Natural Resources Defense Council et al., *Chevron* v. *NRDC*.

115. Brief for the Commonwealth of Pennsylvania, State of Colorado, State of Connecticut, State of Maine, State of New Jersey, State of New York, State of Vermont, and State of Wisconsin, Amici Curiae, *Chevron* v. *NRDC*.

116. *Chevron* v. *NRDC*. The opinion was written by moderate Justice John Paul Stevens. Conservative Justices Sandra Day O'Connor and William H. Rehnquist and liberal Justice Thurgood Marshall did not participate in the decision.

117. Ibid., at 20509. For a brief discussion of how this decision accords with past Supreme Court decisions on judicial review, see James V. DeLong, "The Bubble Case," *Administrative Law News* 10 (Fall 1984). See also Michael H. Levin, "The Supreme Court's 'Bubble' Decision: What It Means," *EPA Journal* 10 (September 1984):10-11, and Phillip D. Reed, "Three Strikes And the Umpire Is Out: The Supreme Court Throws The D.C. Circuit Out of the Bubble Review Game," *Environmental Law Reporter* 14 (1984):10338.

118. The Court cited New York State's brief comment opposing the dual definition and a short report from the Brookings Institution, which simply asserted that bubbles and netting can control pollution more quickly and cheaply than conventional regulation. *Chevron* v. *NRDC*, at 20514.

119. A study of state implementation plans for the National Commission on Air Quality reported that, in 1976, 73 percent of the emissions contributing to Washington's ozone problems came from mobile sources. See Pacific Environmental Services, "Study of the 1979 State Implementation Plan Submittals" (Elmhurst, Ill.: Pacific Environmental Services, 1980), p. 7-14.

120. See testimony of George Carpenter, in U.S. House of Representatives, Committee on Energy and Commerce, Subcommittee on Health and the Environment, *Hearings on Clean Air Act, Part 1*, 97th Cong., 1st Sess. (1981), Serial No. 97-102, pp. 52, 78. The supporting data are found in the research report appended to Carpenter's testimony.

121. Ibid., pp. 53, 80.

122. Kevin G. Croke et al., "An Economic Evaluation of Netting as an Alternative to New Source Review" (Paper delivered at 1984 annual meeting, Air Pollution Control Association, San Francisco), p. 4.

123. Ibid., p. 3.

124. Carpenter testimony, citing Houston data, pp. 62-63, and letter to the author citing San Francisco data, March 26, 1985.

125. There has been little systematic analysis comparing LAER with NSPS.

126. See, for example, Indur Goklany, "Issues Related to the Source Definition for New Source Review in Nonattainment Areas," report to U.S. Environmental Protection Agency, Regulatory Reform Staff (Falls Church, Va.: TRC Consultants, December 1983).

CHAPTER 6. WHERE SHOULD EMISSIONS TRADING GO FROM HERE?

1. John Palmisano, "Emissions Trading Reforms: Successes and Failures" (Paper delivered at 1985 annual meeting, Air Pollution Control Associaton, Detroit), pp. 10-11.

2. Letter from Al Shehadi to the author, February 24, 1985.

3. Conversation with the author, March 14, 1985.

4. See State and Territorial Air Pollution Program Administrators, "Status of State Air Pollution Control Programs" (Washington, D.C.: State and Territorial Air Pollution Program Administrators, 1984), p. 6; and U.S. Environmental Protection Agency, Office of the Comptroller, "Summary of the 1987 Budget" (Washington, D.C.: U.S. Environmental Protection Agency, 1986), p. 77.

5. Leslie Sue Ritts, *State Emissions Trading Regulations* (Washington, D.C.: Environmental Law Institute, forthcoming).

6. See Stephen J. Connolly et al., "Emissions Trading in Selected EPA Regions," report prepared for U.S. Environmental Protection Agency, Regulatory Reform Staff (Washington, D.C.: Jellinek, Schwartz, Connolly, and Freshman, Inc., 1984).

7. Ibid., p. 17.

8. Ibid., pp. 3, 8, 28, 29.

9. U.S. Environmental Protection Agency, Regulatory Reform Staff, "Annual Report—CY 84" (May 1985, processed), p. 5.

10. Ibid.

11. Paul R. Portney, quoted in Rochelle L. Stanfield, "No One Knows for Sure if Pollution Control Programs Are Really Working," *National Journal* 17 (1985):643.

12. "The Dark Side of the Bubble," *The Environmental Forum* 4 (July 1985):32-35.

Selected Bibliography

Ackerman, Bruce A., and William T. Hassler. "Beyond the New Deal: Reply." *Yale Law Journal* 90 (1981):1412-34.

_____. *Clean Coal/Dirty Air*. New Haven: Yale University Press, 1981.

Ackerman, Bruce A., and Richard B. Stewart. "Reforming Environmental Law" *Stanford Law Review* 37 (1985):1333-65.

Air Pollution Control Association. *Proceedings—Economic Incentives for Clean Air Specialty Conference*. Pittsburgh: Air Pollution Control Association, 1981.

American Petroleum Institute. Study Group on Economic Incentives for Environmental Protection. "Background Paper in the Use of Economic Incentives for Environmental Protection." Washington, D.C.: American Petroleum Institute, 1980.

Brady, Gordon L., and Blair T. Bower. "Effectiveness of the U.S. Regulatory Approach to Air Quality Management and Stationary Sources." *Policy Studies Journal* 11 (1982):66-76.

Brady, Gordon L., and Richard Morrison. "Emissions Trading: An Overview of the EPA Policy Statement." Washington, D.C.: National Science Foundation, Office of Policy and Research Analysis, 1982.

Breyer, Stephen. *Regulation and Its Reform*. Cambridge, Mass.: Harvard University Press, 1982.

Bromberg, J. Philip. "Bubbling New Sources with Existing Sources: An Examination of the Environmental and Economic Benefits of an Integrated Approach to Emission Control." Reprinted in U.S. Congress. Senate. Committee on Environment and Public Works. *Hearings on Clean Air Act Oversight, Part I.* 97th Cong., Sess., 1981. Serial No. 97-H12, pp. 528-578.

Brown, Gardner J., Jr., and Ralph W. Johnson. "Pollution Control by Effluent Charges: It Works in the Federal Republic of Germany, Why Not in the U.S." *Natural Resources Journal* 24 (1984):929-66.

"The Bubble Upheld." *Regulation* 8 (May-June 1984):5-7.

Butler, Chad. "New Source Netting in Nonattainment Areas under the Clean Air Act." *Ecology Law Quarterly* 11 (1984):343-72.

Carpenter, G. D., and D. J. Hahn. "The Role of Industrial Growth and Investment on Emission Trends." Cincinnati: Proctor and Gamble Company, Project Engineering Division, 1981. Processed.

"Comment: EPA's Widening Embrace of the 'Bubble' Concept: The Legality and Availability of Intra-Source Trade-Offs," *Environmental Law Reporter* 9 (September 1979):10027-10031.

"Comment: Economic Efficiency in Pollution Control: EPA Issues 'Bubble' Policy for Existing Sources under Clean Air Act." *Environmental Law Reporter* 10 (January 1980):10014-10018.

"Comment: EPA Approves New Jersey Generic Bubble Rules, Develops Consolidated Guidance for Controlled Trading Program." *Environmental Law Reporter* 11 (June 1981):10119-10124.

Connolly, Stephen J., et al. "Emissions Trading in Selected EPA Regions." Report to U.S. Environmental Protection Agency, Regulatory Reform Staff. Washington, D.C.: Jellinek, Schwartz, Connally and Freshman, Inc., 1984.

Cook, Brian J. "The Politics of Regulatory Form: An Analysis of Policy Choice in Environmental Regulation." Doctoral dissertation, University of Maryland, Department of Government and Politics, 1984.

Courant, Carl. "Emission Reductions from Shutdowns: Their Role in Banking and Trading Systems." Washington, D.C.: U.S. Environmental Protection Agency, Economic Analysis Division, 1980. Processed.

Crandall, Robert W. *Controlling Industrial Pollution.* Washington, D.C.: The Brookings Institution, 1983.

Croke, Kevin, Jay Norco, and Ivan Tether. "An Economic Evaluation of Netting as an Alternative to New Source Review." Paper delivered at 1984 annual meeting, Air Pollution Control Association, San Francisco.

Currie, David P. "Direct Federal Regulation of Stationary Sources under the Clean Air Act." *University of Pennsylvania Law Review* 128 (1980):1389-1470.

Cuscino, Thomas, Jr., Gregory Muleski, and Chatten Cowherd, Jr. "Iron and Steel Plant Open Source Fugitive Emission Control Evaluation." Report for U.S. Environmental Protection Agency, Industrial Environmental Research Laboratory. Kansas City, Mo.: Midwest Research Institute, 1984.

DeLong, James V. "The Bubble Case." *Administrative Law News* 10 (Fall 1984):1.

Debusschere, Michael T. "Integrating Emissions Banking and Emission Source Review Processes." Paper delivered at 1984 annual meeting, Air Pollution Control Association, San Francisco.

————. "Section 107 Redesignation: There Must Be a Better Way." Paper delivered at 1984 annual meeting, Air Pollution Control Association, San Francisco.

del Calvo y Gonzalez, Jorge A. "Markets in Air? Problems and Prospects of Controlled Trading." *Harvard Environmental Law Review* 5 (1981):377-430.

Domenici, Pete V. "Emissions Trading: The Subtle Heresy." *The Environmental Forum* 1 (December 1982):15-24.

Doniger, David. "The Bubble on the Cusp." *The Environmental Forum* 4 (March 1986):29, 34.

————. "The Dark Side of the Bubble." *The Environmental Forum* 4 (July 1985):32-35.

Downing, Paul B. "Bargaining in Pollution Control." *Policy Studies Journal* 11 (1983):577-86.

Drayton, William. "Getting Smarter About Regulation." *Harvard Business Review* 59 (July/August 1981):38-52.

Eads, George, and Michael Fix. *Relief or Reform? Reagan's Regulatory Dilemma.* Washington, D.C.: The Urban Institute, 1984.

Elkin, Stephen L., and Brian J. Cook. "The Public Life of Economic Incentives." *Policy Studies Journal* 13 (1985):797-813.

Elliott, William H., Jr. "Dupont Experience—Chambers Works 'Bubble' for Control of Volatile Organic Substances (VOS) under New Jersey Administrative Code 7:27-16.1 et seq." Remarks delivered at Joint U.S. Environmental Protection Agency/Armco Steel Bubble Conference, Philadelphia, December 1981.

"Emission Inventories and Air Quality Management: Selected Papers from an APCA Specialty Meeting." *Journal of the Air Pollution Control Association* 32 (1982):1011-29.

Evans, Jay. *Opportunities for Innovation: Administration of Sections 111(j) and 113(d)(4) of the Clean Air Act and Industry's Development of Innovative Control Technology.* Washington, D.C.: The Performance Development Institute, 1980.

Feldman, Paul S. "Regulatory Reform—Smarter Regulations." Paper delivered at 1984 annual meeting, Air Pollution Control Association, San Francisco.

Fleckenstein, Leonard J. "Modeling Criteria: The Key to Major Reforms for Emissions Trades." Paper delivered at 1984 annual meeting, Air Pollution Control Association, San Francisco.

Foskett, William H., Adrienne Jamieson, and Jay Evans. "Innovation by Regulation: The Administration of Control Technology Requirements Under the Clean Air Act." Report prepared under contract to U.S. Department of Commerce, Experimental Technology Incentives Program. Washington, D.C., March 1981.

Foster, J. David, and Malcolm C. Weiss. "Indirect Offsets: A Supplemental Program to Facilitate Interfirm Trades in Emission Reductions." Paper delivered at 1981 annual meeting, Air Pollution Control Association, Philadelphia.

Friedlaender, Ann F., ed. *Approaches to Controlling Air Pollution.* Cambridge, Mass.: MIT Press, 1978.

Gabe, Jeff. "Tending Accounts at the Emissions Bank and Trust." *CBE Environmental Review*, September/October 1982, pp. 3-6.

Garelick, Barry, and J. David Foster. "Offset Investments and Guarantees: A Program to Provide Incentives for Firms to Deposit and Trade Emission Reductions." Paper delivered at 1985 annual meeting, Air Pollution Control Association, Detroit.

Garelick, Barry, and John Lathrop. "Emission Offsets as an Economic Commodity in California." Paper delivered at 1984 annual meeting, Air Pollution Control Association, San Francisco.

Glass, Adam W. "The EPA's Bubble Concept After *Alabama Power*." *Stanford Law Review* 32 (1980):943-75.

Goklany, Indur. "Improving Pre-Construction Permitting for Air Pollution Sources." Draft report. Washington, D.C.: U.S. Environmental Protection Agency, Regulatory Reform Staff, March 1985).

_____. "Issues Related to the Source Definition for New Source Review in Nonattainment Areas." Report to U.S. Environmental Protection Agency, Regulatory Reform Staff. Falls Church, Va.: TRC Environmental Consultants, December 1983.

Goldstein, Mark. "The Role of Emission Trading Programs in Regional Economic Development." Draft, Baltimore Region Emission Trading Report Series, vol. 2. Baltimore: Regional Planning Council, February 1983.

Greene, Kevin. "Bubble, Bubble, Spoil and Trouble." *CBE Environmental Review*, September/October 1982, pp. 7-10.

_____. "Swapping Particulates at the Steel Mills." *CBE Environmental Review*, (November/December 1983), pp. 5-6.

Hahn, Robert W., and Gregory J. McRae. "Application of Market Mechanisms to Pollution." *Policy Studies Review* 1 (1981-82):470-76.

Hahn, Robert W., and Roger G. Noll. "Barriers to Implementing Tradable Air Pollution Permits: Problems of Regulatory Interactions." *Yale Journal on Regulation* 1 (1983):63-91.

_____. "Implementing Tradeable Emission Permits." In Graymer, LeRoy, and Frederick Thompson. *Reforming Social Regulation*. Beverly Hills, Calif.: Sage Publications, 1982.

Harrison, David, Jr., and Paul R. Portney. "Regulatory Reform in the Large and in the Small," In Graymer, LeRoy, and Frederick Thompson. *Reforming Social Regulation*. Beverly Hills, Calif.: Sage Publications, 1982.

_____. "Who Loses From Reform of Environmental Regulation?" Discussion Paper 113D. Cambridge, Mass.: Harvard University, Kennedy School of Government, Faculty Project on Regulation, 1982. Reprinted in Magat, Wesley, ed. *Reform of Environmental Regulation*. Cambridge, Mass.: Ballinger Publishing Co., 1982.

Healy, Robert G. *America's Industrial Future: An Environmental Perspective*. Washington, D.C.: The Conservation Foundation, 1982.

Hess, Peter F., et al. "Experience of New Source Review in the San Francisco Bay Area." Paper delivered at 1984 annual meeting, Air Pollution Control Association, San Francisco.

Himel, James, and Israel Patoka. "Analysis of the Baltimore City

Industrial Survey: Air Emission Banking, Trading, and Bubbling."
Draft, Baltimore Region Emission Trading Report Series, vol. 3.
Baltimore: Regional Planning Council, March 1982.

Hoff, Paul S. "The Current Status and Future Prospects for EPA's
Bubble Policies." *Environmental Analyst* 4 (October 1983):3-8.

Huber, Peter. "Exorcists vs. Gatekeepers in Risk Regulation." *Regulation* 7 (November/December 1983):23-32.

ICF, Inc. "Memoranda Discussing Preliminary Analysis of Selected
Topics Regarding New Source Emphasis in the Electric Utility Industry." Prepared for U.S. Environmental Protection Agency,
Economic Analysis Division. Washington, D.C., 1984.

Joeres, Erhard, and Martin H. David, eds. *Buying a Better Environment: Cost-Effective Regulation Through Permit Trading*. Madison,
Wisc.: University of Wisconsin Press, 1983.

Kelman, Steven. "Economic Incentives and Environmental Policy:
Politics, Ideology, and Philosophy." In Schelling, Thomas C., ed.
Incentives for Environmental Protection. Cambridge, Mass.: MIT
Press, 1983.

_____. *What Price Incentives?*. Boston: Auburn House Publishing
Co., 1981.

Kontnik, Lewis T. "The Evolving Emission Trading Program: Fish
or Fowl?" *Environmental Analyst* 3 (August 1982):3-6.

Kostow, Lloyd P., and John Kowalczyk. "A Practical Emission
Trading Program." *Journal of the Air Pollution Control Association* 33 (October 1983):982-84.

Krupnick, Alan J. "Costs of Alternative Policies for the Control of
NO_2 in the Baltimore Air Quality Control Region." Washington,
D.C.: Resources for the Future, 1983. Processed.

Landau, Jack L. "*Chevron, U.S.A. v. NRDC*: The Supreme Court
Declines to Burst EPA's Bubble Concept." *Environmental Law* 15
(1985):285-322.

_____. "Economic Dream or Environmental Nightmare? The
Legality of the Bubble Concept in Air and Water Pollution Control." *Boston College Environmental Affairs Law Review* 8
(1980):741-81.

_____. "Who Owns the Air? The Emission Offset Concept and
Its Implications." *Environmental Law* 9 (1979):575-600.

Latin, Howard. "Ideal versus Real Regulatory Efficiency: Implementation of Uniform Standards and 'Fine-Tuning' Regulatory
Reforms." *Stanford Law Review* 37 (1985):1267-1332.

Lave, Lester B., and Gilbert Omenn. *Clearing the Air: Reforming the Clean Air Act*. Washington, D.C.: The Brookings Institution, 1981.

Levin, Michael H. "Building a Better Bubble at EPA." *Regulation* 9 (March/April 1985):33-42.

_____. "The Clean Air Act Needs Sensible Emissions Trading." *The Environmental Forum* 4 (March 1986):29, 32-33.

_____. "Getting There: Implementing the 'Bubble Policy.' " In Bardach, Eugene, and Robert Kagan, eds. *Social Regulation: Strategies for Reform*. San Francisco: Institute for Contemporary Studies, 1982.

_____. "The Supreme Court's 'Bubble' Decision: What It Means." *EPA Journal*, September 1984, pp. 10-11.

Liroff, Richard A. *Air Pollution Offsets: Trading, Selling, and Banking*. Washington, D.C.: The Conservation Foundation, 1980.

_____. "The Bubble Concept for Air Pollution Control: A Political and Administrative Perspective." Paper delivered at 1981 annual meeting, Air Pollution Control Association, Philadelphia.

_____. "The Bubble: Will it Float Free . . . or Deflate?" *The Environmental Forum* 4 (March 1986):28, 30-31.

Majone, Giandomenico. "Choice Among Policy Instruments for Pollution Control." *Policy Analysis* 2 (1976):589-613.

Maloney, M. T., and Bruce Yandle. "Bubbles and Efficiency." *Regulation* 4 (May/June 1980):49-52.

Manown, George A. "Experience of a Coke and Iron Production Facility with Non-Traditional Dust Control." Paper delivered at 1983 annual meeting, Air Pollution Control Association, Atlanta.

Marcus, Alfred A., Paul Sommers, and Frederic A. Morris. "Alternative Arrangements for Cost Effective Pollution Abatement: The Need for Implementation Analysis." *Policy Studies Review* 1 (1981-82):477-83.

Meidinger, Errol. "On Explaining the Development of 'Emissions Trading' in U.S. Air Pollution Regulation." *Law and Policy* 7 (1985):447-79.

Meidinger, Errol. "The Politics of 'Market Mechanisms' in U.S. Air Pollution Policy: On the Emerging Culture of Regulation." Paper delivered at the Conference on Distributional Conflicts in Environmental Resource Policy, Science Center, Berlin, West Germany, March 1984. Revised edition.

Melamed, Dennis. "Shutting Down for Credit." *The Environmental*

Forum 2 (May 1983):29-31.

Melnick, R. Shep. "The Clean Air Program: Options for the Future." *EPA Journal* 10 (September 1984):12-13.

_____. "Deadlines, Common Sense, and Cynicism." *The Brookings Review* 2 (Fall 1983):21-24.

_____. "Pollution Deadlines and the Coalition for Failure" *The Public Interest*, Spring 1984, pp. 123-34.

_____. *Regulation and the Courts: The Case of the Clean Air Act.* Washington, D.C.: The Brookings Institution, 1983.

Miller, Susan E. "The Bubble Concept—A Feasible Emissions Reduction Alternative?" *Dayton Law Review* 9 (1983):65-80.

Muleski, Gregory, Thomas Cuscino, Jr., and Chatten Cowherd, Jr. "Extended Evaluation of Unpaved Road Dust Suppressants in the Iron and Steel Industry." Report for U.S. Environmental Protection Agency, Industrial Environmental Research Laboratory. Kansas City, Mo.: Midwest Research Institute, 1984.

National Commission on Air Quality. *To Breathe Clean Air.* Washington D.C.: U.S. Government Printing Office, 1981.

"Note: Technology-Based Emission and Effluent Standards and the Achievement of Ambient Environmental Objectives." *Yale Law Journal* 91 (1982):792-813.

Palmisano, John. "Emissions Trading Reforms: Successes and Failures." Paper delivered at 1985 annual meeting, Air Pollution Control Association, Detroit.

_____. "An Evaluation of Emissions Trading." Paper delivered at 1983 annual meeting, Air Pollution Control Association, Atlanta.

_____. "Have Markets for Trading Emission Reduction Credits Failed or Succeeded?" Washington, D.C.: U.S. Environmental Protection Agency, Regulatory Reform Staff, 1982. Processed.

Palmisano, John, and Debora Martin. "The Use of Nontraditional Control Strategies in the Iron and Steel Industry: Air Bubbles, Water Bubbles, and Multi-media Based Control Strategies." Paper delivered at 1984 annual meeting, Air Pollution Control Association, San Francisco.

PEDCo Environmental, Inc. "Selective Analysis of the Prevention of Significant Deterioration (PSD) Program." Report to the National Commission on Air Quality. Cincinnati: PEDCo Environmental, December 1980.

Pedersen, William F., Jr. "Pollution Accounting under the Clean Air Act." *The Environmental Forum* 3 (May 1984):36-39.

————. "Why the Clean Air Act Works Badly." *University of Pennsylvania Law Review* 129 (1981):1059-1109.

Phillips, Joseph W. "The Effect of the Existing Regulatory Environment on Emerging Technology." Paper delivered at 1983 annual meeting, Air Pollution Control Association, Atlanta.

Pierce, Alan J. "Emissions Trading and Banking under the Clean Air Act After *NRDC v. Gorsuch*." *Syracuse Law Review* 34 (1983):803-50.

Powers, Thomas B. "Massachusetts' VOC Bubble Regulation: The Daily Cap and Issues It Raises." Paper presented at 1984 annual meeting, Air Pollution Control Association, San Francisco.

Radian Corporation. "Analysis of New Source Review Permitting Experience." Draft final report to the U.S. Environmental Protection Agency. Research Triangle Park, N.C.: Radian Corporation, 1985.

Ramil, John B., and William N. Cantrell. "Application of the 'Bubble Concept' to a Utility Coal Conversion." Paper delivered at the 1981 annual meeting, Air Pollution Control Association, Philadelphia).

Raufer, Roger K., and Stephen L. Feldman. "Emissions Trading and What It May Mean for Acid Deposition Control." *Public Utilities Fortnightly* 114 (August 16, 1984):17-25.

Raufer, Roger K., Stephen L. Feldman, and John A. Jaksch. "The Case for Emission Reduction Credit Leasing." Paper delivered at 1985 annual meeting, Air Pollution Control Association, Detroit.

Reed, Phillip D. "Court Upholds States' Relaxation of SO₂ Controls: Interstate Impacts, Sulfate Pollution Allowable." *Environmental Law Reporter* 13 (February 1983):10036-10042.

————. "*NRDC v. Gorsuch*: D.C. Circuit Bursts EPA's Nonattainment Bubble." *Environmental Law Reporter* 12 (October 1982):10089.

————. "Three Strikes and the Umpire is Out: The Supreme Court Throws the D.C. Circuit Out of the Bubble Review Game." *Environmental Law Reporter* 14 (September 1984):10338.

————. "When Is an Area That Is in Attainment Not an Attainment Area?" *Environmental Law Reporter* 16 (February 1986):10041.

Rehbinder, Eckard, and Rolf-Ulrich Sprenger. "The Emissions Trading

178   RICHARD A. LIROFF

Policy in the United States of America: An Evaluation of its Advantages and Disadvantages and Analysis of its Applicability in the Federal Republic of Germany." Washington, D.C.: U.S. Environmental Protection Agency, Office of Policy Analysis, 1985.

"A Remedy for the Victims of Pollution Permit Markets." *Yale Law Journal* 92 (1983):1022-40.

Rhinelander, Laurens H. "The Bubble Concept: A Pragmatic Approach to Regulation under the Clean Air Act." *Virginia Journal of Natural Resources* 1 (1981):178-228.

_____. "The Proper Place for the Bubble Concept under the Clean Air Act." *Environmental Law Reporter* 13 (1983):10406-10417.

Ritts, Leslie Sue. "State Emissions Trading Regulations." Washington, D.C.: Environmental Law Institute, forthcoming.

_____. "Summary of Comments: August 31, 1983 Shutdown Notice, 48 Fed. Reg. 39579." Report for the U.S. Environmental Protection Agency. Washington, D.C.: Environmental Law Institute, 1984.

Ritts, Leslie Sue, Timothy R. Henderson, and Alysia Watanabe. "Comparison of Selected State Emissions Banking Rules." Washington, D.C.: Environmental Law Institute, 1982.

_____. "Comparison of Selected State Generic Comprehensive Emissions Trading Rules." Washington, D.C.: Environmental Law Institute, 1982.

Roberts, Marc J. "Some Problems of Implementing Marketable Pollution Rights Schemes: The Case of the Clean Air Act." In Magat, Wesley A., *Reform of Environmental Regulation*. Cambridge, Mass.: Ballinger Publishing Co., 1982.

Romaine, Christopher P. "Bubbles or Alternative Control Strategies in Illinois." Paper delivered at 1984 annual meeting, Air Pollution Control Association, San Francisco.

Rose-Ackerman, Susan. "Market Models for Water Pollution Control: Their Strengths and Weaknesses." *Public Policy* 25 (1977):383-406.

Russell, Clifford S. "Controlled Trading of Pollution Permits." *Environmental Science and Technology* 15 (January 1981):24-28.

_____. "What Can We Get from Effluent Charges?" *Policy Analysis* 5 (Spring 1979):155-80.

Schelling, Thomas C. "Prices as Regulatory Instruments." In Schelling, Thomas C., ed. *Incentives for Environmental Protection*. Cambridge, Mass.: MIT Press, 1983.

Simmons, L.L., C.L. Norton, and M.J. DeBiase. "Fugitive Dust Emissions from Roads in Iron and Steel Mills: Compilation of Results and Use under EPA's Emission Trading Policy." Paper delivered at Fourth Symposium on Iron and Steel Pollution Abatement Technology, Pittsburgh, 1982.

Smith, Lowell, and Russell Randle. "Comment on *Beyond the New Deal*." *Yale Law Journal* 90 (1981):1398-1411.

Stander, Leo. "Potential Particle Size Considerations in Developing Emission Trading Proposals." Paper delivered at 1983 annual meeting, Air Pollution Control Association, Atlanta.

Steiner, Bruce. "Armco's Experience with Application of the Bubble Concept." Middletown, Ohio: Armco, Inc., undated.

_____. "Fugitive Dust Control in Iron and Steel Plants." Paper delivered at 31st Ontario Industrial Waste Conference, Toronto, Ontario, Canada, 1984.

Stewart, Richard B. "Economics, Environment, and the Limits of Legal Control." *Harvard Environmental Law Review* 9 (1985):1-22.

Streets, David G., et al. "A Regional New Source Bubble Policy: Its Advantages Illustrated for the State of Illinois." *Journal of the Air Pollution Control Association* 34 (1984):25-31.

Stukane, Thomas J. "EPA's Bubble Concept After *Chevron v. NRDC*: Who Is to Guard the Guards Themselves?" *Natural Resources Lawyer* 17 (1985):647-82.

Tether, Ivan. "Will a Final Policy Rejuvenate the Bubble?" *The Environmental Forum* 4 (March 1986):28, 31-32.

Tietenberg, Thomas H. *Emissions Trading: An Exercise in Reforming Pollution Policy*. Washington, D.C.: Resources for the Future, 1985.

_____. "Transferable Discharge Permits and the Control of Stationary Source Air Pollution: A Survey and Synthesis." *Land Economics* 56 (1980):391-416.

Tobin, Richard J., and John A. Jaksch. "Management Alternatives to the Clean Air Act Amendments of 1977: An Analysis of Regulatory Versus Economic Approaches." Paper delivered at 1981 annual meeting, Air Pollution Control Association, Philadelphia.

Tucker, William. "Marketing Pollution," *Harper's*, May 1981, pp. 31-38.

United States. Comptroller General. *Assessing the Feasibility of Converting Commercial Vehicle Fleets to Use Methanol as an Offset in Urban Areas*. Washington, D.C.: U.S. General Accounting

Office, 1982. Letter Opinion B-207490.

————. *A Market Approach to Air Pollution Control Could Reduce Compliance Costs without Jeopardizing Clean Air Goals.* Washington, D.C.: U.S. General Accounting Office, 1982.

United States. Environmental Protection Agency. Office of Planning and Management. *An Analysis of Economic Incentives to Control Emissions of Nitrogen Oxides from Stationary Sources.* Washington, D.C.: U.S. Environmental Protection Agency, 1981.

United States. Environmental Protection Agency. Office of Planning and Resource Management. "Analysis of New Source Review (NSR) Permitting Experience." Report from TRW. Washington, D.C.: U.S. Environmental Protection Agency, August 1982.

United States. Environmental Protection Agency. Regulatory Reform Staff. "Brokering Emission Reduction Credits—A Handbook." Washington, D.C.: U.S. Environmental Protection Agency, January 1981. Processed.

————. "Creation, Banking and Use of Emission Reduction Credits (ERCs)." Washington, D.C.: U.S. Environmental Protection Agency, May 1982. Processed.

Van de Verg, Eric, and Padraic Frucht. "On Trying to be First: Maryland's Efforts to Implement EPA's Controlled Trading Policy." Paper delivered at 1981 annual meeting, Western Economic Association.

Zosel, Thomas W. "Developing Effective Compliance Alternatives." Paper delivered at 1983 annual meeting, Air Pollution Control Association, Atlanta.

Zwikl, James R. "An Alternative Emission Control Plan for Industrial Plants—Birth of a Concept and Its Regulatory Implications." Paper delivered at 1981 annual meeting, Air Pollution Control Association, Philadelphia.

Index

181